Moral China in the Age of Reform

Three decades of dizzying change in China's economy and society have left a tangible record of successes and failures. Less readily accessible but of no less consequence is the story, as illuminated in this book, of what China's reform has done to its people as moral and spiritual beings. Jiwei Ci examines the moral crisis in post-Mao China as a mirror of deep contradictions in the new self as well as in society. He seeks to show that lack of freedom, understood as the moral and political conditions for subjectivity under modern conditions of life, lies at the root of these contradictions, just as enhanced freedom offers the only appropriate escape from them. Rather than as a ready-made answer, however, freedom is treated throughout as a pressing question in China's search for a better moral and political culture. A probing account of moral China in the age of reform, this book is also an original philosophical inquiry into the relation between moral subjectivity and freedom.

Jiwei Ci is Professor of Philosophy at the University of Hong Kong and the author of *Dialectic of the Chinese Revolution: From Utopianism to Hedonism* (1994) and *The Two Faces of Justice* (2006).

Moral China in the Age of Reform

JIWEI CI
University of Hong Kong

CAMBRIDGE
UNIVERSITY PRESS

32 Avenue of the Americas, New York, NY 10013-2473, USA

Cambridge University Press is part of the University of Cambridge.

It furthers the University's mission by disseminating knowledge in the pursuit of education, learning, and research at the highest international levels of excellence.

www.cambridge.org
Information on this title: www.cambridge.org/9781107646315

© Jiwei Ci 2014

This publication is in copyright. Subject to statutory exception and to the provisions of relevant collective licensing agreements, no reproduction of any part may take place without the written permission of Cambridge University Press.

First published 2014

Printed in the United States of America

A catalog record for this publication is available from the British Library.

Library of Congress Cataloging in Publication Data
Ci, Jiwei, 1955–
Moral China in the age of reform / Jiwei Ci.
pages cm
Includes bibliographical references and index.
ISBN 978-1-107-03866-0 (hardback) – ISBN 978-1-107-64631-5 (paperback)
1. Liberty – Moral and ethical aspects – China. 2. Democracy – Moral and ethical aspects – China. 3. China – Moral conditions. 4. Political culture – China. 5. China – Politics and government – 1976–2002. 6. China – Politics and government – 2002– I. Title.
JC599.C6C6 2014
172.0951–dc23   2014018699

ISBN 978-1-107-03866-0 Hardback
ISBN 978-1-107-64631-5 Paperback

Cambridge University Press has no responsibility for the persistence or accuracy of URLs for external or third-party Internet Web sites referred to in this publication and does not guarantee that any content on such Web sites is, or will remain, accurate or appropriate.

In loving memory of my maternal grandmother

Contents

Acknowledgments	*page* ix
Introduction: Why the Question of Freedom Is Unavoidable	1
1 An Anatomy of the Moral Crisis	12
2 Political Order, Moral Disorder	24
3 Freedom as a Chinese Question	37
4 Freedom and Its Epistemological Conditions	63
5 Freedom and Identification	88
6 Neither Devotion Nor Introjection	108
7 The Insult of Poverty	125
8 Democracy as Unmistakable Reality and Uncertain Prospect	156
9 Freedom's Unfinished Task	182
10 China's Space of Moral Possibilities	187
Index	225

Acknowledgments

I first started paying serious attention to what came to be known as China's moral crisis back in the early 1990s as I was working on an earlier book, *Dialectic of the Chinese Revolution*. It was only much later, around 2005, that it dawned on me that there was, in the Chinese context, an incredibly close link between my interest in the moral crisis and a longstanding preoccupation of mine with the question of freedom. When these hitherto only parallel concerns thus came together, the idea for the present book was born. By a happy coincidence, it was at roughly this time that I began to receive invitations to speak or write about themes in the vicinity of the moral crisis or the question of freedom or both. As this book goes to press, I feel a renewed appreciation of those friends and colleagues who by their invitations and pressures gave me the stimulus to shape inchoate and fragmented inklings into claims, arguments, and narratives. These people include, in alphabetical order, Geremie Barmé, Timothy Cheek, Pochung Chow, Fred Dallmayr, Gloria Davies, Gan Yang, P. J. Ivanhoe, Tao Jiang, Liang Zhiping, Lorenzo Marsili, Thomas Pogge, Q. S. Tong, and Zhao Tingyang.

Some of these initiatives led to particularly useful trial runs, in published form, of ideas that have now found their way into this book. In this connection, I am grateful to several publishers for permission to draw on previously published material. Chapters 1 and 2 are revised and expanded versions, respectively, of "The Moral Crisis in Post-Mao China: Prolegomenon to a Philosophical Analysis," *Diogenes* (Sage Publications), vol. 56 (2009), pp. 19–25, and of "Dialectic of the Chinese Revolution Revisited: Desublimation and Resublimation in Post-Mao China," in Fred Dallmayr and Zhao Tingyang, eds., *Contemporary Chinese Political*

Thought: Debates and Perspectives (Lexington: University of Kentucky Press, 2012), pp. 173–84. Chapter 3 is a substantially revised version of "China and the Question of Freedom," *boundary 2* (Durham: Duke University Press), vol. 38 (2011), pp. 53–76, and Chapter 4 contains, within a new thematic structure, portions of an article that first appeared as "What Is in the Cloud? – A Critical Engagement with Thomas Metzger on 'The Clash between Chinese and Western Political Theories,'" *boundary 2*, vol. 34 (2007), pp. 61–86. Finally, Chapters 6 and 7 are slightly modified versions, respectively, of "Neither Devotion Nor Introjection: Freudian Reflections on China's Moral Crisis," in Tao Jiang and P. J. Ivanhoe, eds., *The Reception and Rendition of Freud in China: China's Freudian Slip* (New York: Routledge, 2013), pp. 103–16, and of "Agency and Other Stakes of Poverty," *Journal of Political Philosophy* (Wiley-Blackwell), vol. 21 (2013), pp. 125–50.

It has not been an easy time writing this book, especially emotionally, as I am not only an observer but also a participant in relation to the subject matter, and prolonged reflection on the deep roots of the moral crisis and the huge obstacles to freedom as its solution is bound to take its toll on the participant in the author. All the more invaluable under such circumstances has been the intellectual and moral company of friends, which gives constant life to the simple truth that passionate critique is a labor of love. Thus, without mentioning these friends by name, as they know best who they are, I thank them both for helping keep me sober and for making me dare to be more hopeful than I would otherwise be.

It gives me special pleasure to express my deep appreciation of the two anonymous readers for Cambridge University Press for their engaged commentary and thoughtful suggestions. Last, but not least, I am greatly indebted to Robert Dreesen, my editor at Cambridge University Press, for his good judgment and enthusiastic support from the very start, and to Elizabeth Janetschek, Robert's assistant, for taking patient care of the details.

Introduction

Why the Question of Freedom Is Unavoidable

A little more than three decades ago, China embarked upon a course of fundamental change in its economy and society, and we now have a tangible record, positive and negative, of what has transpired on these fronts. The trajectory of subjectivity – of moral life and life of the spirit – belongs to a rather different part of the larger story: more than thirty years after the winds of change started sweeping across the moral and spiritual landscape of China, the dust is still swirling around, and what has taken temporary shape is a veritable morass. All members of Chinese society, including myself, are part of this dust, this morass, and our understanding of our own situation is, for the most part, no less unsettled and confused.

One sign of this confusion is the way in which the question of political reform is typically approached and lack of progress and its consequences comprehended. It is a commonplace of both Chinese and Western analyses of the matter that political reform has lagged far behind economic reform and that political reform must catch up soon if China is to maintain its momentum of economic growth and prevent problems such as official corruption and social injustice from going completely out of control. While it contains a grain of truth, this piece of received wisdom only scratches the surface. Political reform is a value-laden process, and, as such, it can achieve a real breakthrough only if a corresponding breakthrough in values – even perhaps a revolution in values – takes place in Chinese society at the same time. What is the infrastructure of values that must exist if political reform is to make *moral* sense and command more than opportunistic support? What is it about the structure of Chinese society and its political system that stands in the way, not so much of political reform, as of the more fundamental transformation in values?

Deeper if more elusive questions such as these must be addressed if we are to understand the tortured process of political reform and what is necessary for its prospects to improve. But these questions are also worth pursuing in their own right – as questions about the state of morality, subjectivity, and life of the spirit in China today. Indeed, they must be pursued in their own right if we look for answers of adequate depth and scope.

In the book before you, I seek to provide such answers in their own right but also in the hope that the results can serve as the basis for a deeper understanding of the quandary of China's political reform, among other things, although I will not directly pursue this understanding myself. I will attempt, that is, to cut one path through the moral and spiritual morass of China's reform in search of a clear and steady if necessarily partial view of it from the inside. My point of entry is the *moral crisis* that has dogged China throughout the three decades of reform, while my diagnosis, including the route of escape from the crisis implicit in this diagnosis, has *freedom* as its central term of reference. Behind such problems as pervasive official corruption and gross social injustice is the moral crisis, according to my diagnosis, and behind the intractable question of political reform is the more fundamental question of freedom.

My choice of the moral crisis as the point of entry is, in the present context, entirely motivated by the search for understanding. There is, to be sure, much about the moral crisis to lament and indeed to condemn, and, as a member of the society whose crisis it is rather than as an outside observer, I cannot write about it without emotional or existential involvement. But what causes me to attach so much importance to the moral crisis is the realization that this crisis is a symptom of fissures in the deep structure of Chinese society and its body politic that we might not otherwise be led to investigate. The moral crisis is a mirror, if we look carefully, not only of failures but also of successes (as viewed within a commonsense frame of reference), not only of changes that have failed to materialize but also of transformations that add up to a different way of life, both outer and inner. And thus it is a mirror of the entire reform – most importantly of the tensions and contradictions that have given China today its distinctive shape and out of which the future of China will unfold.

If the moral crisis reveals one thing most *immediately* and consequentially, it must be that China today lacks a new moral subject, a kind of subject that is fit to act morally and meaningfully in the new society that the three decades of reform have brought into being – and fit to make this a better society. The moral crisis reveals this immediately because this is what can be inferred from the very fact of a moral crisis: a moral crisis is nothing but a crisis of moral subjectivity. What it also reveals, by the same token, is that the old moral subject, of the Maoist mold, is defunct, or – what amounts to the same thing – that the conditions for the preservation of that kind of moral subject have largely disappeared. The new conditions of life, however we care to characterize them and whether we like them or not, call for a different kind of moral subject.

This new subject has no moral leader to follow, no moral exemplar to emulate, because it finds itself under conditions of life – economic, social, cultural, and otherwise – in which the very categories of moral leader and moral exemplar no longer make sense. It must assume responsibility for itself as a moral subject, a subject among equal subjects. Even if it still wants to defer to moral leaders or exemplars or indeed relies on such deference, if only unknowingly, it will insist on one condition, namely, that it defers only if it chooses to do so. It will not accept high-handed exhortation or open propaganda.

This is no prescription but what is made necessary by the collapse of the old communist-style, totally organized way of life and its replacement, in the course of the reform, by an increasing and by now deeply entrenched individualization of everyday life. Choice and responsibility, by and for individuals qua individuals, pervade this new form of life in place of the obedience and overt conformism that served in the old one. The one thing that is lacking is what can bring separate acts of choice and responsibility together into some semblance of moral and volitional unity: a new moral subject appropriately individuated and made fit for the radically new form of life that made its initial appearance in China as if by a surprise attack and has since conquered most of it by stealth. Until this new moral subject takes shape, we shall remain in the grip of the moral crisis. The moral crisis is a constant reminder that, barring the extremely improbable restoration of the collective form of life with its communist telos, there is no avoiding the need to create a new moral subject.

This new moral subject is defined, above all, by freedom. For responsibility for oneself as a moral subject, even when it takes the form of deciding to defer to others, presupposes freedom. And the freedom thus presupposed is not just actual or de facto freedom, of which there is plenty in China already, but a conscious, valorized entitlement to freedom as commensurate with one's responsibility, and hence freedom raised to the level of a value. Thus understood, freedom is the sum total of conditions, moral and political, that allow one to make choices for oneself and assume responsibility for oneself in all relevant domains of life and, above all, to become the kind of self that is capable of doing so, with its concomitant dignity and worthiness of respect. Since the need to make choices for oneself and assume responsibility for oneself is already a fact of life in China today, the call for freedom is simply a demand to make possible what is already necessary. A moral crisis is nothing but the disjunction of the necessary and the possible.

Thus freedom is unavoidable as a presupposition of a certain kind of moral subject, and this moral subject in turn is necessary because a new way of life has sprung up around us and is here to stay. Must we accept or acquiesce in this new way of life, such as it is, in the first place? We need not, and I myself do not find the balance sheet of the three decades of reform readily endorsable – given, on the negative side, the unchecked corruption and collusion between power and capital, the runaway inequality inexcusable in a society still with so much poverty, the environmental degradation, and, most pervasive and immensurable, the near-destruction of the moral and spiritual ecology of an entire people. Nor is freedom a simple and innocuous concept or practice (what kind of freedom? whose freedom? freedom for what?), and that is why I have been careful to say about freedom only what strictly needs to be said as a presupposition of a kind of moral subject that has to be significantly more individuated than its counterpart in Mao's China. While I have deep reservations about what I have roughly called the new form of life in China, I do not see, and do not want to see, a return to the old communist-style, totally organized form of life. The latter form of life may have been necessary once, and, if one is to wax normative about it, even to some extent desirable in its time. But it is no longer, as a whole, necessary and desirable. Whatever alternative to this life we find attractive and feasible, I for one believe that a radically more individuated moral subject must figure in it and so, correspondingly, must a kind of freedom that makes such a moral subject possible. Only this kind of moral subject can give us any hope of making the best of the new form of life in China today and, if necessary, transcending it through critique and struggle from within.

This is not to accept the new realities of China as we find them; nor to take on board the vision of the bourgeois atomistic, possessive, and increasingly consumerist individual along with its ideologically defined and restricted freedoms; nor to accentuate, in the Chinese context and as a corrective, individual freedom at the expense of values and practices of solidarity. On the contrary, only by becoming clear about the need for greater individuation and greater freedom and by confronting the questions posed by this need can we hope to raise apposite warnings against the prospect of the conception and codification of freedom being overwhelmingly shaped by the dominant power of capital and against the pitting of the lonely and alienated individual against forms of solidarity and community essential for good human life.

In this light, what I call freedom is nothing more and nothing less than the room we need, as individuals and as members of communities, to be meaningfully and responsibly human under modern conditions of life. As dwellers in the modern world, we should have no trouble or qualm endorsing this room as such. What precise form, ethical and institutional, this room takes is another matter, subject to political contestation and especially the quieter, less visible struggles to shape the social imaginary. I will not join such contestation or struggle, for the most part, in the present book. I am concerned with the prior task of showing, mainly for the Chinese context but with resonance beyond it, that the question of freedom is unavoidable, that it is unavoidable because it is internal to Chinese society as we now find it, and that it is internal in that the lack of freedom (in the sense I have described) lies at the root of the prolonged moral crisis in post-Mao China, just as enhanced freedom offers the only promise of escape from this crisis.

It is one thing, however, to make the case that freedom is necessary in China today, in the sense and for the reasons I have set out, and something else altogether to show how freedom thus understood is to be achieved, or, harder still, to prove that it will be achieved. That freedom is a necessary condition for overcoming the moral crisis does not tell us whether it will materialize. Indeed, a special feature of the moral crisis in post-Mao China, and an important reason for its staying power, is precisely the existence of durable political forces with a vested interest in preventing the materialization of the necessary. The Chinese political structure as it has evolved in the past six decades or more has been consistently devoid of internal incentives to promote or allow incremental growth in those virtues and capacities associated with freedom and self-government, and this remains largely true today. It should therefore come as no surprise if initial increases in freedom, if and when central control slackens in one way or another, are accompanied by displays of confusion, crude egoism, sheer irresponsibility, and even new forms of corruption and lawlessness. Nor should it be surprising, in such an event, if the immediate consequences of increased freedom are taken to show that freedom is what China can ill afford. So I do not think for a moment that our path to freedom will be straight and easy: we have been lurching toward freedom, and we know not exactly what it is. I have tried only to show that it is necessary, in the hope that knowledge of this necessity combined with awareness of the difficulties and dangers of acting on this necessity will produce in us both the moral motivation to strive for freedom and the political prudence to go about it in the right way. The test of freedom is one we will have to pass sooner or later if we are to extricate ourselves from the moral crisis that signals our entrapment in the thwarted transition from the old to the new. Only then will we have moved properly – that is, as modern subjects – into the modern world, with its fair share of problems and fair chance to cope with them.

The line of thinking just sketched is one that informs, in one way or another, all the chapters of this book. This does not mean, however, that these chapters are neatly constructed to give substance and cogency to this line of thinking and do nothing else. If the chapters hang together around the twin themes of moral crisis and escape through freedom, most of them take up other issues along the way. These other issues invariably bear to one degree or another on the main thematic thread. Even when they appear to do so less directly, they belong to the larger picture of the moral, political, and spiritual landscape of the reform, which, as I have said, I am also concerned to capture, especially as refracted by the mirror of the moral crisis. As a result, each chapter, although animated and shaped by the overarching themes of moral crisis and freedom, is nevertheless largely independent and freestanding, treating a set of problems with a self-contained subject matter and logic of its own.

In Chapter 1, I provide a reasonably comprehensive, if somewhat schematic, account of the moral crisis. In this account I touch on many other things, both conceptual and substantive, than is directly relevant to the theme of freedom because it is only in the context of some such richer account that the theme of freedom can naturally and accurately emerge. If this chapter provides an anatomy of the moral crisis itself and is in this sense a treatment of the purely *moral* dimension of the crisis, Chapter 2, also devoted entirely to the moral crisis, probes its political dimension and gives a glimpse of how the moral vacuum, as the moral crisis is sometimes called, is to a large degree politically created. In these first two chapters, the idea that a new kind of moral subject is needed to fill the moral vacuum makes its initial appearance, as does the related idea that this new moral subject in turn needs greatly expanded opportunities for choice and responsibility. The stage is thus set for the theme of freedom to come to the fore, and so it does in the next chapter.

Introduction

Chapter 3 has what I intend to be a very deliberate title, for we have come to a point in China, as the moral crisis tells us, where we must confront the question of freedom, but it is, first and foremost, as a question that we must consider it. Freedom is an ideologically loaded concept – as much an indispensable value under modern conditions of life as it is a highly plastic notion that lends itself to all kinds of questionable conceptions and uses. There is no ready-made notion of freedom, in either moral or institutional terms, that we can simply pick up and, as it were, apply to Chinese society. It is in this spirit that I approach the question of freedom in Chapter 3, both conceptually and substantively, and if there is one thing central to this approach, it is the realization that freedom must be understood and appraised within the larger framework of agency.

By agency I mean the distinctively human way of acting and acquiring subjectivity in and through acting, including the values that make such action and subjectivity possible. Thus understood, agency is a common denominator of all forms of human life as *human* life, whether or not the value of freedom has a place in them. To think about freedom in the larger and deeper terms of agency is not to deny the pivotal role of freedom as a set of values and institutional forms in which agency must find expression under modern conditions of life but precisely to understand freedom as such. Adoption of this broader approach also allows us to examine within the same conceptual framework a very different configuration of agency, which I call identification, as it figures in both traditional China and Mao's China. Thus, in Chapter 5, I give a comparative account of freedom and identification as two major, alternative configurations of agency. Although it is perhaps only natural that in this account I associate freedom with the modern West, for the most part, and identification with traditional and Mao's China, the most important comparison I am pursuing is typological. There is no reason why freedom cannot present itself as a question in the context of Chinese moral and political culture and become part of that culture. Thus, while the cross-cultural dimension of the comparison is not without its interest, my deeper aim is to outline the two paradigms of agency – freedom and identification – in terms of which we can more precisely understand not only the kind of moral subject that is called for by the new realities of Chinese society (as discussed in Chapter 3) but also the old Maoist moral subject it is meant to replace. In this, Chapter 5 serves as a necessary complement to Chapter 3.

This approach to freedom is quite far removed from the prevailing one, so I devote a part of Chapter 4 to showing why it is to be preferred. I do so in the form of a commentary on Thomas Metzger's account of freedom, both because this account is representative of the prevailing view and because Metzger addresses the question of freedom in a comparative context involving China. In this regard, my polemic against Metzger is intended to serve as a natural bridge to Chapter 5. But there is an even more important reason to subject Metzger's account of freedom to critical discussion, for Metzger takes with uncommon seriousness what one may call the epistemological conditions of freedom and, to my knowledge, his is the only extensive treatment of such conditions that places the Chinese and Western traditions and current realities in a comparative context. Thus, I can think of no better way to take up this important dimension of the question of freedom than through an engagement with Metzger, and the bulk of Chapter 4 serves this purpose.

In some ways Chapter 6 brings together the treatment of the moral crisis in Chapters 1 and 2 and the examination of freedom and identification and agency in Chapters 3 to 5, but with a Freudian slant. In this chapter I draw on Freud's ideas of the superego and group psychology, among other things, to provide an analysis of the moral crisis that is less comprehensive than that found in Chapter 1 but that goes deeper into the structure of the crisis. In the process of doing so, I find it useful to work with a distinction between what I call the leader-centered and the superego-centered morality, based on devotion and introjection, respectively, which match quite well the two paradigms of agency called freedom and identification. The result is a reinforcement and enrichment of the earlier analyses, linking the moral crisis with the two kinds of agency and of moral subjectivity in one unified frame of reference and, unlike in Chapter 5, doing so entirely within the Chinese context. It is worth emphasizing here, as I do in the chapter itself, that my Freudian or Freud-inspired reflections on China's moral crisis and on the two kinds of morality and moral subjectivity are meant to be judged on their cogency and explanatory power and not on their accuracy as an interpretation of Freud.

On the face of it, Chapter 7, an analysis of poverty in terms of agency, has little to do with either the theme of moral crisis or the theme of freedom, except that it shares with my treatment of these themes a theoretical underpinning in the concept of agency. But closer inspection will reveal that it actually stands in a significant relation to both, quite apart from the fact that the issue of poverty in China today is worth examining in its own right. There is a sense in which the alarming gap between the rich and the poor that has opened up in the course of the reform and shows no signs of narrowing is both an outcome of the moral crisis and one of its aggravating conditions: an outcome in that the unchecked and ill-regulated scramble for wealth is a mirror of the soullessness and meaninglessness of the human condition in China; and an aggravating condition because the resentment of the poor against the rich, so often for good reason given the extent of social injustice but with no effective outlet, adds limitless fuel to the burning down of trust and law-abidingness that is part of the moral crisis. There is also a sense in which the lack of freedom for other things – above all, for the emergence of a new, self-governing moral subject – is what lies behind the desperate concentration of energy on the quest for wealth as an escape from the otherwise empty and meaningless condition of life. The gap between rich and poor in China today, with its devastating effect on the social and moral fabric of Chinese society, is thus part of a larger picture in which poverty, moral crisis, and lack of freedom stand in a mutually causal relationship with one another.

Next, in Chapter 8, as another kind of complement to Chapter 3, I take up the question of democracy. As in my account of freedom, I see and present democracy as a problem that is entirely internal to the condition and dynamic of Chinese society. Whereas the title of the chapter refers only to democracy, the actual treatment of the subject cannot but give almost equal weight to the question of freedom: democracy is understood in terms of agency, just as freedom is, and the two are inextricably linked in that uneasy combination known as liberal democracy. In this chapter, as in almost all the chapters preceding it, what emerges above all is a sense of the new realities of Chinese society and of what it takes to respond adequately at the level of moral and political culture to such realities. As I make clear in this chapter, and this applies equally elsewhere in the book, I do not affirm these new realities or, by the same token, any specific vision of what China should be like in its moral and political culture, let alone in the institutional realization of any such vision, given such realities. But two things I do believe: namely, that these new realities must be confronted at the level of moral and political culture; and that, whatever one may think about such realities in their specific, contingent form in China today, we, as inhabitants of the modern world, have no choice but to embrace (the need for) much greater freedom than we have been accustomed to in Mao's China and since and to accept, wherever they may lead, the challenges and risks of this new freedom.

In the specific context of China today, these challenges and risks resist any comfortable expectations of freedom as a ready solution to our problems. For freedom is above all a question, and to speak of it as a solution, as I have frequently done in this book, is actually to think of it as an especially necessary question. How we approach and answer this question will help determine whether we will be able to come up with what can reasonably qualify as a solution, and, if so, what that solution is like. Chapter 9, much briefer than all the others, serves as a reminder of the status of freedom as a question. And it does so by showing, in general terms, that modern liberty raises deeper issues than the mainstream, liberal democratic conception of freedom is able or concerned to address, and, in the specific context of post-communist China, that one essential task, and hence test, of freedom is as an adequate response to the moral crisis and to the need for a new kind of moral subject.

Finally, in Chapter 10, I attempt to provide a tentative answer to the questions of freedom raised in Chapter 9 and indeed throughout the book – or rather a tentative framework or line of approach for thinking about potential answers. To this end, and in order to set the normative quest for the most apposite freedom on a reasonably solid footing, I seek to combine a rough sketch of the normative contours of the modern world and of China as part of it with a brief consideration of the relevant political and cultural realities in China today. The result is a relatively comprehensive, if necessarily schematic, view of what I call the space of moral possibilities in the foreseeable future of China. If one thing stands out in this space as both needful and realistic in principle, however difficult in practice, it is the prospect of finding a symbiotic relation between freedom and the good. If this is too much to hope for, as yet, I hope at least to have shown the point of embarking on the quest.

As this glimpse of its individual chapters makes clear, the book is essentially about China. It may therefore come as a surprise that, here and there, fairly long stretches of text are devoted to theoretical issues, such as the structure and configurations of human agency, with no immediate mention of China. This is true, for example, of Chapters 3, 5, and especially 7 and 10. In most cases of this kind, I allow myself a certain leeway in pursuing theoretical issues because this seems to me the best way of shedding light on the problems of China under discussion.

While relevance to these problems supplies the motivation and the necessary discipline, as well as a test of effectiveness, it would not be far wrong to say, of the more philosophical parts of my undertaking, that I have also intended this book as a work of theory (especially of moral psychology and political philosophy) – theory developed in response to China's problems and thus a kind of explicitly situated theory. As I conceive of my undertaking, while the immediate and main object under discussion is freedom in China, this is also an occasion for reflecting on the question of freedom in general. The same is true, at the level of specific topics, of my discussion of democracy, equality, modern nihilism, the nature of moral subjectivity, identification as a configuration of agency, the stakes of poverty, the character of modernity, and so on, in portions of Chapters 3, 5, 6, 7, 8, and 10. The fact that this book is intended in this sense as a work of theory, in addition to being a study of China, does not make it better or worse; it only calls for a more open or patient approach to it on the part of the reader and, as is only fair and appropriate, a correspondingly more complex and more stringent standard of judgment.

It is in part from its structure as a work of theory that the book derives its cohesion, just as, thematically and as a work on China, the book has another source of unity in the twin themes of moral crisis and escape through freedom. By design, the ten chapters cohere along these structural and thematic threads, but each chapter also, as I have noted, has an agenda of its own, as it takes in its scope other issues, big and small, that belong in the larger moral and spiritual landscape of China today. This balance of unity and variation will, I hope, make for a more expansive and more stimulating exploration than the book would otherwise afford. Also on the positive side, each chapter can be read largely on its own, as desired, although the ten chapters taken together mean considerably more than the sum of the chapters taken individually. But, slightly on the negative side and I hope only slightly, the relative independence of the chapters makes a small amount of overlap unavoidable, especially considering that some chapters – 3, 5, 7, and 10 – draw for their theoretical basis on the same account of agency. I have treated all such overlaps as leitmotifs and tried to approach them each time with different formulations and nuances beyond stylistic variations.

In the end, if I do not want to sound unduly apologetic about this, it is because in any case the book is bound to contain many flaws both larger and more substantive. Thus I offer the book, flaws and all, as an interim report of my reflections on what I believe is a shared question of freedom, in what I hope is a common struggle, not only in China but everywhere else, for the best freedom we can imagine and realize.

I

An Anatomy of the Moral Crisis

I

Morality and life of the spirit in China today are widely, and quite correctly, viewed as being in a state of crisis.[1] This perception finds support even at the highest level of the Chinese leadership, which one would have thought would normally be the last to own up to such a crisis given its delegitimating implications. Although this moral crisis is only one constituent of life in China today, it casts an ever-darkening shadow over almost everything else and suffuses all things otherwise good and worth celebrating with its corrosive atmosphere of an unspeakable wrongness of the whole.

Thus, any adequate understanding of China today, whatever one's perspective or interest, requires an effort to make sense of its moral crisis. To assess the achievements and costs of the three decades of economic and social reform, it is necessary to reckon with this moral crisis. Likewise, to make any informed conjecture about what shape China is likely to take in the foreseeable future and how this shape might impinge on the world at large, it is necessary to grasp the inner workings of this crisis.

---

[1] See, for example, Liu Zhifeng, ed., *Daode Zhongguo* (Moral China) (Beijing: Zhongguo shehui kexue chubanshe, 1999); and Shao Daosheng, *Zhongguo shehui de kunhuo* (Quandaries Confronting Chinese Society) (Beijing: Shehui kexue wenxian chubanshe, 1996). For accounts of this crisis in English, see Xiaoying Wang, "The Post-communist Personality: The Spectre of China's Capitalist Market Reforms," *The China Journal* 47 (2002): 1–17; and Yunxiang Yan, "Immorality and Its Moral Implications in Contemporary Chinese Society," *Journal of Religious Ethics*, forthcoming.

For it is only through an examination of the moral crisis that we can hope to form an adequate idea of what China's recent transformation has done to its *people* or, more precisely, of what the people have done to themselves as part of this transformation. An attempt to make sense of the moral crisis is a necessary part of any larger effort to figure out the meaning and consequences of the reform in human terms: what the Chinese, as individuals and as a people, have come to be like, not just in their so-called standard of living but comprehensively, especially in their moral and spiritual existence; how they are likely to act and fare in the future as long as they stay as they are; and what changes in China's political structure and moral culture are necessary for them to change collectively and individually and to act and fare better.

To study the moral crisis, then, is to study China's social and economic transformation in terms of what surely lies at the heart of this process: the people as agents, as beings who change themselves internally as they change their country and the world at large. This is my first reason for taking a serious interest in China's moral crisis – to understand China and its people as they have evolved as a result of the three decades of reform. I should emphasize that I pursue this understanding as an "insider," as a member of Chinese society, with all the advantages and limitations that come with this relationship to the subject matter and with this self-understanding.

To go beneath the surface of China's moral crisis, however, I must aim to provide more than an intellectually distilled empirical account informed by an ad hoc admixture of refined common sense and occasional philosophical insight. I must, that is, pursue theoretical reflection on, among other things and above all, the nature of moral subjectivity: its constitution, its different types, and its political, epistemic, and other conditions. A sustained probe into China's moral crisis presents a nearly ideal occasion for theorizing about such matters as well as a good test for the accuracy and explanatory power of such theorizing. This then gives me a second reason for undertaking a theoretical inquiry into the moral crisis.

I have yet a third motivation, in that I pursue this inquiry in part as an act of intellectual and civic intervention. Aware that an attempt at scholarly understanding is extremely limited in its power to insert itself into the chains of causality that make up the "real world," I nevertheless want to contribute in a small way by shedding light on the inner workings of the moral crisis and, in a disciplined and responsible manner, imagining a way out of it.

In this chapter, however, I can make only a modest beginning. Although I attempt to provide a reasonably comprehensive analysis of the moral crisis, I will do so with the brevity and dearth of elaboration typical of an outline. The term "anatomy" in the chapter's title is meant to hint at these two features of the treatment. It is also intended to reflect a third. Because the analysis provided is of a crisis, it is naturally critical of those factors that are identified as contributing to the crisis. In the face of a crisis there is no avoiding the need for critique. But such critique, aimed at understanding the crisis as a precondition for overcoming it, is distinct from moralistic condemnation, the mere passing of negative judgment. I stand not on moral high ground but on the level of the crisis itself: the critique here is internal critique, and internal critique is a form of self-critique.

I first explain why it is appropriate to speak of a moral crisis and then examine the nature of the crisis. This examination is partly conceptual and partly causal. In the conceptual part, I discuss terms frequently used in reference to the crisis and introduce some analytical terms and distinctions of my own for further clarity. In the causal part, I trace the moral crisis to a crisis of identification with moral authority and exemplars, the latter crisis in turn containing important clues to the structure of self and agency in Chinese moral culture.

2

Is it not true, a skeptic might ask at the very outset, that every society has its share of moral problems, often serious and intractable? If so, why conceive of such problems in post-Mao China as amounting to a moral *crisis*? On what grounds can it plausibly be said that what China is going through in its moral domain has the proportions of a crisis?

One kind of answer lies in some account of the various phenomena that make up what is called a moral crisis and give one reason to speak of a moral crisis in the first place. Such an account will be in part descriptive, generalizing from the empirical, and in part analytical, drawing on more or less explicit standards of what counts as a state of affairs that is relatively free of crisis. The aim is to pin down, at the level of phenomena, what one means in adopting the discourse of crisis, and to give as comprehensive, precise, and balanced a picture as possible of what the moral crisis is like in its content, atmosphere, and consequences when approached in a reflective yet everyday, intuitive way.

I cannot hope to present anything like such a picture in this chapter, nor even in any of the later chapters, although details of one kind or another will be added to the sketchy account given here. I see four phenomena, however, in view of which, especially when taken together, the perception of a moral crisis in post-Mao China is appropriate and unexaggerated. First, everyday norms of coexistence and cooperation – be they moral, legal, or regulatory – are breached on a massive scale. The sheer scale in question is astonishing. Second, every sector of society, including officialdom and the academic community, is implicated in a big way, with no single institution or profession able to maintain a semblance of moral respectability. It is no longer remotely alarmist to speak of the corruption of an entire people (*quanmin fubai*), although this is no doubt an exaggeration if taken literally to cover all individual members of society. Third, the norms that are violated by so many in every walk of life are very elementary ones indeed (*dixian lunli*, as they are called in Chinese), not ones that require altruism or the adoption of perfectionist conceptions of the good. Violations of such elementary norms have resulted in all too many instances of unsafe food (infant formula and so-called gutter oil among the most prominent examples), medicine, water, and traffic, not to mention coal mines – the last item the most visible example until some time ago of what has gone wrong and how difficult it is to fix and, one might add, also of how easily public sensitivity can wear off.[2] Fourth, and finally, this state of affairs has become increasingly normal. Watch programs like *Jiaodian fangtan* (Today's Focus), *Zhongguo fazhi baodao* (Reporting on Law and Order in China), and *Daode guancha* (Moral Watch) on CCTV or *Shehui nengjiandu* (Society under the Spotlight) on Phoenix TV or read newspapers such as *Beijing qingnianbao* (Beijing Youth Daily) and *Nanfang zhoumo* (Southern Weekend), to name just a few, and it would be hard to resist the conclusion that norm-breaching

---

[2] Another large and important category is what may be called callous omissions, in which onlookers make no effort to help victims of crime or accidents when they could do so at little or no cost to themselves. See Yunxiang Yan, "The Good Samaritan's New Trouble: A Study of the Changing Moral Landscape in Contemporary China," *Social Anthropology* 17 (2009): 19–24. The most notorious example involves a two-year-old girl popularly known as Xiao Yueyue who was run over by reckless motor traffic and then left to die until help came from the nineteenth passerby, by which time it was already too late to save the little girl's life. For an academic discussion of this incident, see Wenqing Zhao, "Is Contemporary Chinese Society Inhumane? What Mencius and Empirical Psychology Have to Say," *Dao*, forthcoming. On problems of food safety with "Chinese characteristics," see Yunxiang Yan, "Food Safety and Social Risk in Contemporary China," *The Journal of Asian Studies* 71 (2012): 705–29.

behaviors one has every reason to wish were rare exceptions have come dangerously close to forming part of the order of the day. Even as official media report all kinds of blatantly unacceptable behavior with a view to stopping or reducing them, they turn such reporting, willy-nilly, into an entertainment of sorts or at best produce a kind of routinized exposure, a way for society to confront and digest the moral crisis through the enactment and channeling of outrage without providing real solutions. With this kind of normalization, the *sense* of moral crisis has diminished and may diminish even further. Upon reflection, however, this is cause for a deeper sense of crisis.

It could appear from this account that what I call China's moral crisis is such only in that it exhibits more seriously and pervasively problems that are otherwise the familiar stuff of human society. I believe such an impression would be mistaken. But it is an impression, if only hypothetical, that is worth responding to by way of better identifying those features that are truly distinctive of China's moral crisis. To this end, it may be helpful to carry out comparisons of post-Mao China, the focus of the present study, with, say, China in the decades (or centuries) before 1949, for example as the character of the Chinese people and society was seen by Lu Xun, the writer who is believed to have shown the deepest insight into this subject; or with American society in the Gilded Age, when it went through what may be thought of as a moral crisis, until the Progressive Era; or, finally, with those formerly communist societies in Russia and Eastern Europe that have made a morally disorienting transition to openly affirmed capitalism. I will not pursue any of these comparisons, however, in the pages of this book. I will try instead, in a small way in this chapter and with a gradually refined analytical apparatus in later chapters, to locate the specificity of China's moral crisis in the distinctive structure of the Chinese moral self – the kind of moral subjectivity that is in crisis – especially as this structure still combines elements of both Maoism and the Confucian tradition.

3

The notion of elementary norms to which I have appealed requires clarification, and here we immediately encounter something that sets China apart, at least from the typical modern liberal society, with respect to its moral culture and such a culture's liability to crisis. It is necessary to distinguish between norms of right (or justice) that govern relations among members of society on the one hand and standards of the good life that inform individual or collective choice of ends on the other. By elementary norms I mean the former, and thus the moral crisis in post-Mao China that I am talking about is, in the first instance, a crisis involving the right (or justice) rather than the good. In other words, by moral crisis I refer to a state of affairs in which large numbers of people fail to comply with more or less acceptable rules of social coexistence and cooperation rather than a situation in which large numbers of people pursue legally and morally permissible but arguably less than admirable conceptions of the good. Given this notion of a moral crisis, it is not surprising that the moral crisis in post-Mao China is at the same time a crisis of social order.

It is worth noting that the distinction between the right and the good is not one that informs the basic structure of Chinese moral culture. I say this for three reasons. First, the list of activities that members of Chinese society are routinely enjoined to do or to refrain from doing is a mixed bag of (what could be distinguished as) commendable/noncommendable conceptions of the good and just/unjust courses of action. Second, the motivation to choose just courses of action and avoid unjust courses of action (insofar as such courses of action are distinguishable from those pertaining to the good) is explicitly based on subscription to an overarching conception of the good couched in teleological terms of socialism and communism. Third, the process of striving to realize this overarching conception of the good is in turn meant to be presided over exclusively and to the very end by the Communist Party, and in this sense morality in China is explicitly continuous with politics.

Strictly speaking, then, there is no structural distinction in Chinese moral culture between the good and the right, between morality and politics. This fact is important: it yields a sense in which China's moral crisis is a crisis of the whole, that is, a crisis that does not admit of straightforward compartmentalization in the way, say, that a moral crisis in a modern Western society would.

This need not prevent us, however, from drawing a second-order, analytical distinction between the good and the right, morality and politics, with a view to clarifying the distinct locus of China's moral crisis and even its distinct causal story. Having claimed that the locus of China's moral crisis is in the first instance the domain of right, I hasten to add, as a hypothesis about its causal story, that this crisis has its origin in a crisis of the good, that is, a crisis of the socialist-communist conception of the good.[3] I would indeed suggest that the heavy dependence of the

---

[3] See my *Dialectic of the Chinese Revolution: From Utopianism to Hedonism* (Stanford: Stanford University Press, 1994), chap. 3.

right on the good, of morality on politics, to the point of allowing little room for these distinctions (at the first-order level), is itself a structural root cause of China's current moral crisis. It is also worth adding that the crisis of the socialist-communist conception of the good is in turn much aggravated by the rise of capitalist desires with few corresponding values to regulate them, or the influx of capitalist values without the benefit of critical examination, because this aspect of the reform has never been publicly confronted in a society that still officially calls itself socialist.

Given the causal hypothesis just put forward, why do I not speak of a crisis of the good, in the first instance, and then say that this crisis of the good has given rise to a crisis of justice and social order? This is because a crisis of the good in and of itself does not give us sufficient reason to get so worked up about the state of moral affairs in post-Mao China and describe it in such alarming terms as a moral crisis. No modern, pluralistic society is ever free of a crisis of the good in the eyes of a significant number of its members. By putting the crisis of justice and social order at the front end of China's moral crisis, I mean to differentiate China's moral crisis from a lesser, self-contained crisis of the good – self-contained in the sense of leaving justice and social order more or less intact. It is for this reason that I say that China's moral crisis is in the first instance a crisis of justice and social order.

I hasten to add that it is such only in the first instance. As soon as we look at the causal picture, it is important to see, as I have suggested, that the crisis of justice and social order in China is of a kind that is largely caused by a crisis of the good. Not only does this causal story give a distinctive character to China's crisis of justice and social order, it also reveals as special China's crisis of the good, for the latter is of a kind that has a built-in tendency to cause a crisis of justice and social order. Especially for this reason but almost equally in its own right, China's crisis of the good is no less important in its stakes and consequences than the conceptually distinct moral crisis. It goes to the heart of the moral crisis and afflicts not only the social fabric but the soul of all who breathe its leaden air.

Although its reality is thus not in doubt, we do not actually hear of a crisis of the good in popular discourse about China's moral crisis: "crisis of the good" belongs to the analytical vocabulary that I have adopted to make sense of the moral crisis, not to everyday discourse. What we come across in everyday discourse instead are references to a "crisis of the spirit" (*jingshen weiji*) or a "crisis of belief" (*xinyang weiji*). These terms lack sharpness, to be sure, and yet they point, if only vaguely, to something that runs through the more mundane problems of justice and social order. We can thus usefully retain these terms by making their referent more specific and precise, that is, by understanding them as representing different ways of trying to capture what I have been calling the crisis of the good. A crisis of the spirit or of belief occurs when the good that forms the content of the spirit or belief loses its power to convince and inspire. In the case of post-Mao China, such a crisis is, as I have already noted with respect to the good, more than a crisis involving the spirit or belief, for it leads directly to a crisis of justice and social order. This says something about the internal, causal structure of Chinese moral culture, making what we mean by crisis of the spirit and crisis of belief in the Chinese context very different from what we would mean by superficially similar terms in, say, the context of a modern Western society.

4

Having looked into the relation between the crisis of justice and the crisis of the good within China's overall moral crisis, I now want to return to the former for further elaboration. For there is yet another reason for which I want to treat China's moral crisis as, in the first instance, a crisis of justice and social order that is conceptually distinct from a crisis of the good. Once a crisis of justice and social order is under way, whatever its causes, it has a tendency to sustain and even aggravate itself. This is because noncompliance with norms of justice by some members of society, unless corrected in an effective and timely fashion, tends to weaken the motive of compliance on the part of others, thus leading to progressively worse overall noncompliance. This simple logic has clearly been set in motion in post-Mao China: very large numbers of people who otherwise would be perfectly willing to abide by elementary norms of justice have lost that willingness to one degree or another because so many other people, themselves perfectly willing at one time, have done so, violating norms with impunity and gaining unfair advantage. In this way, the perception that society is seriously lacking in predictable compliance with norms of justice, without the prospect of significant improvement in the foreseeable future, breeds more and more noncompliance until the whole society is enveloped in an atmosphere of mistrust and resentment and sheer ill temper. This kind of atmosphere does not depend on the majority of people being guilty of noncompliance; it requires only a certain critical mass, which has no doubt been reached in China.

When I say that injustice unstopped or unpunished breeds more injustice, I need to be more specific about the nature of the injustice involved. Does the injustice I have in mind result from the implementation of norms that are themselves seriously flawed or from the failure of large numbers of people to comply with more or less acceptable norms? It is for the most part the second scenario that is characteristic of the moral crisis in post-Mao China.

One example of the first scenario is the enforcement of laws and regulations that maintain the city/countryside divide, another the dismantling of the old socialist system of virtually universal, albeit very basic, health care.[4] In both of these cases, highly questionable norms are effectively put into practice. There is no shortage of unjust norms like these, and the effective implementation of any of them is a source of injustice. This kind of scenario, though highly problematic, is not what I chiefly mean when I speak of China's moral crisis.

Most of the injustices that make up what I am calling the crisis of justice belong rather to the second scenario. The norms breached by so many with such cumulatively disturbing consequences are for the most part not objects of moral disagreement. The crisis of justice consists instead in the routine violation of norms by people who do not object to the norms themselves and who definitely do not violate the norms *because* they object to them.

Why do so many people fail to comply with norms to which they take no exception as norms? A large part of the answer, as I have already suggested, is that too many *other* people did the same, and this in turn because yet too many other people had done the same before them, in a vicious cycle. There is nothing surprising about this phenomenon, for the disposition to be just is a conditional disposition. Such a disposition is marked by the willingness to comply with norms, as laid down in a given conception of justice, on condition that other members of society do the same. Each act in keeping with a norm is not only an instance of compliance but also a token of reciprocation.[5] There are thus two necessary conditions (among others, as we shall see) for a just person's willingness to follow a norm: first, that the norm is regarded as reasonably just, and second, that most people comply with it most of the time. When the first condition (call it *the validity condition*) is seriously unsatisfied,

---

[4] There has been a public outcry against the latter and something is being done about it.
[5] See my *The Two Faces of Justice* (Cambridge, MA: Harvard University Press, 2006), pp. 1–2, 13–25.

the typical reaction informed by a sense of justice ranges from moral outrage through attempts at reform to civil disobedience or even revolt. When the second condition (call it *the reciprocity condition*) is seriously unsatisfied, what happens, in keeping with the conditional nature of the disposition to be just, is the gradual erosion of the willingness to comply with norms that are themselves regarded as largely unproblematic. In post-Mao China, we are witnessing a serious failure to satisfy the second condition, and thus China's crisis of justice is essentially a breakdown of reciprocity. As such, the crisis manifests itself in a widespread lack of trust both in other members of society to comply with basic norms of social coexistence and cooperation and in the ability of the state to enforce compliance with such norms where enforcement is appropriate. The presence of so many free riders who routinely get away with free riding exacts too high a material and psychological cost on others, and, not surprisingly, people of ordinary moral caliber who otherwise would be quite willing to follow basic norms of justice gradually shed that willingness in the absence of secure expectation of reciprocation from other members of society.

5

We have seen that the validity condition is not a sufficient condition of willingness to comply with norms. Such willingness requires further support in the shape of one or more other necessary conditions. One such further condition is the reciprocity condition just considered. There is yet another condition, one that has played an even bigger part in China's moral crisis. This condition has two components. The first – call it *the authority condition* – is the ungrudging acceptance of the authority that stands behind norms. This condition, though by no means unique to communist China, nevertheless figures with special prominence in it, in that the Party-Government is the only institutional initiator and authorizer of moral norms, not just legal norms. The second component, of equal importance in the Chinese context, involves the role of exemplars and the general perception that those who are supposed to be exemplars are living up to this role. Call this *the exemplar condition*. This condition, though conceptually distinct, is substantively continuous with the authority condition in China, in that those who make up the authority behind the norms, that is, the Party-Government as embodied in its officials at various levels, are the same people who must play the role of exemplars in acting on the norms.

The authority condition and the exemplar condition have an important feature in common, namely, that they both explicitly place an institutional intermediary between norms and ordinary moral agents. For this reason, we can think of these two conditions as components of one larger condition, which may be called *the identification condition*. It is through identification with moral authority and moral exemplars that ordinary moral agents in a moral culture like China's acquire an understanding of norms and the motivation to act in accordance with them. What is important in the notion of identification here is that ordinary moral agents' access to norms is understood as necessarily mediated by the relation in which they stand to moral authority and moral exemplars. This relation has gone awry in post-Mao China, and we can see the resultant crisis of identification in its two component crises – a crisis of authority and a crisis of exemplification.

It is not difficult to infer a crisis of authority from the fact that the Party-Government, the sole institutional source of moral norms, actively engages in various forms of moral exhortation and yet there is no shortage of people who act in disregard of such exhortation. Given the crucial role of political authority in Chinese moral culture, the high incidence of norm-violating behavior tells a special story.

Nor is it difficult to detect a crisis of exemplification in a lack of exemplars who command public credence. This is one of the gravest consequences of widespread official corruption and public knowledge of it. Corruption – by no means necessarily present everywhere in Chinese officialdom and yet well in excess of a minimal critical mass sufficient to cause alarm – looms large in the public perception of officials, and because the reliance on exemplars remains largely unchanged in Chinese moral culture and public officials are exemplars par excellence, the effect of this perception is one of rampant negative exemplification. Official corruption is imitated, as it were, in countless ways by people who are not in a position to practice corruption but who nevertheless follow the example of corrupt officials in throwing moral scruples and fear of sanctions to the wind.

From this fact something of fundamental importance about Chinese moral culture can be extrapolated, namely, that in this moral culture the moral self is formed on the basis of identification. Ultimately, a moral crisis is a crisis of the moral self, a crisis of moral willingness or moral agency. Where such willingness is undermined by a crisis of identification, it can be inferred that the very formation of the moral self in question rests on what I have called the identification condition, comprising the authority condition and the exemplar condition. I shall have more to say on this subject in Chapters 4 and 6.

6

More generally, whatever social or psychological mechanisms are involved in the formation of a moral self, they must somehow produce that element of willingness which defines a *moral* self. It is this element of willingness characteristic of a moral self that makes a crisis otherwise involving mere behavior a moral crisis. A moral crisis is a crisis of willingness to act in conformity to moral norms for moral reasons. As such, a moral crisis is distinct from a pure crisis of enforcement of norms and calls for a distinct kind of explanation. Indeed, some significant degree of moral willingness is constitutive of strictly moral behavior and therefore is constitutive of the very possibility of a moral crisis. I have hypothesized that the social production of this moral willingness in Chinese moral culture depends on a distinctive mechanism of identification. This hypothesis needs elaboration and testing, and other mechanisms may play a part as well. At the core of this effort to make sense of China's moral crisis is the idea that moral willingness must be produced somehow, or else there would be no moral self, moral behavior, or moral crisis to speak of.

Not surprisingly, Chinese moral vocabulary contains an apt term for this willingness: *zijue*. *Zi* means the self and *jue* the sort of awareness and motivation that is part and parcel of being a moral self or agent. The moral crisis we are talking about is nothing but a crisis of *zijue* thus understood. To get to the bottom of China's moral crisis, therefore, we must give a reasonably accurate account of the structure of the Chinese moral self, that is, an account of the kind of *zijue* that is now in crisis. Only such an account will put us in a position to render a philosophically informed and culturally nuanced understanding of the moral crisis as a crisis of a distinctively Chinese moral subjectivity that happens under specific social, economic, and political conditions. Because there is no ready-made account of moral subjectivity fit for this purpose, I have to propose one of my own, at least in a rough and ready fashion, as I shall do step by step in some of the chapters that follow. It has been a major part of my aim in this chapter to set the stage for such an account so that I will be able to work on different aspects of it with the benefit of an overview, if only a very partial one.

2

Political Order, Moral Disorder

I

Thirty years after China set off on the path of reform that has changed it beyond recognition in so many ways, what I have called the dialectic of the Chinese revolution is yet to run its full course.[1] The contradictions that make up this dialectic – between the lingering idealism of a moribund socialism and the ascendant materialism of a brave new quasi-capitalist world – retain much of their potency, and in this sense China is still very much in the transition from Mao's social order to a new one. We live amidst the ever renewed fallout of that transition, one of the most telling manifestations of which is a moral crisis with no end in sight. A phenomenon worth serious reflection in its own right, this moral crisis is also a point of entry into other problems, such as that of legitimacy, that have dogged China's reform from its start to the present day. It is for its significance on both counts, and especially with a view to comprehending the relation between its moral and political dimensions, that I shall examine the moral crisis again in this chapter.

What is particularly striking about this moral crisis is that it has endured and even worsened alongside determined attempts by the party in power to maintain leadership and monopoly in the propagation of systems of belief and meaning. Despite the gradual relaxation of central control in the economic sphere and in many aspects of everyday life, the propagation of systems of belief and meaning, in morality no less than

---

[1] See *Dialectic of the Chinese Revolution: From Utopianism to Hedonism* (Stanford: Stanford University Press, 1994).

in politics, remains the prerogative of the state alone. It is one of the few crucial domains of life on which state political control is still strictly imposed.

This domain is distinctive, however, in that it has an internal dimension – the more or less active appropriation, or "internalization," of belief and meaning – as well as an external one – the propagation itself – and yet only its external dimension is amenable to effective monitoring and management. Not surprisingly, such management has succeeded in one way but failed, or succeeded far less, in another. It has succeeded in preventing alternative systems of belief and meaning from emerging in the jealously guarded public domain of morality and ideology or at least from acquiring sufficient critical mass to compete with the official one. Yet it has fallen some way short of getting the official system of belief and meaning understood, accepted, and absorbed – in a word, internalized – by the populace. Up to a point, but increasingly less so, people still have to act, in public, as if they embraced this official system, but more and more of them have learned to cope by going through the motions without taking up the spirit. What is the spirit anyway? This creates a troubling situation: systems of belief and meaning that might have a chance to be internalized and help give significance and direction to everyday life are not allowed much room to develop, on the one hand, and the only system that is given free rein offers little that lends itself to internalization, on the other, and the result is an *inner* vacuum of belief and meaning.

2

This situation has been much analyzed in terms of "moral vacuum" (*daode zhenkong*), "crisis of belief" (*xinyang weiji*), and so on, and various official solutions have been tried. I do not disagree with this line of analysis, which I myself follow to some degree in Chapter 1, but I want to push it further by working with a more expansive sense of what a moral crisis involves and thus providing a new perspective on the composition of the crisis and on the logic of the official attempts to cope with it. To this end, I want to begin by reproducing here a set of claims I first made in 1994 – claims that can usefully serve as a point of departure for this chapter and which it is part of my purpose to refine and modify.

In *Dialectic of the Chinese Revolution*, I proposed an account of the Chinese communist experiment in terms of a movement from utopianism to hedonism via nihilism. By utopianism, I meant, simply put, the whole system of beliefs and practices informed by the communist ideal. By hedonism, I had in mind the increasingly openly acknowledged and guilt-free pursuit of wealth and pleasure that was set in motion by the initiation of economic reform in the late 1970s. With the term nihilism, I designated the erosion of belief in communism that paved the way to hedonism. By the late 1970s, there could be little doubt that utopianism had largely ended up in nihilism. Nor was there much doubt that nihilism had in turn somehow contributed to the burst of hedonism. The really tough question had to do with the relation between utopianism and hedonism: Is this relation best understood predominantly in terms of continuity or break? I came down in favor of continuity, and among my most important reasons for doing so was the realization that, despite its ascetic appearance, Maoist utopianism was actually the sublimation of hedonism – a sublimation that was made necessary by conditions of dire poverty and made possible, and given direction, by belief in a communist future. By the same token, the outbreak of hedonism in post-Mao China was nothing but the desublimation of the original utopianism – the undoing of the original sublimation – thanks at once to a significant reduction of poverty, with the realistic prospect of yet further reduction, and to the loss of belief in the communist future that had earlier sustained the sublimation. In the context of this trajectory, desublimation means, then, the descent of utopianism into hedonism via a combination of nihilism and improved material conditions.[2]

When I first presented such an account of the dialectic of the Chinese revolution back in the early 1990s, I thought that China's problems had been greatly simplified – which is not to say improved – by the desublimation of utopianism into hedonism. On the basis of this assessment, I located the prospect of future crises almost entirely within the framework of the new hedonism – in terms of a possible "management crisis of hedonism," as I called it.[3] With the benefit of twenty years of hindsight, it is now clear to me that I seriously underestimated potential contradictions between the economic and the political imperatives of the order that was then emerging, or, put another way, between the radically new organization of desires and the in part (though only in part) old organization of power relations. These contradictions have come to the fore since, in the form of the simultaneous intensification of propaganda drawing on slogans and practices reminiscent of the Mao era on the one hand

---

[2] For a more detailed account of this process as well as the antecedent process of sublimation, see ibid., introduction and chap. 4.
[3] Ibid., pp. 241–42.

and the unimpeded growth of the hedonistic and consumerist ethos on the other. In view of this development, I now find it necessary to revisit the subject of desublimation and couple it with the idea, as it were, of resublimation.

3

But first I want to present three reasons why I think desublimation remains a useful concept for understanding the nature of the transition from Mao's China to the era of reform, despite the need for a more sophisticated treatment. First, the concept is that of an integral process involving three distinct dimensions of equal importance, epistemic, moral, and corporeal, so that through it we can grasp the unity of these distinct dimensions of the moral-political trajectory of post-Mao China. The *epistemic* dimension has to do with belief in the truth – the correctness and the feasibility – of communism as a moral-political system. The *moral* dimension is a matter of the stringency of that system's moral codes and practices, that is, of the degree to which they require self-denial and self-sacrifice in favor of collective interests. The *corporeal* dimension pertains to the organization of desires, in ways that are more or less ascetic or hedonistic. The unity of these dimensions of desublimation – and of sublimation in the opposite direction – lies in the fact that all living and effectual worldviews and moral beliefs must command the credence of those involved and be embodied in everyday corporeal practices.

Second, the very concept of desublimation helps draw attention to the otherwise easily neglected corporeal dimension of practices that are all too often apprehended in overly conceptual moral or political terms. When we put the accent on this corporeal dimension, we think of the reorganization of desires, in post-Mao China, in increasingly hedonistic rather than ascetic ways. If we replace "hedonistic" with "self-regarding" and "ascetic" with "other-regarding" (or "collective-regarding"), we will be shifting our attention to the moral dimension of desublimation. On this dimension we are concerned directly not with the organization of desires (or relation with oneself) but with the organization of power relations (or relation with others). The organization of desires and the organization of power relations are closely linked, of course, and it would be interesting to examine this link in the context of Mao's China and after. But undertaking this task (although I will not do it here) presupposes identifying the organization of desires as a distinct dimension in the first place. The concept of desublimation helps us do just that.

Third, and especially important for my purposes in this chapter, by distinguishing the three dimensions of desublimation and yet taking careful note of their close relationship, we will be able to spot contradictions in attempts to reverse desublimation in one or two but not all three dimensions. This is not to suggest that it would be better or wiser to reverse desublimation comprehensively, in all three dimensions at once. As far as present-day China is concerned, a comprehensive reversal of desublimation is simply not on the cards, and this is (arguably) a good thing, too. What *is* being attempted, as we shall see, is a selective or partial reversal of desublimation. To understand and assess this selective or partial reversal, we cannot do without a clear distinction between the three dimensions of desublimation. Indeed, only on the basis of this distinction are we able to understand what is going on as a selective or partial reversal of desublimation.

4

Let me say a little more about each of the three dimensions of desublimation in order then to say something about why they tend to go together. By the epistemic dimension of desublimation I mean the decline of belief in the truth of communism as a system of action-guiding (and state-legitimating) ideals, ideals that used to make the sublimation of hedonism into utopianism possible. This decline is not a purely epistemic matter but an integral part of the process of desublimation: it is the devaluation not of an epistemic system as such but of the epistemic *basis* of what happens in the moral-political and the corporeal spheres.

By the moral dimension of desublimation, I have in mind the relaxation of state prescriptions of altruism, collectivism, and so on, on the one hand, and the reduction of behavior in keeping with such prescriptions, on the other. This change in moral standards and behavior is bound to affect moral agents in both body and soul.

Finally, by the corporeal dimension of desublimation I refer to the gradual replacement of the ascetic organization of desires with a more and more hedonistic one. This replacement goes hand in hand with the gradual withdrawal of negative moral and political judgment on the expression and satisfaction of desires, not least the desire for pleasure and consumer goods.

To see how the three dimensions of desublimation implicate one another, take the moral dimension, for example, and start with the antecedent process of sublimation. If people are to act on a moral code that enjoins altruism and collectivism, both of which involve a high degree of self-denial, they must be presented with a set of reasons for doing so, reasons to which they are able to give credence. In Mao's China, those reasons took the form of the whole belief system known as communism. At the same time, people must be able to control their own desires in order to act in altruistic ways: it is much easier for them to practice altruism or collectivism if they are also schooled in asceticism. Every member of a revolutionary collective "carries within himself a small traitor who wants to eat, drink, make love," as Elias Canetti colorfully puts it,[4] and this hedonism, rather than any so-called egoism or individualism per se, is the archenemy of altruism and collectivism. This explains why in Mao's time asceticism (*jianku pusu*) and altruism-collectivism were almost always preached in the same breath, and – to bring in the epistemic dimension as well – almost always with some reference to communism. Now, once the belief system on which prescriptions of altruism and collectivism rest is weakened, and once asceticism ceases to be a regular feature of everyday life, the practice of altruism and collectivism begins to lose not only its rationale but also what we may call its corporeal condition of possibility. Thus unfolds the multidimensional process of desublimation.

That we must see sublimation and desublimation in this comprehensive way is because a certain way of organizing power relations (in terms of altruism and collectivism, and ultimately, of denial of self and obedience to authority) has a close affinity with a certain (ascetic) way of organizing desires, and because both in turn must, short of relying exclusively on coercion, rest to some degree on belief in the truth of a certain (communist) doctrine. Thus we tend to encounter sublimation in all three dimensions at once, and the same is true of desublimation.

5

It is one thing to suggest, as I have just done, that the three dimensions of desublimation – and of the antecedent process of sublimation – go naturally together. It would be something altogether different to say, however, that those who preside over the massive social transformation I am calling desublimation must think and act accordingly and hence proceed along all three dimensions at once and to the same degree. As a matter of fact, there is every indication that they have been trying to halt

---

[4] Elias Canetti, *Crowds and Power*, trans. Carol Steward (New York: Farrar Straus Giroux, 1984), p. 23.

or slow down desublimation in its epistemic and moral dimensions while actively promoting desublimation in its corporeal (not least consumerist) dimension. What has resulted from such attempts is an uneven process of desublimation that is rich in contradictions. This unevenness, or the effort to produce it, is dictated by the overriding need to maintain a semblance of public belief in the legitimacy of the political order, on the one hand, and by the almost equally pressing systemic need for heightened consumerism as part of the new economic order, on the other. At bottom, the contradictions that mark the uneven process of desublimation are contradictions between the political and the economic imperatives of the brand-new type of society that has taken shape, gradually but inexorably, since the start of the reform.

How to keep these contradictions in check – as it is impossible to resolve them without fundamentally changing the new dispensation itself – is one of the toughest challenges for present-day Chinese politics. The fact of the matter is that desublimation has actually occurred quite evenly in all three dimensions, to a degree sufficient to give rise to the "moral vacuum" or the "crisis of belief" referred to at the start of this chapter as symptoms of a systemic breakdown. Thus, the relative evenness of desublimation, or comprehensive desublimation, is the problem, to begin with, and what I have called *uneven* desublimation, with all the contradictions it entails, has resulted understandably, as it were, from official attempts to tackle this problem. Maintaining the existing political system in the face of an increasingly even or comprehensive desublimation no longer seems a viable or safe option. The officially preferred state of affairs, it appears, is one that may be described in terms of a partial resublimation – *resublimation* in the sense of undoing some of the desublimation that has occurred or restoring some of the sublimation that has been lost, and *partial* because this resublimation applies only or chiefly to the epistemic and moral dimensions. This has been attempted for some years now, with apparent ups and downs, to be sure, but more recently with an increasingly clear-sighted and firm sense of the necessity of the task.

If an even process of desublimation is fraught with risks, not least political ones, the attempt to counter such risks through partial resublimation is in danger of looking like a farce. Given, as I have noted, that the three dimensions of sublimation and desublimation have a natural tendency to happen together, *partial* resublimation, however expedient, is doomed to frustration. In the case of current attempts at partial resublimation, it should come as no surprise, with the corporeal dimension missing, if resublimation does not materialize in the epistemic and moral dimensions, either. Nor should it be a cause for surprise if this kind of selective resublimation does not make any but the most superficial sense to those generations of people who never went through the process of sublimation in the first place and cannot rely on their memory to understand what is going on in the current experiments with partial resublimation.

6

In such moves, resublimation takes the form of a seeming revival, the bringing back of the substance or spirit of an earlier sublimation that has unraveled during the reform. It is arguable, of course, that what is being revived is not so much the old system of belief and meaning as the old ethos of conformism and mass allegiance, together with the institutional means of creating and sustaining this ethos. Whatever the case may be, the important thing is that what is being revived depends for its meaning and possibility of internalization on the old social and political context, marked as it was by a future-oriented asceticism. That context alone made sublimation in the epistemic and moral dimensions both necessary and possible and helped give substance and motivational force to those moral and political values that were part and parcel of this process of sublimation. There is little doubt that that context itself is not being brought back, and this is clear from the absence of the corporeal dimension from the current attempt at resublimation. For those with no experience and memory of that context, what the current partial resublimation is reviving are mere discourses, discourses that bear little relation to a *habitus*, a concrete way of life with its real pressures for sublimation. Just imagine how little sense it would make to try and force the younger generations to understand and act on the moral-political imperative "Serve the people," a dictum that used to be meaningfully embedded only in an ascetic, anti-consumerist form of life, itself in turn (we must not forget) an integral part of a communist project in full swing.

What about those who went through the original process of sublimation and can draw on their memory to understand what is being revived? Major difficulties stand in the way even of their *re-internalizing* the old values now. Obviously, the attempt at resublimation is being made in a social and political context that is very far removed from the original one in which those ideals used to make some kind of sense to them by serving as more or less plausible interpretations of their everyday ascetic and state-controlled existence. It could even be argued that those ideals were but ways of making a virtue of the necessity of a materially impoverished life as organized in a holistic and future-oriented fashion. Now that that kind of life is no longer either a matter of necessity or an expression of virtuousness, any attempt to bring back the old moral and political values that had their meaning and function only in that life is likely to strike those who used to live by those values as pure propaganda. Those who have memories of the old values are of course perfectly capable of going through the (discursive) motions, with a little updating here and there, if they wish to or have to, but they can no longer embody those values because the living context of those values belongs to the past, and most have no desire to return to that past.

7

None of this is contradicted by the seemingly widespread nostalgia for the Mao era. The main objects of nostalgia, the sort of things many people seem to hark back to with approval, are certain features of the Mao era – such as a guaranteed livelihood, relative equality of income, and low incidence of monetary corruption – that are often exaggerated or taken out of context in response to the perceived lack of these features in the post-Mao period. The nostalgia appears to be real, however, much of it having some easily appreciable point and at least some basis in reality regarding aspects of the past and contrasting aspects of the present.

Even so, there is little evidence to suggest a widespread desire to return wholesale to the Mao era – to its kind of life and the spirit and ethos appropriate to it. Most of those who remember Mao with reverence or affection are no keener than anyone else to relearn the ascetic values Mao espoused, still less to go back to the highly regimented life in a closed and comprehensively state-controlled society. It is their sense of being unfairly left out, or left behind, rather than any conscientious refusal to join the new form of life that breeds their resentment and nostalgia. One should not be surprised if the selective nostalgia thus motivated is more likely to be found among the worse-off, especially among those who have joined the ranks of the worse-off since the reform. This is a dark spot on the record of the post-Mao reform and speaks volumes about the class character of the reform. Among the not so badly-off, nostalgia carries a rather different meaning, bespeaking their desire to have the best of both worlds or else expressing a measure of dissatisfaction with their relative place in a new form of life which they otherwise prefer to the Maoist one.

Distinct from such intuitive and personally motivated nostalgia are more politically conscious and more organized ways of appropriating the Maoist past in which nostalgia sometimes plays a part. But these latter moves show a similar ambiguity and, upon scrutiny, no more resolute desire to return to the Maoist organization of life with its integrity intact. There is, for example, a certain effort to conceive forms of production and shared life, in opposition to the current largely capitalist regime of atomistic and consumerist individualism, on the model, say, of working-class agency supposedly found in factory life in the Mao era. While this kind of attempt is wholly admirable in its normative quest and social imagination, it must be said that the room for spontaneous grassroots agency in Mao's time – spontaneous not only in the sense of not being orchestrated from above but also in the sense of being allowed to happen without fear of politically colored punishment – is hugely exaggerated and misunderstood. But then this too is partly understandable, in the spirit of the proverbial tiger's leap, as the aim of the new utopian experimenters is not to restore a past, with its unique conditions of possibility and its share of problems, but only to retrieve fragments of the past with sufficient plausibility (or sufficient vigilance against wishful reconstruction) to serve as hints for an exercise of the imagination focused on the present.

Such preoccupation with the present is even more obvious in the case of a certain defense of Mao's achievements as a nationalist and state-builder, as the founding father, one might say, of what has come to be conceived in current political parlance as China's grand project of national revival, or as a champion of equality and the rights of working people. Conspicuously absent from these lines of defense are even vague references to Mao as leader of the communist project. This should leave us in no doubt that the point of invoking Mao is not to pit the supposedly communist China under Mao against the increasingly capitalist China after Mao. Rather, the point is precisely to claim credit for the achievements of the latter on behalf of the former and, on this basis of reinterpreted causality and continuity, to make the case and mobilize public sentiment in favor of more state-centered or more egalitarian agendas for the future. Whatever one may think of such agendas, one has little reason to regard them as truly radical: there is no negation of the reform as a whole, no attempt to revive the communist project or even to appropriate the reform in its name, and no clarion call to arms against what in Mao's books would today more than qualify as oppressors and exploiters. There is no telling whether Mao himself would appreciate his renewed relevance in an increasingly depoliticized cause of national revival and social justice that has left his vision of society and the China shaped in his image irrevocably behind.

8

As long as the desire for a wholesale return to the Mao era is lacking, there is an obvious limit to how much can be accomplished by heightened attempts in the media (e.g., TV dramatization or re-dramatization of wartime and peacetime "revolutionary" heroes or events) to construct memory for those who lack the experience presupposed by resublimation and to reconstruct the memory of those whose recall of the Maoist past is too negative to serve as an aid to resublimation. To be sure, the old experience of poverty, hardship, and struggle is recaptured to some degree in the media representation of revolutionary deeds and personalities in the past. And implicit in that representation is a re-valorization of those ascetic and combative values that served as the vehicle for sublimating the unfortunate experience of poverty into the willing embrace of an ascetic existence for the sake of posterity's eventual enjoyment of material and spiritual plenitude in a communist society. What is missing is any relevant similarity between that past experience and people's experience today. Equally missing, by the same token, is any connection between the old values – values that used to sublimate that experience – and a present experience that clearly does not call for the same kind or degree of sublimation. In the absence of such a connection, the implicit re-valorization is only of disembodied values, values that have outlived their usefulness and can no longer inform everyday, corporeal practices. Memory can be created and re-created through media representation, up to a point, but such representation cannot by itself create the relevance of such memory for the context of life today, still less that context itself.

In this way, partial resublimation can easily end up as resublimation out of context. If such resublimation is unlikely to give a new lease of life to old moral and political values, what can it possibly accomplish? One of the things it can do, perhaps even effectively, is to keep the public space of belief and meaning occupied and to send a "hands off" signal to all alternative sources of belief and meaning that might otherwise expand and compete with the official one. In view of the internalization requirement for any system of belief and meaning, some may regard the increased levels of official propaganda as amounting to little more than going through the motions – and this on the part of initiators and recipients alike. Yet these motions are by no means idle, for they may succeed in the external dimension of political management despite lack of success in the internal one. The result of this combination of success and lack of success is, predictably, the vacuum of belief and meaning that is so often talked about.

It is possible that those who are presiding over the project of partial resublimation are not unaware of the likely outcome of their efforts. Should this be the case, it is not inconceivable that current ideological operations not only tend to perpetuate the vacuum they are supposed to fill but are designed to achieve this second-best result.

9

There is even a sense in which this second-best outcome appears to dissolve, or at any rate render harmless, the contradictions between the intensified propaganda of socialist values (resublimation) and the increasingly entrenched reality of hedonism and consumerism (continued desublimation). The latter, after all, is where the real action takes place and what does the real work of legitimation – of sorts – in that the Communist Party's ability to maintain popular acceptance depends more than anything else on uninterrupted economic growth and ever rising standards of living. While the idealistic-sounding propaganda on its own commands little attention and even less credence, it is nevertheless the only discourse in terms of which the economic achievements of the reform and the material basis of political legitimacy are publicly interpreted. And as long as the real goods are delivered, few have the incentive to subject the interpretation to serious challenge, and many have indeed come to believe it, if only half-heartedly, at least to the extent of seeing the Communist Party as the only political agent capable of leading the China it has single-handedly created and presiding over its continuing prosperity and stability, for all the corruption and social injustice.

It may seem that such skewed legitimation is innocuous, with both parties to the process getting what they are after. Indeed it is, from the narrowly political point of view, as long as the economy keeps growing at the requisite pace and something is done and seen to be done about the gross social injustice and staggering relative poverty that are raising mass resentment close to boiling point. But success at this kind of legitimation – supposing it can last – is one thing, and internalization of its constitutive values quite another. So we have an ambiguous and volatile state of affairs: the political power of the Communist Party is more or less happily taken for granted, and yet the values that ostensibly underwrite the Party's distinctive claim to that power and are ostensibly meant to inform the ethical and moral life of China's new breed of wealth-chasing and pleasure-seeking subjects fall on cynical ears. If this diagnosis is roughly correct, we are in for a protracted moral crisis in the form of a disjunction, that is, of a superficial legitimacy without internalization of its ostensibly constitutive values. It would take extraordinary moral imagination and political ingenuity, and much else, to steer China out of this crisis toward a new conjunction of political and moral order.

3

Freedom as a Chinese Question

1

It is a sad comment on the character of political discourse in our time that freedom, expressive in one form or another of a general human need under modern conditions of life, has become an increasingly debased currency through relentless ideological exploitation. This is manifest as much in the superficial criticisms of China for its supposed lack of freedom in comparison with Western societies – the latter all too often taken for granted as lands of freedom – as in the predictable retorts that China has no shortage of freedom or that too much freedom would lead to social chaos. I have no wish to join the chorus of such criticisms or to leap to China's defense. The question worth our while is whether there is a real problem of freedom, that is, lack of freedom, as viewed from within the Chinese context and, if so, how the problem can be fruitfully formulated and approached. I believe there is, and I also believe that any reasonably open-minded approach to the problem must be free of the assumption that such a problem does not exist, or exists only to a lesser degree, in other, especially Western societies. This means, in turn, that we must work with a general understanding of freedom that steers clear of this assumption and is able to delve deeper into the nature and constitution of freedom than this assumption makes possible.

2

As a starting point, it seems safe to say that freedom is a value. But even this barest of claims immediately prompts a question with no straightforward answer, indeed a question that seldom presents itself, namely: what is freedom a value *for*? We are often given to understand that freedom is something so basic that it does not serve anything larger or deeper than itself. This does not seem right, if only because many forms of human life have existed without the value of freedom playing any role in them, and yet we are inclined to grant that these are valuable forms of recognizably human life. Unless we deny that these forms of human life have anything of importance in common with those other forms of human life that are informed by the value of freedom, we are left with an unavoidable assignment, that of searching for the most humanly significant common denominator among different forms of human life. And *that*, whatever it may turn out to be, is what freedom as a value is valuable for. The most promising candidate for this most significant common denominator, I want to suggest, is agency, and thus our attempt to come up with a general understanding of freedom unencumbered with partisan presuppositions must take a detour through a discussion of agency.

By agency I mean, roughly, a distinctively human form of meaningful causality in which causal efficacy (or power, as I prefer to call it) is appropriated through, and in the service of, a self or center of meaning (or subjectivity, as I prefer to call it). To capture this notion of agency in a serviceable formula, we can think of agency in terms of "power organized as subjectivity," or "subjectivity achieved through power."[1]

Power is to be understood in a broad sense to cover all instances of human causal efficacy. Nietzsche's account of agency is an obvious point of reference here, but only provided that the term *power* as used by Nietzsche is given a more abstract construal than some of his remarks appear to suggest. This is especially necessary in view of Nietzsche's claim that "life itself is *essentially* appropriation, injury, overpowering of what is alien and weaker; suppression, hardness, imposition of one's own forms, incorporation and at least, at its mildest, exploitation."[2] For our purposes, this claim needs to be taken more abstractly so that power means human causal efficacy in general and may or may not literally take the

---

[1] This concept of agency is largely a Nietzschean one, of which Mark Warren has given an excellent exposition. See Mark Warren, *Nietzsche and Political Thought* (Cambridge, Mass.: MIT Press, 1988). The expression "power organized as subjectivity" is taken from p. 59. My own account of agency here draws on Nietzsche and Warren, especially at the early stages, but is meant to be judged on its own merit rather than in terms of accuracy of representation of either source.

[2] Friedrich Nietzsche, *Beyond Good and Evil*, trans. Walter Kaufmann (New York: Random House, 1966), aphorism 259.

form of injury, suppression, or exploitation. As a characterization of power rather than particular instantiations of power, Nietzsche's formulation "overpowering of what is alien" is accurate only if taken in this more abstract sense.

Power as such is indiscriminate, or without object, and meaningless, or without subject, until it is organized as subjectivity, until it contributes to and issues from a self. We might indeed say that the distinctively human significance of power lies in the formation and maintenance of a self as a center of meaning and subjectivity, along with its reflexive dimension in the shape of a sense of self. Neither power nor subjectivity exists by itself for a human being. A self is not anything like a metaphysical essence but rather a human capacity that comes to be realized only through concrete activities or, in the terms we are using, experiences of power. Only through such experiences, cumulatively and unceasingly, is a self able to emerge and persist: a subject who forms so-called intentions and causes things to happen in accord with such intentions, registers such intentions and the effects of carrying them out as emanating from and belonging to a self, attaches value to this self and its activities through interpretation, and, of course, who does all these things as a subject among subjects. Thus, distinctively human power always means the power of a self, or else power would be an instance of causal efficacy or expenditure of energy that is devoid of all distinctively human significance and motivation. On the other hand, a self cannot be formed or sustained independently of experiences of power, or else it would be no more than a potential. It is this active constitution of the self that I mean to capture by the idea of agency in terms of power organized as subjectivity. To put this point in more explicitly Nietzschean terms, we might say that what Nietzsche calls the will to power is, in the human case, the will to selfhood through power.[3]

Crucial to the organization of power as subjectivity is a mechanism we may call *attribution*. Organizing power as subjectivity is, in an important sense, a matter of attributing power to someone who thereby becomes, or continues to be, a subject. A subject, an "I," is formed and sustained

---

[3] Nietzsche's insight here is twofold: seeing selfhood as systematically dependent on power and, more radically, showing that even the self, not just our picture of the external world, is in an important sense a construction. Nietzsche writes, for example, that "the 'subject' is not something given, it is something added and invented and projected behind what there is" (Friedrich Nietzsche, *The Will to Power*, ed. Walter Kaufmann, trans. Walter Kaufmann and R. J. Hollingdale [New York: Random House, 1967], sec. 481).

on the basis of an ongoing series of such attributions. Not all attributions will do, of course, but only those that are to one degree or another socially sanctioned or normalized. A "normal" self, then, is one who is capable of making and accepting "normal" attributions. Such attributions take the form of praise and blame, reward and punishment, and, in general, of holding individuals responsible for certain classes of happenings and creating a memory and conscience commensurate with such responsibility.[4]

That certain attributions regularly succeed and serve well enough as the basis of a certain type of subjectivity does not make these attributions true, however. Attributions are acts of interpretation, and, as such, are plausible or implausible, rather than true or false. Humans are not agents by virtue of some a priori, inalienable property but rather constitute themselves as agents through systems of attributions that are somehow plausible to themselves and members of their relevant group. Accordingly, agency is not a fact of human experience that is amenable to empirical proof but an interpretation of experience that is subject to conditions of plausibility. Its proper mode of vindication, of the kind that matters to what Kierkegaard calls "existing" human beings, lies in the feeling of power and, ultimately, the constitution of self that such feeling makes possible.

3

Power attribution and subjectivity constitution take place through values, and, as we may expect, all human societies have values that perform this function in one way or another. Freedom (or, more precisely, individual freedom) is one such value: it is distinctive in that it makes possible and valuable the direct and explicit attribution of power to the individual qua individual and the formation of a corresponding type of subjectivity. Thus, it would be a mistake to reduce agency to freedom or to equate agency with freedom. While all humans constitute themselves as agents through attributions of power, only in some societies do they accomplish this task by invoking values such as freedom. Because the constitution of subjectivity through attribution of power is a defining feature of human

---

[4] See, for example, Friedrich Nietzsche, *On the Genealogy of Morals* (and *Ecce Homo*), trans. Walter Kaufmann and R. J. Hollingdale (New York: Random House, 1967), second essay, secs. 1–3; *The Gay Science*, trans. Walter Kaufmann (New York: Random House, 1974), aphorism 354.

being as such rather than only of human being in, say, a liberal society, it is necessary to think of freedom as but one strategy for the execution of this task, a strategy we may call *agency-through-freedom*. What is unique about this strategy is the attribution of a very significant, even sometimes an unbearable, amount of power to the individual under such familiar descriptions as autonomy, liberty, and choice, and the formation of a type of subjectivity supposedly belonging to the sovereign individual. Whether this strategy works, and how it works when it does, is a matter of the relation between the uses of freedom as an interpretation and the everyday practices to which this interpretation is applied. Given this way of looking at freedom, two questions present themselves as especially pertinent: first, of what everyday practices, exactly, does the value of freedom serve as an interpretation; and, second, under what conditions does this interpretation acquire plausibility in the eyes of those who are subjects of this freedom?

Since freedom is a value, that is, a *valorizing* interpretation, it is not meant to apply to activities that are unimpeded or unconstrained in a merely de facto sense. As a value, freedom serves to organize power as subjectivity, and it does so through the more or less plausible subsumption of activities under the valorizing description of freedom. It is through the regular performance of such subsumptions that agents come to think of themselves as *acting* freely (power) and *being* free persons (subjectivity).

This does not mean that such agents act truly freely and are truly free persons in some objective or realist sense. The notion of freedom used here is social or cultural, not metaphysical. Thus understood, freedom is a constructed and acquired property of members of a society in which freedom happens to be a value. Members of such a society act freely and are free persons to the extent that they are able to make attributions of power, to one another and each to oneself, under the plausible rubric of self-determination, as opposed to social (as distinct from natural) external determination, and to form and sustain a corresponding type of subjectivity in which one is able to see oneself as the sum total, as it were, of one's freely chosen and freely performed actions.

The extent in question is subject to two general limitations that inhere in the very nature of human beings as social beings. Our notion of freedom is of the freedom of such beings, and this freedom is intrinsically constrained by two forms of social external determination: identification and subjection.

Identification is built into the social form of human freedom in that, barring the rarest of exceptions, the identity of a subject, no matter how freely chosen, depends on identification with some social category of being that is prior to the act of choice. By identity I mean the concrete form that subjectivity takes. A subject that forms and sustains itself through experiences of power is always a specific kind of subject, that is, a subject with a particular identity. Identity picks out those domains of activity in which experiences of power are meaningfully organized as subjectivity. These identity-relevant domains of activity are, in turn, socially rather than individually established and sustained. Thus, when we act as so-called free individuals we actually, for the most part, choose our projects from among those that are already constituted as valuable or meaningful by our society, or at least by a portion of our society. Only by carrying out such *socially* valorized projects or choosing from socially valorized categories of being are we able to act freely and be free *individuals*. If freedom receives its direction from identity, identity is acquired through *identification*.

There is a sense in which identification itself is made possible by subjection as something both prior and ongoing. It is the process of subjection that creates subjects in the first place, subjects capable of realizing freedom through identification.[5] When individuals reach a point at which they are able, and can be trusted, to be free and to act freely, they will have already been shaped in a particular way – down to their innermost being, including their desire for freedom and their tendency to act on this desire in particular ways. It is a basic fact of the human form of life that, even in the most liberal of societies, individuals are determined before they can come to determine themselves, and how they proceed to determine themselves cannot but forever stand in a causal relationship to the prior determination from the outside. The notion of subjection brings out the fact that individuals have *no choice* but to be so determined from the outside and *no other way* to acquire any form of subjectivity at all. Thus, acting freely and being a free person, no less than acting in any other way and being any other kind of person, rely on a background of compulsion, and this is as true of the nature of subjectivity itself as it is of the empirical process of socialization. There is no way, in principle or in practice, that freedom can bypass subjection.

Identification and subjection make up a social background of irremovable limitations against which freedom can be intelligibly conceived and practiced as a value. Any interpretation of human acting and being

---

[5] See Louis Althusser, "Ideological State Apparatuses," in *Lenin and Philosophy and Other Essays*, trans. Ben Brewster (New York: Monthly Review Press, 1971), pp. 127–86 at p. 182.

in terms of freedom that does not take cognizance of this background must be considered an overinterpretation, an interpretation that makes people out to be freer than they are or could be. And such overinterpretation is ideological if it can be shown to serve some reprehensible cause, such as domination, by placating the dominated with illusions of freedom.[6]

4

It is essential to bear in mind the notion of freedom as a value as we approach the question of freedom in the Chinese context (or in any other context, for that matter). It is not freedom in some de facto sense but freedom as a value interpreting and shaping reality that is the proper object of scrutiny and appraisal. If China lacks freedom, the freedom it lacks is not de facto freedom – negatively, the absence of obstacles to whatever people may want to do, or, positively, the presence of abilities to do whatever people may want to do. It is impossible to measure de facto freedom, for there is simply too much of it to measure and there is no way of being selective without relying on some notion of *meaningful* freedom. And, of course, as long as a notion of meaningful freedom is lacking, there would be no point in measuring de facto freedom in the first place. If we are to measure instances of de facto freedom at random, on the other hand, a society like China may well have more of them than a so-called free society does, and this abundance of de facto freedom may not be a good thing by either society's standard of meaningful freedom. So, once again, de facto freedom is not an appropriate object of measurement. What about approaching de facto freedom in a qualitative rather than quantitative fashion, that is, by focusing on specific freedoms that are regarded as important or salient in some way? The problem, of course, is that freedom in this qualitative sense already presupposes some notion of meaningfulness and thus takes us beyond freedom in a purely de facto sense. It makes no sense to talk about freedom in a society or to compare one society with another in terms of freedom as if it is some objective set of facts that we are measuring or appraising. It does not make sense to say, for example, that China lacks freedom in some objective, de facto sense.

---

[6] For an account of ideology as a combination of epistemic confusion and service to reprehensible ends, see Raymond Geuss, *The Idea of a Critical Theory: Habermas and the Frankfurt School* (Cambridge: Cambridge University Press, 1981), p. 13.

Nor does China lack the *concept* of freedom. Indeed, China *cannot* lack such a concept, for the simple reason that, as what we may call a normal human society, China abounds in practices in which people hold one another responsible and, by implication, treat one another as free, and vice versa.[7] However, it is one thing for a society to have the concept of freedom in the sense of having a practice whose idea presupposes it and something very different for that society to have the concept of freedom as an interpretation of reality that is thematized and valorized. It is one thing for freedom to figure as a necessary condition of responsibility and something very different for freedom to be considered important in its own right. In Chinese moral culture, the idea of freedom (say, in the shape of *zijue*, meaning a certain conscientiousness) is present in the first sense, as it has to be if moral life is to be at all possible, but not, for the most part, in the second.

What China lacks, then, is the *value* of freedom – freedom thematized and valorized in such a way as to inform how people conduct and see their lives. This is what makes freedom important, and with this notion of freedom in place, we can begin to make worthwhile observations about de facto freedom in relation and in contrast to it.

It is a fact of enormous significance and consequence that certain de facto freedoms began to exist in the People's Republic of China for the first time with the launch of market reform and have been allowed to expand, especially since the early 1990s, at a pace that is nothing short of breathtaking. Chief among these are the freedom to acquire private wealth, the freedom to indulge one's desires (for sex, for consumption, for information, and so on), and the freedom to live in another country out of preference or discontent. It is difficult to overstate the amount of energy, individual and collective, that has been poured into activities made possible by these de facto freedoms. There is also the thrill, again hard to exaggerate, that comes from the reduction of material scarcity and the lifting of moral inhibitions after decades of asceticism and of the highly moralized regimentation of everyday life. Finally, with the dizzying rise in material standards of living and the corresponding enlargement of the scope for material inequality, more and more people, but especially the new rich, have discovered in wealth and material gratification the new symbols of prestige and power.

---

[7] On the relation between the concepts of freedom and responsibility, see Philip Pettit, *A Theory of Freedom: From the Psychology to the Politics of Agency* (New York: Oxford University Press, 2001).

What is particularly striking against this background is that no value of freedom (or, as one might say, culture of freedom) has emerged whereby people can interpret their new experiences and thus further empower themselves or enrich their lives, *in terms of freedom*. The de facto freedoms remain mostly just that, and, at least partly for this reason, of a kind that is strongly resistant to sublimation and internal evolution according to the naturally expansive logic of freedom. Given the context and trajectory of the reform, it is not surprising that these de facto freedoms, rather than others, have taken center stage in the political reorganization of libido. The headlong compulsiveness with which people have availed themselves of these freedoms suggests that something crucial is missing from their enjoyment of these unsublimated, de facto freedoms. Those who are free and understand themselves as free do not behave as if they were propelled from behind by an irresistible force. Precisely for this reason, as long as the merely de facto freedoms exist in abundance – freedoms that are part of the new social order with its hedonistic and consumerist ethos – and as long as the political order is inhospitable to the *value* of freedom, it is easy to predict that the absorption of libido into these de facto freedoms will continue to weaken the desire for the construction of freedom as a value. If indulgence in de facto freedoms still leaves something to be desired, then the only safe solution in this politically constrained setting is ever more of the same indulgence.

5

To get a more exact sense of what de facto freedoms cannot deliver, we will need a closer look at what it means for a society to lack freedom as a value. It means, first, that freedom is not available to help give meaning to what people do, such that what they do, over and above its content or substance, can be construed as an exercise of initiative and choice and indeed of self-making, and, as such, as contributing a surplus value, as it were, to what they do and who they are. In other words, freedom is not available as a *moral resource*. It means, second, that freedom is not available as a moral limit to power, as a legitimate title in the name of which we can keep others and especially the otherwise inordinate power of the state and of capital from unduly interfering with how we see and conduct our lives. In other words, freedom is not available as a socially recognized means of self-protection, in short, as a *right*.

Given that freedom is unavailable as either a moral resource or the title to rights in a society, it is only natural, third, that there are in that society no institutionally guaranteed freedoms, such as freedom of expression and freedom of the press, whose function it is to facilitate the employment of the moral resource or of the right. Such freedoms may exist on paper, to be sure, but they will be predictably idle as long as freedom is not recognized as a value in the first two senses just enumerated. It is even possible, in this context, that the existence of certain standard freedoms on paper serves less to thematize and valorize freedom than to preempt its real or effective thematization and valorization. There is no shortage of people, to be sure, who *personally* find such freedoms important and who even take it upon themselves to struggle for their realization. But until the value of freedom finds sufficient resonance in Chinese society at large, through such struggles but much more, these people have no basis yet in Chinese moral and political culture, beyond futile references to the letter of the constitution, from which to press for the implementation of specific freedoms, and it is not hard to understand why all too often they are perceived by the state as people who are only out to create trouble.

This perception in itself signals something extremely important about the relation between freedom and order in Chinese moral and political culture. Before I take up this question, however, I will need to bring up, in general terms, the securing of social order as a cultural-political task that is as essential for human society as the promotion of agency. This will pave the way for the introduction of a further, fourth dimension of the value of freedom that can be grasped only with reference to agency and order at the same time.

6

I have so far characterized freedom solely in terms of agency. Such an understanding of freedom is incomplete in that it leaves out the positive relation in which freedom can stand to the preservation of social order. The latter is not only a matter of first importance in constituting human society but also a precondition for agency, and, as such, is a cultural and political task on a par with the promotion of agency. Thus, we need an account of moral and political culture that comprises both the promotion of agency and the securing of social order. On this expanded view, we are to understand and appraise different ways of organizing moral and political life – for example, Chinese versus modern Western ways – as different paradigms for giving cultural shape to human agency in a manner compatible with meeting the need for social order, or, to shift the emphasis, as different paradigms for securing social order while simultaneously taking care of the human need for agency. The complex character of a moral and political culture derives from the duality of its functions and from the different kinds of relation in which one function can stand to the other.

On this view of moral and political culture, a value such as freedom can be properly understood only in terms of the *combination* of the two primary functions of moral and political culture rather than in terms of its agency-related function alone. This point is worth emphasizing, as it is all too easy for common sense to misconceive the relation between freedom and order as if freedom had everything to do with agency but none at all with order. What is often missing even from better informed accounts of freedom, both in Western societies and among Chinese proponents of the value of freedom, is any inkling that freedom – the valorizing interpretation of certain human practices under the notion of freedom – may play a crucial role in securing (a particular kind of) social order and, in so doing, serve as a recipe for conformity no less than for spontaneity.[8] Think of those societies that promote freedom as a central moral and political value and are also among the most predictable. It is a remarkable feature of such societies that individual freedom goes together not only with a certain orderliness in human interaction but also sometimes with a considerable degree of conformity and even uniformity, in such matters as political opinion, lifestyle, and so on, notwithstanding certain conventional divisions along lines of class, race, and gender. That order and conformity can be secured in this way, often more effectively and always less obtrusively than is possible in a society that pits order against individual freedom, suggests the need for a different explanatory framework for approaching the relation between freedom and order, a framework that will disabuse us of the understanding of freedom in terms of agency alone.

Michel Foucault's idea of a "mode of subjection" points us in a useful direction for building such a framework. According to Foucault, every morality, whatever content it has as a moral code and whatever actual behavior it helps produce, must rely on what he calls an ethics or ascetics, that is, the way in which individuals constitute themselves as "subjects" of the moral code. A mode of subjection is a dimension of ethics thus understood, and by it Foucault means "the way in which the individual

---

[8] This idea is made familiar by Michel Foucault, among others. For a useful Foucauldian account, see Nikolas Rose, *Powers of Freedom: Reframing Political Thought* (Cambridge: Cambridge University Press, 1999).

establishes his relation to the rule and recognizes himself as obliged to put it into practice,"[9] or "the way in which people are invited or incited to recognize their moral obligations."[10]

I believe we can capture an essential aspect of freedom in a liberal order if we think of freedom in such an order as a mode of subjection. The idea here is that a valorizing interpretation of human activities in terms of freedom works as the central device of the mode of subjection suitable for a liberal order, that is, as the chief manner in which individuals are brought to act willingly in accordance with the kind of moral and political code that defines a liberal order.[11] This way of thinking about freedom shifts our attention from the misleading question of whether people, say in a liberal order, *are* free to a more appropriate and fruitful question, namely: under what conditions may people come to think of themselves as free or self-determining, while happily and unknowingly allowing themselves to be so massively determined by forces from the outside?

The all-important thing is that those who subject themselves to social external determination under the description of freedom must find the description itself plausible as an interpretation of their real existence – or, as Louis Althusser would have it, of their imaginary relationship to their real conditions of existence. Clearly, obliviousness of external determination is a condition of the experience of freedom, and in this sense freedom is an illusion, a misrecognition of external determination as self-determination. Full obliviousness is both cognitive and affective, that is, marked by the simultaneous absence of knowledge and concern, but merely affective obliviousness – the inability or unwillingness to take certain kinds of social external determination with moral seriousness – may be enough to do the trick. In either case, it is a no less profound truth

---

[9] Michel Foucault, *History of Sexuality*, vol. 2, *The Use of Pleasure*, trans. Robert Hurley (New York: Vintage Books, 1990), p. 27.

[10] Michel Foucault, "On the Genealogy of Ethics: An Overview of Work in Progress," in *The Foucault Reader*, ed. Paul Rabinow (New York: Pantheon Books, 1984), pp. 340–72 at p. 353.

[11] The kind of moral and political code typical of a liberal order has at its center the idea that it is up to individuals to decide how best to lead their lives. To be sure, people want this kind of freedom not only for its own sake but in order to pursue one conception of the good or another. But it is to be expected, in any liberal order, that people will pursue diverse, often conflicting conceptions of the good, and that many will value the possibility of revising their conceptions of the good. Thus, a shared and enduring identification with a liberal order cannot come from any particular conception of the good, or even from any particular set of conceptions of the good, but must come from the more abstract notion of freedom to pursue and revise conceptions of the good. In other words, the mode of subjection must take the form of freedom, not the good.

than is found in the unmasking of freedom as illusion that such illusion or misrecognition has *real* conditions of possibility. Indeed, other things being equal, the more obvious (to observers) it is that the application of the value of freedom to certain or all activities involves misrecognition, the more demanding or substantial must be those conditions that need to exist if such misrecognition is to be plausible (to the participants).

There must thus be something real about freedom in a liberal order – not about freedom itself but about the conditions for the plausibility of the value of freedom as an interpretation of a way of life. On the other hand, that certain real conditions – such as a significant amount of discretion in the domain of private life, along with a modicum of participation or consent in the choice of government – must exist in order for the misrecognition of external determination as freedom to be possible does not change the fact that in an undeniably significant sense it is misrecognition. The important thing, then, is to recognize the reality of *the conditions for the plausibility of the value of freedom* and yet avoid the mistake of equating the presence of such conditions with freedom itself.

It is only when we think of freedom as belonging to a mode of subjection with its own conditions of plausibility that it is possible to accommodate in our account both aspects of freedom in a liberal order: its moment of illusion and its moment of reality. At the level of phenomena, these moments translate into the experience of freedom, on the one hand, and the seemingly contradictory practice of conformity, on the other, but it is the seamless conjunction of these that is truly the hallmark of a liberal society. Indeed, the conjunction is so seamless that we should speak of freedom and subjection not as if they are separate moments but, more precisely, of freedom as a mode of subjection. As such, freedom *simultaneously* helps give a specific expression to the human need for agency and bring agents into line with the particular kind of order that prevails in their society.

This, one might say, is the "secret" of a liberal society, the formula that makes a liberal society seemingly the least coercively governed large-scale society hitherto invented. The subsumption of human activity under the description of freedom, matched by conditions that render such a description plausible, allows individuals to participate willingly and even actively in their subjection and conformity to a social order that supposedly rests on their untrammeled freedom. The element of willingness in such participation has the magical effect of changing the psychological character of subjection itself, turning the process of identification with and subjection to social categories of being into an *experience* of freedom.[12] When individuals think of themselves and their conduct as free, this will make a world of difference in how they relate to mechanisms of social control, for they will act in socially expected ways under the description of freedom and therefore take initiative and pleasure in doing so. And because they derive pleasure, and indeed a sense of identity and self-worth, from what they regard as exercises in freedom, they will dispense with much of the need for external supervision and enforcement. Thus, the idea of liberal government consists essentially in creating and maintaining conditions that render plausible the interpretation of individual conduct in terms of freedom. Part of this involves the proliferation of everyday practices to which the value of freedom can be applied, and another part involves making invisible the background of identification and subjection as forms of social external determination. To the significant if never anywhere near complete extent that this idea is matched by reality, the rest of government is self-government, unsurprisingly the most reliable and the least psychologically costly form of government there is.[13]

Nor should it be surprising that, given the background of social external determination, such self-government does not necessarily promote the flourishing of individuality as it is supposed to do. Individuality and spontaneity are often no more present in a liberal society than they are in societies in which the value of freedom does not figure so prominently or at all. The reason why we need to treat freedom as a mode of subjection in order to make sense of this fact is that freedom and subjection are utterly inseparable in those phenomena that stand in the way of individuality and spontaneity in a liberal society. Without the idea of freedom (as subjection), we would be at a loss to explain how liberal government mostly takes the form of self-government. Conversely, without the idea of subjection (through freedom), we would be helplessly baffled by the degree of uniformity and conformism in societies that pride themselves on how much liberty their members enjoy.[14] Once we think of freedom

---

[12] As Rose puts it, "What began as a social norm...ends up as a personal desire" (*Powers*, p. 88).

[13] See Mitchell Dean, *Governmentality: Power and Rule in Modern Society* (New York: Sage Publications, 1999), p. 12.

[14] As Pierre Manent writes, "The experience of modern democracy puts before us a strange contradiction: democratic man is the freest man to have ever lived and at the same time the most domesticated," and he goes on to ask, "how, since the dog whose contentment the wolf envies is not unaware of the collar to which it is tethered, modern man is so

as a mode of subjection, it should not be hard even to see that there is no great difference between an exercise in freedom and the practice of conformism as long as the background of social external determination is made invisible and ordinary individuals play no significant part in shaping it.

We catch a salutary glimpse here of negative lessons that we shall ignore at our peril if we truly set great store by freedom. But before attending to such lessons (in terms of the notion of critical plausibility), I must first explore the positive potential in our discovery that freedom as a mode of subjection is capable of catering to agency and social order at the same time.

7

The unique advantage of freedom as a mode of subjection is that it makes possible one unified formula for carrying out the twin social tasks of providing for individual agency and securing social order and is more effective than any other approach at preempting what might otherwise be an implacable tension or conflict between these equally important tasks. For this reason, it is only when freedom serves as a mode of subjection that it can *safely* serve also as a moral resource and as a right. A peculiar invention of modern Western societies, this use of freedom is entirely foreign to mainstream Chinese moral culture, both past and present. Far from being a mode of subjection and hence compatible with and indeed systematically productive of order, freedom is typically pitted against order in Chinese moral culture. Behind this understanding of freedom is an idea that has profoundly informed mainstream Chinese moral and political culture to this day, namely, that the two primary tasks of society – the promotion of agency and the establishment of order – are to be so conceived that they must be carried out separately.

Because of this separation and of the assignment of freedom to the category of agency, there is a built-in tension between freedom and order. Order is always achieved at the expense of freedom, even if this sacrifice

---

sure of being ever more free if in reality he is ever more subjected?" (*The City of Man*, trans. Marc A. LePain [Princeton: Princeton University Press, 1998], p. 181). Manent immediately proceeds to give one answer. Across the ideological spectrum, Herbert Marcuse gives another, in *One-Dimensional Man: Studies in the Ideology of Advanced Industrial Society* (Boston: Beacon Press, 1964). On a more empirical plane, see David Riesman's classic account of "other-direction" in *The Lonely Crowd* (New Haven: Yale University Press, 1950).

of freedom for order is considered a matter of course. Likewise, freedom is always permitted at some cost of order, even if it must be permitted to some degree given the human need for agency and even if the degree in question is so determined as not to pose any serious threat to order. The proper solution, according to this way of thinking, is conceived in terms of balance, but the underlying logic remains that the more there is of one, the less there is of the other.

When order and freedom are thus separated, there is no question which should come first. Insofar as it is granted that freedom is necessary for agency, freedom is something positive that must not be denied outright or denied qua freedom. But freedom must be put in its place, for freedom is also pitted against order, and in case of serious conflict it is easy to decide that order must take priority over freedom. After all, order is a precondition of agency, and freedom can effectively contribute to agency only with the secure fulfillment of this precondition. Thus the crucial fact of Chinese moral and political culture in this regard is the understanding of agency and order as separate tasks and of freedom and order as pulling in different directions. The rest follows from this understanding.

Given that freedom is perceived as somehow opposed to order, and given that in view of this opposition, order will understandably have priority, society must guard against the possibility of *too much* freedom. Too much freedom is whatever degree of freedom happens to pose a threat to order, as determined especially by those with the authority to impose order. Too much freedom means not enough order, and lack of order is, without question, a bad thing – bad in itself and bad also because it undermines agency. So while freedom is not to be completely denied, it needs to be constantly kept in check in the interest of order. When this fails, so the logic continues, chaos will result.

The specter of chaos thus hovers with unpredictable menace over this understanding of order and freedom. Among the imperatives of government, nothing is more important than keeping this specter from descending upon the ever fragile human order of rulers and the ruled, and so the correct balance between order and freedom must always be struck with generous margin on the side of order. The permissible amount of freedom is subject to this margin. Any freedom that seems to intrude into this margin will smack of chaos, and those who agitate for such freedom will incur the charge of stirring up trouble from ulterior motives.

There is even a sense in which this charge has an element of truth. In keeping with the understanding of order and freedom as being necessarily in conflict, China's political system is so arranged that order is indeed incapable of withstanding certain freedoms that figure prominently in societies where freedom is not pitted against order but serves as a mode of subjection. Just as this understanding is a fact of Chinese moral and political culture, so the vulnerability of order in the face of freedom is a fact of the Chinese political system. These are man-made facts, of course, but facts nevertheless, and, as long as these facts do not change, freedom – in the shape of freedoms of speech, of the press, of association, and so on – poses a *real* threat to order, and, accordingly, order must be preserved at the expense of such freedoms. There is thus an ever present need to curtail, and at times to suppress, such freedoms, but this is a *systemic* need and, as such, has little to do with the whims or authoritarian tendencies of holders of political office, although, needless to say, the politically powerful are among the first beneficiaries of the system that has this need and would be the first to defend it. By the same token, those who act in such ways as to hamper the system as it goes about maintaining order in its own distinctive manner are, wittingly or unwittingly, challenging the system itself. And, until the system is changed, they are, wittingly or unwittingly, undermining the social order that the system knows how to procure only in its own way.

So why not change the system? Why not, indeed! But first we need to understand exactly what fundamentally needs to be changed, and, moreover, we need to understand with similar rigor and freedom from illusion whatever alternative arrangement we might hope to put in its place. What fundamentally needs to be changed is not merely a political arrangement but, at a deeper level, the conception of freedom and order that informs it. This conception must be abandoned for setting freedom and order at loggerheads, but what we can responsibly envisage as a replacement is not going to be the promise of untrammeled possibilities of agency but must instead be a conception of freedom that is capable of answering the twin human needs for agency and order at the same time. As we have seen, however, freedom thus conceived has its liabilities as well as advantages. If we are to prefer this conception of freedom because it secures more freedom for all and not because it happens to advance our narrow interests given our place in society, then we must do so with sober cognizance not only of the advantages but also of the liabilities of freedom as a mode of subjection.

8

This preference is far from being a normative luxury. In an important sense, the profound social transformation of China in recent decades has overtaken us, to the point where we risk permanent moral crisis as a society if we do not begin to find a place for freedom in our moral and political culture – freedom as a mode of subjection and, either as part of this mode of subjection or in tandem with it, as a moral resource, as a right, and as concrete liberties.

The qualitatively different role of freedom in everyday life in recent decades and the correspondingly greater fear of freedom as a threat to order are symptomatic of this profound change. In Mao's China, freedom did not figure as a vehicle either for channeling agency or, still less, for securing order. It might indeed be said that within the social system that had taken shape by the late 1950s there was no need for freedom, in that any such need was preempted by a combination of social and ideological factors. Chief among the social factors was the successful monopolization by the state of almost all the means of production. This allowed the state to assume the role of sole provider of livelihood for virtually the entire population while, in tandem with this arrangement, the system of work units enabled the state to exercise nearly total control over the life of each and every member of society. As far as ideological factors were concerned, none was more important than the state's ability to induce and sustain, against a background of considerable terror directed at any hint of heterodoxy, the population's belief in the prospect of an ideal, communist society. These two factors went hand in hand, the social factor creating a way of life in which the ideal of communism made sense, and the ideological factor serving in turn to provide the principal justification for the social system.

The fact that every person belonged to a work unit and acquired not only a livelihood but also an identity from such belonging meant that people had no choice but to submit themselves to the almost total control by the state. Obedience to authority was an economic and existential necessity within this arrangement and provided the essential basis for social order. But this was far from being merely an imposed necessity. The ideology of a communist future and the charisma of Mao combined to make a virtue of such necessity and to turn a de facto lack of choice into an active pursuit of the collective cause of communism. In this way, control was made seamlessly continuous with mobilization, and the need for social order was satisfied simultaneously with the need for agency. As long as this state of affairs continued, freedom had no raison d'être *within* it, and those who wanted to go outside of it were easily enough shown to be enemies of the socialist order – and indeed of socialist agency, for freedom had little to contribute to such agency. As a collective project, communism was supposed to rely on solidarity rather than individual freedom. As a project initiated and led by a vanguard, it needed single-minded loyalty and obedience to the leader and the party rather than room for independent judgment and action. Given this conception of the communist project, insistence on individual freedom was, first and foremost, a threat to the configuration of agency in Mao's China rather than, as may be thought of China today, only to social order.

This configuration of agency – agency in the form of active obedience in pursuing a collective cause – seemed perfectly natural, except to those who tragically refused to be assimilated, as long as its social and ideological conditions remained. The success of the Mao era, while it lasted, lay precisely in creating and maintaining these conditions and thereby sustaining a distinctive form of agency. This form of agency became increasingly difficult to sustain toward the end of the Mao era.[15] The death of Mao was followed by what has come to be known as the reform, which, in three decades, has completely eroded the social and ideological conditions that once made possible the Maoist form of agency. The state's control over the means of production, especially as regards its share in providing employment and livelihood, and hence over the lives of the population, has diminished drastically, and this means nothing less than the irrevocable loss of the material basis on which the state used to demand absolute loyalty and obedience from all its citizens. Once people are left to make a living for themselves and, in effect if not in official rhetoric, to find their own identity and meaning in life, it becomes possible, for the first time under the rule of the Communist Party, to think of the state as interfering with how they choose to do so. On this momentous account, individual freedom has acquired an undeniable raison d'être it never quite had before. On the ideological front, meanwhile, communist values have made a decisive, though never officially acknowledged, retreat in favor of their exact opposites in hedonism, individualism, and consumerism, and no trace is left of the old belief in communism that was able to reduce morality to political loyalty and happily dispense with any independently based moral agency.[16]

The upshot is that the configuration of agency that flourished in the Mao era has no more life in it today, and a new configuration has to take its place. Whatever concrete form the latter will take, it will definitely

[15] See my *Dialectic of the Chinese Revolution: From Utopianism to Hedonism* (Stanford: Stanford University Press, 1994).
[16] On the reduction of morality to politics, see ibid., chap. 3.

not center around the pursuit of a collective cause with its valorization of asceticism, altruism, and obedience to the leader. In fact, a new configuration of agency, with its focus on individual prosperity and pleasure and security, has already established a firm foothold; only it has not been allowed to run its natural course. A symptom of this thwarted transition is the moral crisis that has gripped China since the start of the reform and is still everywhere in evidence.[17] With the loss of belief in communism, China stands in desperate need of a new mode of subjection for purposes of both agency and order. There is little doubt that this new mode of subjection will have to include some value of freedom, given the increasingly entrenched socioeconomic reality in which members of Chinese society have to fend for themselves as individuals, and given the growing ethos of individualism that has been an integral part of this reality. If this is so, then unless the value of freedom finds ample room for endogenous growth, there can be no fitting general rationale for willing subjection to moral norms and no end in sight to the moral crisis. In this sense, the construction of freedom as a value is an unavoidable challenge for China, a necessary condition for meeting the dual need for agency and order in the type of society that China has undoubtedly become.

There is no less urgent a need in China today for freedom as a moral resource – as a value that helps give meaning to what people do, such that what they do, over and above the achievement of concrete goals or functions, can be appropriated as an exercise in freedom, in self-making. Earlier, I distinguished between de facto freedom and the value of freedom. Since the start of the economic reform in the late 1970s, the state has gradually loosened its control over (and, in the process, shed much of its responsibility for) people's lives and, as a result, there now exists a great deal of de facto freedom, especially in economic activity and in private life. Yet there is no officially affirmed or even permitted value that, supported by a suitable institutional framework and a minimum of social justice, enables people to interpret their experiences *in terms of* freedom and thereby find meaning in their activities through the relatively smooth and morally unproblematic attribution of initiative and efficacy to themselves. It is for this reason, more than any other, that the nihilism that first arose in response to the failure of the communist experiment of the Mao era is showing no signs of abating more than three decades after the death of Mao and the introduction of the economic reform. This

---

[17] See Chapters 1 and 2 of this book.

kind of nihilism means a moral and spiritual vacuum for which no amount of material prosperity can compensate. What has been sorely lacking is not more material prosperity but more moral resources for giving meaning and more equality to such prosperity. With the dearth of moral resources, it is no wonder that the nationwide quest for individual wealth and pleasure has acquired an otherwise baffling air of desperation, with so much newly mobilized or released energy having no other channels of expression or objects to pursue. Although this frantic quest has effectively diverted energy from deliberate challenges to the political system, it has done so, and is continuing to do so, at a huge cost to the moral health of China as a culture and a society.

It would be naive to think, however, that the need for the value of freedom as a mode of subjection and as a moral resource will by itself produce an irresistible momentum toward the endogenous development of the value of freedom. Freedom, as we have seen, also constitutes a legitimate title or a right in the name of which we can claim a certain status and a certain space for action in relation to political authority. Such a value of freedom is a weapon of self-assertion and self-defense vis-à-vis political authority, and thus its introduction will entail a profound change in the political arrangement, a radical remaking of relations of power. It is difficult to say whether this will happen in the foreseeable future, and if so, how. But until this happens, Chinese society will continue to suffer from a deep contradiction: the current political arrangement is incompatible with an officially sanctioned, full-fledged value of freedom, and yet, unless such a value is developed, China will not be able effectively to meet its dual need for agency and order under its new social and economic conditions. This, I would suggest, is one of the most daunting challenges for those who want to see China thrive comprehensively and perhaps even for those who are only narrowly interested in China's sustained prosperity.

9

Implicit in our earlier discussion of the role of freedom in a liberal society are negative as well as positive lessons. Having weaved the positive lessons into my case for the endogenous growth of freedom in China, I must now respond to the negative lesson regarding the undercutting of freedom by conformism. I was at pains to show, in that earlier discussion, that there must exist in a liberal society real conditions that lend a measure of plausibility to the application of the notion of freedom to human experience. It is important not to underestimate how high this measure of plausibility can be and the significant role it plays in sustaining a liberal order. In my concern to give due credit as it were to such plausibility, however, I am according it a largely empirical status as distinct from a normative one. To say, as I have been doing, that the plausibility rests in part on conditions that are themselves real is, of course, already to grant some normative status to it as being to some degree properly grounded. But, as it happens, the plausibility in question does not quite withstand critical reflection as informed by the rationale that is internal to the liberal notion of freedom itself. So I say that the plausibility of the notion of freedom as used in a liberal society is plausible, and understandably so, but only up to a point; it does not deserve to be considered nearly as plausible as it is often made out to be. There is ample room to call into question the plausibility in the eyes of the average member of a liberal society, and thus I distinguish between empirical and critical plausibility.[18]

With this distinction, I want to suggest that in developing the value of freedom in China we should aim to do more than replicate the conditions that make empirical plausibility possible in existing liberal societies. We should, that is, have as our normative point of reference a conception of freedom that meets the standard of critical plausibility so that we have reason to *think* ourselves free instead of merely somehow *feeling* free or not feeling unfree.

What, then, is critical plausibility? And why is empirical plausibility not enough? To answer these questions, we need to pick up two concepts introduced earlier as making up an unavoidable background for the exercise of freedom. If, as we have seen, freedom necessarily involves an element of identification, indeed subjection, is there anything that distinguishes the exercise of freedom against the background of identification and subjection from lack of freedom? One thought is that where freedom is present, it redeems the identification, as it were – and by the same token the identity that rests on it – through an exercise of individual judgment and endorsement, which is itself a manifestation of agency. Likewise, the presence of freedom serves to redeem subjection if it can be brought about that those who begin as the largely passive recipients of subjection gradually grow into, as in any successful process of socialization, its active and willing subjects. In either case, what defines an exercise of freedom is not that it excludes identification or subjection but that the identification or

---

[18] I have drawn on Geuss's discussion of the "reflectively acceptable" in developing my notion of critical plausibility. See his *Idea of a Critical Theory*, chap. 3, sec. 1.

subjection leaves sufficient room for initiative and discretion to be compatible with being a subject and feeling like one. It is this fact that gives a measure of normative validity as well as psychological reality to the exercise of freedom despite its moments of identification and subjection.

Still, freedom thus construed is a matter of the choice of individual or collective projects *within* an existing framework of liberties and social necessities. Is it possible to extend the value of freedom so that it also covers our relation to this very framework? Is it possible, that is, for there to be a democratic moment to subjection? If subjection, as a precondition for the formation of subjects, is prior to any exercise of democratic intersubjectivity, is it at least possible for subjection – both its form and its substance – to be revised through the ongoing exercise of democratic intersubjectivity?

To be sure, given the very nature of subjection, it is impossible for democratic intersubjectivity to shape or reshape it in a wholesale fashion. But, just as surely, the fact that subjects are always already shaped by subjection does not preclude the possibility that they can reflect on it and reshape it in significant ways, if necessarily in the manner of internal critique and revision. The true spirit of democracy lies in exploring this possibility, in taking as far as possible the intersubjective determination of the *framework* for the exercise of freedom. Thus, the less the democratic process accepts as given, the more it will live up to the spirit of democracy.

The problem with existing liberal democracies is that questions about the framework of subjection and subjectivity are generally bracketed in the exercise of freedom and democracy alike. As a result, freedom seldom goes beyond choosing from and identifying with existing categories of being, no matter how these categories have come about, and democracy is mostly confined at best to representative majoritarian decision-making within the parameters of the given. It is an important feature of the given, of the existing background of identification and subjection, that all too often it is shaped in ways that reflect relations of domination. This political fact about the background, rather than the existence of a background as such, is what is problematic and in need of ideology critique as a test of critical plausibility.

Let us first be clear about what need *not* be ideological here. What need not be ideological is that there is something arbitrary about the liberal framework or horizon of subjection and about the particular set of freedoms to which liberalism attaches so much prominence and importance, for arbitrariness is a characteristic of all horizons. Closer to being ideological is the concealment – or perhaps more precisely the motivated lack of acknowledgment – of the arbitrariness of those freedoms that are visible on the liberal horizon, of the possibility of potentially significant freedoms that are not visible on the liberal horizon, and, not least, of the liberal horizon itself as a horizon. This lack of acknowledgment largely takes the form of naturalizing what is social, but this too is a feature of horizons in general, as is the largely unquestioning acceptance of social, in principle alterable, constraints by mistaking them, for all practical purposes, for natural, inevitable ones.

Such lack of acknowledgment becomes fully ideological, however, when it is accompanied by the refusal to contemplate alternative horizons, alternative thematizations, and valorizations, even when serious candidates of such alternatives are put on the table, along with the naturalistic defense of the liberal horizon and the freedoms rendered visible and important by it whenever the latter are under challenge. Such stubbornness of vision and epistemic confusion raise the suspicion that there is something to hide, not in the sense that those involved, knowing it themselves, consciously hide it from others, but in the sense that they benefit from that which is hidden and from its being hidden. What is hidden in this sense is that the liberal horizon, as historically and currently constituted, systematically goes together with a distinctive set of unequal relations of power. These relations of power involve the all too well-known domination of capital over labor, of administration over people, and the priority of the imperative of profit and efficiency over all human needs that are incompatible with it. It is becoming increasingly true that the freedom permitted by such relations is freedom *within* a totally commodified and administered society and thus freedom without spontaneity and freedom as a form of control. In the final analysis, what is concealed or not acknowledged is just the set of unequal relations of power that has helped give shape to the background of identification and subjection – as well as the ever present possibility of reshaping that background if a society were really open and democratic.

What is thus ideological about the liberal use of the value of freedom is that the liberties that are rendered visible and important by the liberal horizon, and the liberal horizon itself, are guarded with a close-mindedness that befits the defense of vested interests in maintaining relations of domination. Accordingly, what is nonideological or anti-ideological is not the defense of an alternative set of liberties and an alternative horizon, but rather the willingness to acknowledge the socially framed character of liberties, to be as open as possible about any construction of liberties, not least when alternative constructions are proposed, and to render any such construction as free of domination as possible. The antidote to the ideological use of the notion of freedom is the attempt to redeem the identification and subjection that make up its necessary background – to redeem identification, itself unavoidable, by making it amenable to endorsement that is as free and informed as possible within the context of the subjection that is given, and, going a step further, to redeem subjection itself, also unavoidable, by making it maximally amenable to democratic discussion and revision.

On this view of freedom, we have no reason to take any existing societies, including liberal ones, as setting a sound enough example of how to conceive and realize freedom, although some societies must be credited with invention of an idea of freedom that is capable of attaining sufficient empirical plausibility to serve as an important value. Empirical plausibility is double-edged, however. Insofar as it rests on real conditions that are sufficient for the creation and continuation of the plausibility in question, it is commendable. But insofar as it conceals relations of domination, it is deceptive, indeed deceptive just to the degree that it is plausible.

It is an important fact of Chinese perceptions of the value of freedom that such perceptions are heavily influenced by what is taken to be the state of freedom in Western, liberal societies. Two mistakes are equally to be avoided in this regard. The first is the mistake of taking the empirical plausibility of the notion of freedom to be sufficient and promoting in China conditions that, in Western liberal societies, serve to maintain such plausibility. The other mistake is to correctly see through the partial deceptiveness of such empirical plausibility only to conclude, erroneously and even dangerously, that there is no more to freedom than ideologically engendered appearance and therefore freedom is not worth having. What people of both persuasions miss is that the cause of freedom can be conceived as a constant struggle for the creation or renewal of social conditions that render the value of freedom critically plausible.

This is unfortunate; the more so because there is no denying that China has become sufficiently like modern, liberal societies in relevant respects that *some* value of freedom is unavoidable if the dual task of providing for individual agency and social order is to be properly fulfilled. Equally, China has become sufficiently like modern, liberal societies in relevant respects that, if we are not extremely careful and vigilant, we could easily end up in a totally commodified and administered society the moment we think we have brought about Western-style freedom. Perhaps worse, in that the liberal (or neoliberal) style of total administration could be compounded by our legacy of the communist variation on the same theme. In this context of possibility and danger, our best bet is to recognize the empirical plausibility of the liberal value of freedom for the achievement that it is and at the same time to let our awareness of its limitation and deceptiveness motivate us in our struggle for *real* freedom – for freedom that can stand the test of critical plausibility.

4

Freedom and Its Epistemological Conditions

I

The account of freedom in the last chapter is informed by the idea that freedom is (the name of) a configuration of agency, a culturally specific way of giving form to the human need for agency while catering to the no less basic human need for order. This is not a familiar approach to freedom, still less a standard one, and I will need to say more about it by way of elaboration and justification, especially by considering freedom alongside another, very different configuration of agency. Before I do so in the next chapter, I want to discuss in this chapter a more familiar or standard approach to freedom as presented by Thomas Metzger in his important book, *A Cloud across the Pacific*.[1]

There are two reasons why this work by Metzger is a particularly suitable object for analysis in this context. First, Metzger addresses with considerable incisiveness and intellectual daring what one may call the background discursive conditions of freedom, especially as they pertain to epistemology, and such conditions must figure in any effective attempt to shed light on freedom as a human construction. Indeed, Metzger devotes most of his book to a wide-ranging treatment of such, especially epistemological, conditions, and in commenting on him I shall cover roughly the same issues. Second, Metzger pursues the question of freedom in a comparative context involving China and the West. This is exactly the kind of comparative context in which I myself find it necessary to take

---

[1] Thomas A. Metzger, *A Cloud Across the Pacific: Essays on the Clash between Chinese and Western Political Theories* (Shatin, Hong Kong: The Chinese University Press, 2005). Hereafter cited parenthetically by page number only.

up the issue of freedom again in Chapter 5 as a complement to my own account of freedom in Chapter 3.

Metzger thinks quite conventionally in terms of the presence (in the modern West) or relative absence (in China) of freedom but thought-provokingly understands this difference in turn as deriving from or belonging to the larger difference between epistemological pessimism (in the West) and epistemological optimism (in China). I think Metzger is wrong at both steps, but importantly and instructively so. In this chapter, I provide a critical response, to be followed in the next chapter by my own alternative account. But even in my critical discussion of Metzger, my aim is not only to pave the way for my alternative account but, just as importantly, to examine Metzger's work in its own right.

2

A menacing cloud hangs across the Pacific, over relations between China and the United States, according to the title of Metzger's book. The book's subtitle, however, refers to a clash between China and the West as a whole. In the book itself Metzger shifts flexibly, often imperceptibly, between these two distinct loci of tension, motivated by two closely related concerns. On the one hand, he is interested in actual political conflicts, especially those that cast "a deep shadow over the prospects for world peace in the next century" (2). There is little doubt that such conflicts exist more between China and the United States than between China and Europe (or loosely speaking, between China and the West as a whole); in any case two distinct if related sets of conflicts are identifiable here. On the other hand, Metzger takes actual political conflicts to result in large part from philosophical differences over how to think about politics, about knowledge, and especially about the relationship between the two – with freedom (politics) and its epistemological conditions (knowledge) making up a prominent case in point. In addressing such philosophical differences, the subject matter of his book, Metzger speaks of China and the West, and in this context there is something to be said for this pairing.

Metzger's highly sustained attempt to probe beneath conflicts of national interests in search of underlying epistemic differences – in his own words, "to uncover the epistemological basis of a major pattern of international tension today" (147) – yields a number of claims that are of uncommon interest for comparative political philosophy. According to Metzger, China and the West are separated by an epistemic divide, above all, a divide created by a modern Western paradigm shift in the conception of knowledge that has yet to take place in China. Metzger calls this paradigm shift the Great Modern Western Epistemological Revolution (GMWER), claiming that the paradigmatic epistemic differences that result from embracing or rejecting this revolution are the root cause of more tangible conflicts of interests between China and the West, especially between China and the United States. It is on account of these fundamental epistemic differences, and of the central political values that go together with them, such as freedom and its opposite, that each side views the other not as a competitor in a shared game but, at worst, as a force that is immoral and irrational (2–3). This unnecessary elevation of the stakes, in Metzger's view, is what makes for the depth and intensity of the clash between China and the United States.

It follows that the key to improved political relations is to clarify and resolve the fundamental epistemic differences that underlie the surface conflict of national interests, making it resistant to pragmatic calculation and compromise. In other words, the best way to approach the actual political conflicts between China and the United States is to look at the clash between Chinese and Western political *theories* as repositories of ways of conceiving knowledge, politics, and the relation between them. What, then, is the clash between Chinese and Western political theories referred to in the subtitle of the book?

3

Metzger wisely approaches this clash in terms of differences between discourses rather than differences between entire cultures.

A large population regarded as "a society" or "a culture" typically consists of a number of such we-groups [a we-group being a set of people who share the same basic premises and can speak in terms of "we"]. The discourse of each partly overlaps, partly conflicts with the discourses of other we-groups, and the degree of overall integration varies greatly from society to society. Unless one can demonstrate a high degree of such integration or show that a population possesses only one discourse, one cannot precisely describe "a culture." That is, one can precisely describe only particular discourses. (76)

The discourses that are the main objects of Metzger's analysis are mainstream modern Chinese political thought (dubbed discourse #1) and mainstream modern Western political thought (dubbed discourse #2), discourses in which, according to Metzger, can be found the epistemic clashes that inform the political conflicts between China and the United States.

Metzger finds the central epistemic clash in the opposition between the epistemological optimism of discourse #1 and the epistemological pessimism of discourse #2, and he sees the chief political implications of this opposition as bearing on the issue of freedom. As he puts it with a disarming boldness, "discourse #1 and discourse #2 clash especially in that the former correlates epistemological optimism with thick parameters of individual freedom, while discourse #2 correlates epistemological pessimism with thin parameters of individual freedom" (25). His line of explanation for these correlations is just as bold:

> According to discourse #1,... the knowledge with which spiritually to transform the citizenry is available; the corrigible state can be expected eventually to respect the moral-intellectual virtuosi with this knowledge; and propagation of this knowledge through education can produce the thick moral parameters that will prevent the freedom of the three marketplaces [economic, intellectual, and political] from turning into license. According to discourse #2, however, maximizing this freedom even at the risk of its turning into license is the only hopeful way to try to improve society, because the knowledge needed to transform human nature and create thick parameters is unavailable, not to mention the Jacobinic dangers in trying to solder any such knowledge into an incorrigible political center. (26; see also 30, 40, 67)

Immediately obvious is the sheer importance of these claims regarding the correlations, and I shall devote the bulk of this chapter to unpacking these claims by examining the wealth of arguments Metzger provides in their support. But first it is worth noting that Metzger's *political* take on freedom, as distinct from his approach to freedom's epistemological dimensions, falls into a rather conventional and not particularly illuminating mold. The underlying idea is that freedom is largely the opposite of conformity, while the underlying political value is that, as such, freedom should be maximized and conformity minimized, though by no means eliminated. Metzger's detailed descriptions and analyses add up to a picture that is more complex than this, of course. Still, missing from that picture is any realization that as a value, that is, as the valorizing interpretation of certain human practices under a certain description, freedom is neither synonymous or continuous with license nor opposed to conformity. As we saw in Chapter 3, when freedom serves as a moral resource and as a mode of subjection in a society (and this is what freedom typically does in a liberal society), not only does it usually keep license well at bay,

Freedom and Its Epistemological Conditions

but it can contribute to conformity with an ease or excess that is one of its liabilities. This undeniable and yet seemingly counterintuitive relation in which the value of freedom stands to license and conformity suggests the need to suspend conventional wisdom and carefully unpack the notion of freedom, including Metzger's specific notion of parameters of freedom, and, above all, the need for a different explanatory framework within which to place these notions.

The central question in thinking about this framework should be conceived not in terms of more freedom or less freedom but in terms of how it comes to pass that members of a society are subjected to a social order in a manner that meets the individual's need for agency, in individual and collective forms, sufficiently for the social order to be acceptable and stable. Given this way of posing the question, what Metzger calls thin- and thick parameters of freedom can be interpreted as representing two different social paradigms for satisfying the twin needs for individual agency and for social order. It is an oversimplification and, if carried too far, an illusion, that thin parameters of freedom favor individual agency, while thick parameters of freedom are conducive to social order. Both are ways of *simultaneously* meeting the need for individual agency and the need for social order. In catering to the latter need, both involve the production of conformity, just as in serving the former need, both must allow room for individual initiative and subjectivity. Thus, we need to counterbalance the conventional way of thinking about such issues by asking, with regard to those societies marked by so-called thin parameters of freedom, in what ways such notions as freedom and autonomy figure in conformity-producing social practices, and, with regard to societies marked by so-called thick parameters of freedom, how agents are constituted if not through such notions as freedom and autonomy.

Whatever one's answer may turn out to be, it must not only address the question of how moral and political values correlate with social practices but also, and just as important, treat whatever correlations happen to exist as answering to the dual need for individual agency and social order. Therefore, if modern Chinese and Western political philosophies differ profoundly (I, like Metzger, believe they do), they do so as comprehensive strategies for meeting the dual need for individual agency and social order, not simply as doctrines regarding parameters of freedom.[2]

---

[2] It is possible that, while, say, China and the United States today have profoundly different moral cultures (as well as political systems), they nevertheless increasingly share the same capitalist economic structure. To the extent that this is the case, the two societies may be

Placing freedom within some such framework and seeing it as answering to needs even more basic or general than itself will allow us to take a much-needed step back from claims about freedom that are self-evident only to oneself and one's own side. The alternative is ideological confrontation without end. We know all too well how futile and obfuscating such confrontation tends to be and how predictably it arises whenever freedom is treated as a first premise so that any proposed alternative premise must be either positively mistaken or else privative and hence deficient. The fact that differences between Chinese and Western political values are so often represented as conflicting positions on freedom, even by as thoughtful a thinker as Metzger, shows the fatal attraction of precisely such ideological confrontation. To me, this fact suggests that one or both sides are involved in an ideological clash with a rather low moral or intellectual content. The Cold War may be dead, but the old rhetoric is not, and there is nothing like a big political entity like China that still calls itself socialist to help keep that rhetoric alive, with its rich store of memories and affects. Though largely a misrepresentation of China in relation to the United States and the West at large, the continuing ideological discourse in terms of freedom is itself an *ideological reality* and, as such, a contributing or complicating factor in conflicts between the two sides. All the more reason, then, to try and suspend all ideological investment in the value of freedom and dispassionately examine what freedom is, how it works, and, especially important for this chapter, under what conditions it is possible or seems most sensible and attractive. In the last regard, his ideological investment notwithstanding, Metzger has performed an invaluable intellectual service through his cross-cultural comparison of the epistemological conditions for what he calls thin and thick parameters of freedom.

4

It is interesting that Metzger uses as a neutral, common denominator between discourses #1 and #2 a concept that fits discourse #2 much more

---

said to have distinct capitalist orders, each deriving its character from the articulation of moral culture and economic structure, among other things. Thus the difference in moral culture tells only part of the story. In a similar spirit, Kenneth Surin sees in China today a capitalist "mode of production" that goes together, with respect to the "system of regulation," with "a putatively communist mode of societal regulation combined with a capitalist mode of economic regulation," in *Freedom Not Yet: Liberation and the Next World Order* (Durham, NC: Duke University Press, 2009), p. 39.

comfortably than it does discourse #1. For Metzger, "the discourse of any we-group is based on ideas regarded as indisputable by that we-group, and... we-groups loosely use generic labels like 'reasonable,' 'truth,' and 'knowledge' to lump together all the kinds of thinking based on these indisputables and to reject all the kinds that are not" (78). A substantive doubt rather than a terminological quibble is in order here, for, in all seriousness, it does not seem indisputable to me that the premises upon which a group of people thinks and acts have to be indisputable to them. Often, when such premises do not appear disputable to the people whose premises they are, this is not because the premises have been subjected to scrutiny and found to be indisputable but because they have *not* been and thus the question of their disputability or indisputability simply does not arise. In the event that the question has arisen and received a positive answer, all that seems to be necessary for such premises to serve as a basis of thinking and acting is for them to be considered plausible or not too implausible. In either case, the concept of indisputability misses what is going on, and *nondisputability* seems more appropriate: Something is nondisputable either in the sense that it is simply not called into dispute or in the sense that it is considered sufficiently plausible not to make (further) dispute imperative or necessary.

This way of looking at the matter should help rather than undermine Metzger's comparative project. For one of the things that set discourse #1 and discourse #2 radically apart is precisely whether and to what extent such nondisputables (I use this term to match Metzger's "indisputables") are subjected to scrutiny and critique. Discourse #2 may be said to represent the limit case, in which the standard used in such scrutiny and critique is nothing less than indisputability. Metzger's notion of indisputables is quite apt with regard to this particular attitude toward nondisputables but, by the same token, inappropriate for describing the much less unyielding attitude that is characteristic of discourse #1. "Nondisputables," then, can serve as a neutral term for a minimal epistemic threshold and a common denominator, with "indisputables" reserved for a more stringent epistemic demand well beyond the minimum. There is a sense in which the readiness and severity with which nondisputables, or nondisputable claims, are subjected to critical dispute are a measure of how seriously the claims are intended to be taken and are in fact taken – as illocutionary rather than perlocutionary acts. The more seriously they are taken by addresser and addressee alike, the stronger the incentive to prove that they are indeed *in*disputable, and so the greater the readiness to place them under scrutiny and to perfect the intellectual apparatus needed for the task. Paradoxically, all this increases the probability that ideas that have been nondisputable hitherto will turn out *not* to be indisputable and that what is treated as indisputable today will prove to be less than indisputable tomorrow. This profound paradox lies at the heart of what Metzger calls epistemological pessimism, for him the preeminent feature of discourse #2, just as the absence of this paradox marks the epistemological optimism of discourse #1.

5

The distinction between epistemological optimism and epistemological pessimism was first drawn by Karl Popper to describe two opposite mistakes of thinking. Metzger adopts these terms not to refer, as Popper does, to the extreme readiness to believe or not to believe, but rather to designate two ways of balancing credulity and skepticism (22). Still, in Metzger's scheme of things, discourse #1 (mainstream modern Chinese political thought) is essentially optimistic, and discourse #2 (mainstream modern Western political thought) essentially pessimistic, and this, according to Metzger, is a fundamental epistemic difference with, as we have seen, highly important implications for the place of freedom in moral and political life.

The first obvious question is what epistemological optimism is exactly optimistic about, and, as part of this question, how much of the optimism is strictly epistemological. Discourse #1 is optimistic, or so it appears, about a wide range of things, as Metzger's discussion shows but does not explicitly say, a range that includes the power of human understanding, the goodness of human nature, the efficacy of education, the feasibility of implementing moral ideals, the incorruptibility of good leaders, and so on. Within this mix, at least three broad categories need to be distinguished. The first is a purely or largely *epistemic optimism*, which places huge confidence in human epistemic powers. This optimism is supposedly reflected in such features of Chinese thought as the obliviousness of the historicity of knowledge, the treatment of all aspects of the world as forming a unity accessible to human comprehension, and the concomitant absence of the fact/value distinction (53, 66, 127–28). Distinct from, though obviously related to, this epistemic optimism is a *moral-political optimism*, an optimism about human moral powers, not least the ability to overcome selfishness, and about the kind of political institutions that presuppose such moral powers. It does not follow either from epistemic optimism or from moral-political optimism, or indeed from their combination, however, that government should take the form of "top-down control," that is, "a corrigible political center" presided over by "moral-intellectual virtuosi" (24). The preference for this kind of government must rest on a further premise, namely, the natural superiority of a select few in epistemic and moral powers to ordinary people who have enough ability only to follow. What this premise is optimistic about is not some generic human power, whether epistemic or moral, but the greater share of such power by an oligarchic or aristocratic minority that gives it the title to rule. An optimism about the epistemic and moral superiority of a ruling elite, then, or *narrow epistemic-moral optimism*, is a third element that needs to be identified.

Thus, when Metzger asks, "Is the kind of knowledge needed fully and perfectly to organize society available? Or, to put the matter more modestly, *to what extent* should people such as children, students, and ordinary citizens believe that there are people who have more knowledge than they about how they should think and live, and whose authority over them should therefore be respected?" (21), he is conflating questions of epistemic power, moral power, and epistemic-moral inequality. Once we keep these questions separate and bear in mind the three distinct elements that make up Chinese epistemological optimism, we see more clearly the tensions and possibilities that exist in this complex position. Metzger is quite right, for example, to distinguish between "(a) the belief in blind, unconditional compliance with the commands of persons occupying socially established positions of authority, such as parents, teachers, and government officials, and (b) the belief that one should autonomously search in one's own conscience for the universally true principles of life (the *tao*) and then completely obey anyone who knows what these principles are" (20). However, if such a distinction in favor of (b) as a description of discourse #1 goes together well enough with epistemic and moral optimism in theory, it nevertheless tends in practice to be more or less neutralized by narrow epistemic-moral optimism, especially by the political culture and institutions that rest on such optimism. Thus, it is a considerable exaggeration to say, as Metzger does, that the Chinese brand of authoritarianism based on (b) "legitimizes defiance of conventionally established political leaders *as easily* as it does respect for them" (20, emphasis added), although one should obviously not be surprised if this potential for defiance is realized once in a while.

The most important question here is why the epistemological optimism of discourse #1 has not led to the establishment of what Metzger calls thin parameters of freedom. This question presents itself with a compelling logic in view of the first two strands of optimism we have identified, namely, a generic epistemic optimism and an equally generic moral optimism. Since the object of these two kinds of optimism is human nature, the nature of all human beings, it follows that all human beings have it in them to direct their own lives and that it is the task of politics to create a favorable social setting in which they can do so. There is no straighter intellectual path leading from a general belief about human nature to universal moral entitlement to freedom, and, according to the sheer logic of the matter, it should not take anything more than political trial and error to move from moral entitlement to freedom to the institutionalization of this entitlement in one form or another of thin parameters of freedom. As we know only too well, things do not work this way in discourse #1, and this should give us pause. It is hard to resist the suspicion that what Metzger calls the epistemological optimism of discourse #1 is so internally balanced as to give decisive weight to narrow optimism over generic optimism. Thanks to this balance, the optimism about human nature is emptied of its radical implications and made socially and politically safe by a more pronounced optimism about elites. This marriage of optimism and elitism is perfectly illustrated by the otherwise egalitarian-sounding belief, which is part (b) of Metzger's distinction cited earlier, that "one should autonomously search in one's own conscience for the universally true principles of life (the *tao*) and then completely obey anyone who knows what these principles are" (20). So, strictly speaking, it is not epistemological optimism as such but an elitism that does not have to be part of it that stands in the way of what Metzger calls thin parameters of freedom. This is tantamount to saying that oligarchy stands in the way of freedom.

Insofar as the optimism of discourse #1 is chiefly confined to elites, then, it is little different from elitism in general as one can count on all elitism to be optimistic about the relevant capacities of elites. The question therefore is not so much whether the epistemological optimism of discourse #1 is optimistic as the degree to which it is properly epistemological in the sense of being well-grounded. Since optimism stands in a unique relationship to both future and past, it is not a simple and straightforward matter to decide when it is well-grounded. Insofar as optimism is prospective, it does not lend itself to appraisal in terms of being true or false, but insofar as it is retrospective, in the sense that all optimistic goals or aspirations will sooner or later have had enough exposure to the future to be held to retrospective account, it is perfectly fair game for judgment of its truth value. One familiar and still serviceable way of rendering this kind of judgment is in terms of the distinction between ideology and utopia.

6

The rareness with which the radical potential of the epistemological optimism of discourse #1 – not least its potential for benevolent government and equal citizenship – is realized should alert us to the possibility that this epistemological optimism, including even its more innocuous generic components, is not utopian but ideological. I am drawing here on Karl Mannheim's well-known distinction. According to Mannheim, "Only those orientations transcending reality will be referred to by us as utopian which, when they pass over into conduct, tend to shatter, either partially or wholly, the order of things prevailing at the time." And he continues:

> In limiting the meaning of the term "utopia" to that type of orientation which transcends reality and which at the same time breaks the bonds of the existing order, a distinction is set up between the utopian and the ideological states of mind. One can orient himself to objects that are alien to reality and which transcend actual existence – and nevertheless still be effective in the realization and the maintenance of the existing order of things. In the course of history, man has occupied himself more frequently with objects transcending his scope of existence than with those immanent in his existence and, despite this, actual and concrete forms of social life have been built upon the basis of such "ideological" states of mind which were congruent with reality.[3]

In the light of Mannheim's still highly illuminating distinction, I have serious reservations about Metzger's description of Chinese epistemological optimism as a species of utopianism. According to Metzger, "Chinese utopianism... differs from the Platonic idea of a perfect state imagined by someone realizing it is impracticable. This concept is missing in the history of Chinese political thought. What is basic to this history is a concept of political perfection put forward by Chinese believing it is practicable" (20). The crux of the matter is *practicability*, as claims about the relation between imagination and reality must be subjected to falsification (for all practical purposes) over time just as they must be allowed to prove themselves in the fullness of time. There is in principle some point, sooner or later, at which the past must be allowed to speak more loudly than the future and optimism must be judged to have lost its

---

[3] Karl Mannheim, *Ideology and Utopia*, trans. Louis Wirth and Edward Shils (New York: Harcourt, Brace and World, 1936), p. 192.

right to dwell in its comfortable prospectiveness. At this point, however indefinite, one must have the sobriety and courage to say "enough is enough," for or against. In the enormously long time span of the Chinese tradition, belief in the practicability of some perfectionist vision may have been held at one point or another, indeed at many points, without overstretching credulity, in which case the discourse of optimism would indeed have bespoken a utopian mentality. But it is surely implausible to ascribe a utopian mentality to purveyors of an optimistic discourse who came much later in the same tradition and enjoyed the benefit of extended hindsight, who saw the supposed practicability of the tradition's optimistic vision fail to prove itself generation after generation, who had little evidence that the political and educational institutions erected on the basis of belief in this practicability had really worked, and yet who, apparently immune to disillusionment, continued to propagate their vision of an ideal society and of ideal rulers and speak of both in seemingly practicable terms. The only plausible explanation for this otherwise mind-boggling phenomenon, it seems to me, is that the optimistic discourse must have at some point turned into an ideological discourse, assuming that it had started life as a utopian one. There is no better proof than in the fact that "the situationally transcendent ideas... never succeed *de facto* in the realization of their projected contents"[4] – the more definitively the longer the time span in question. This applies not only to the better part of the immensely long (loosely called) Confucian tradition (Metzger calls it discourse #6) but also to the selective continuation of socialist-communist rhetoric after the demise of Maoism.[5]

Metzger gives the impression that what he calls Chinese utopianism is an *enduring* feature of the Chinese tradition, a moral and political ideal that has informed the actions and tempers of generation after generation of Chinese.

One can (1) be determined to act decisively to end completely all this moral-intellectual dissonance [i.e., selfishness, corruption, irrationality, etc.]; (2) give up this radical, transformative hope but still denounce the dissonance as inexcusable

---

[4] Mannheim, *Ideology*, p. 194.
[5] For Metzger, utopianism is a thread that runs through the entire Chinese tradition right up to the present. "I would especially emphasize," he writes, "the continuity of a Chinese epistemological scene free of epistemological pessimism, the utopian belief in the political practicability of greatly reducing the role of selfishness in political-economic life, and the belief that societal transformation can be accomplished by intellectual virtuosi as super-citizens working with a corrigible political center. All these ideas were central equally to the modern Chinese discourse #1 and the Confucian discourse #6" (88).

and intolerable; (3) regard this dissonance as the normal medium of accommodative, peaceful, piecemeal, gradualistic, progressive political efforts; (4) deplore but opportunistically accommodate this dissonance; or (5) fatalistically accept it.

Certainly all five attitudes can be found in China today or perhaps even in any major society. In China, however, the four premises above [see p. 695] made up a coherent, widespread intellectual standpoint morally legitimizing options #1 and #2 and utterly incompatible with the moral legitimization of option #3. It is this extremely prominent and optimistic concept of political practicability for which the term "Chinese utopianism" is suitable (700).

If this picture of Chinese utopianism is true, the Chinese must be utterly irrational, the "moderate realism" noted by Metzger notwithstanding. The worst enemy of minimally rational belief in the practicability of a perfectionist vision is time, and more than enough time has passed and setbacks occurred to make continuing belief in the political practicability of realizing either Confucian or communist ideals utterly risible – the risible imperviousness of those who are stubbornly incapable of telling reality from fantasy. To show something to be risible is not strictly to prove it untrue, to be sure, but this does make it advisable to seek an alternative explanation compatible with the Chinese being minimally rational.

It is in the search for such an explanation that the hypothesis of an ideological use of utopian-sounding discourse presents itself. To call an optimistic or utopian-sounding discourse ideological is to suggest that its function is not that of informing radical change but that of legitimating the status quo and the rule of those who preside over it, with or without moderate improvement of the status quo on its own terms. We know for certain that optimism about elites – whether in the shape of the Confucian doctrine of sagely government or in the guise of the Leninist idea of a revolutionary vanguard – is serving this function whenever it blurs the distinction between fantasy and reality by pushing the moment of truth ever further into the future and renders itself once more immune to falsification. As long as it is believed that some human beings are endowed with the epistemic and moral capacity for an exemplary kind of rule, there can be little doubt that this kind of rule is to be preferred to any that turns a blind eye to this positive capacity in favor of checks and balances more suitable for knaves than sages. And once this kind of rule becomes a settled cultural preference and a legitimating article of faith, it is ripe for abuse as all rulers will claim to be exercising this kind of rule, or at least trying their best, happily unencumbered with all the nuisance of checks and balances fit only for morally flawed rulers. In this context, the generic optimism with its otherwise radical implications is reduced to serving as a general anthropological supplement to the politically motivated optimism about elites, enhancing the latter's credibility and satisfying the need of ideology for subtle and not so subtle slippages between the few and the many. Such ideological employment of a tamed moral optimism has been a fixture in Chinese political culture.[6]

7

There is a sense, then, in which an ideological discourse says one thing and does another without ever intending either to close the gap or else give up its claims. For an ideological discourse to function, this gap must be kept from conscious and clear view, and for this condition to be met, a discursive habit must be formed that preempts skepticism and subversion by ridding ideological speech acts, especially at the receiving end, of all intellectual seriousness. Thus, while an ideological discourse has content, this content is not meant to be taken seriously at face value. As competent speakers of a language, we all know intuitively how to react to ideological discourses, that is, how not to take the ostensible content of such discourses as an invitation for a properly epistemic response, that is, the kind of response that has the potential, a dangerous potential, to overturn the ostensible content of the discourse on epistemic grounds. What renders such a response irrelevant and futile is an unspoken aim that is fixed in advance and never intended for serious revision or abandonment should its presentable grounds fail to withstand critical scrutiny. In this sense, an ideological discourse is *nonepistemic* despite its epistemic surface, and thus to regard a discourse as ideological is, among other things, to regard it as nonepistemic.

This brief clarification allows me to venture the observation that what Metzger calls discourse #1, especially in its communist version, is predominantly nonepistemic. This is the case even when, sometimes especially when, these discourses invoke some notion of truth; here, strikingly, the very employment of the language of truth is nonepistemic. To be a competent participant in Chinese political culture is to have learned how to

---

[6] This also helps explain the dearth of systematic reflections on "moral darkness" (781) in the Chinese tradition. Rather than put lack of discussion of "moral darkness" down to lack of insight into it, it seems more plausible to suggest that such discussion would sit ill not only with the odd utopian discourse, for obvious reasons, but also with the mainstream ideological discourses of legitimation that have always rested on a highly positive account of the moral capacity of leaders regardless of the actual record.

relate to official invocations of truth. When one encounters an official appeal to objective truth (*keguan zhenli*), universally valid truth (*pubian zhenli*), laws of historical development (*lishi guilü*), science (*kexue*) in the broad sense of the true and the correct, and so on, one knows, pretheoretically but surely, that this is not an invitation for discussion of the epistemic merits of the case in question but a conversation stopper, with varying degrees of risk involved if one reacts publicly as if it were such an invitation. To respond to such an appeal with an epistemic challenge or even query is to misconstrue the official speech act and commit a category mistake. To do so knowingly rather than naively is to commit a political mistake. Small wonder, then, that in the course of their political socialization most people learn soon enough how to behave in the appropriate way: it is not a matter of daring to tell the truth as one sees it, nor a matter of having to lie against one's conscience; it is simply a matter of comporting oneself nonepistemically by going through certain expected linguistic motions, notwithstanding occasional displays of sophistication and commitment.

8

If I am right in my claim (in Section 6) that discourse #1 is largely ideological rather than utopian and in my further claim (in Section 7) that such ideological discourse is largely nonepistemic, then it follows that, even if we are still inclined to follow Metzger in seeing some kind of optimism in discourse #1, this optimism is no longer fit to be called *epistemological* as it is by Metzger. There is indeed a reason to call into question the epistemic credentials of discourse #1 even as *utopian* discourse (as we grant or suspect that it once was). If this reason stands, it should help further explain why discourse #1 (mainstream modern Chinese political thought) and discourse #6 (Confucian political thought) before it have enjoyed such longevity as ideological discourses, and help explain why in both cases the evolution of a utopian discourse into an ideological one should prove so easy, so seamless, and so unobtrusive.

The reason I have in mind is an important feature of the Chinese intellectual tradition common to discourses #1 and #6, namely, a certain practice and spirit of working with nondisputables instead of subjecting nondisputables to the test of indisputability before they are allowed to count as knowledge. I briefly discussed this feature earlier when I explained why it was necessary to distinguish between what Metzger calls indisputables and what I proposed to add in the shape of nondisputables, and it is now worth spelling out more fully.

To begin with, if in a certain way of thinking the standard of knowledge is undemanding and therefore relatively easily met, it is hardly accurate to characterize this way of thinking in terms of *epistemological* optimism. Rather, for an epistemology to be really optimistic, it must contain a belief in the possibility of knowledge *by a highly demanding standard*. This kind of optimism is a central constituent of what has come to be known as the Western philosophical tradition, beginning with Socrates' introduction of certainty as the standard that distinguishes knowledge from mere opinion. Not surprisingly, epistemological optimism thus understood can lead over time to pessimistic conclusions about the scope and even the possibility of knowledge. But without epistemological optimism to begin with, how could there be epistemological pessimism as the disappointment of initial hopes?[7]

In the Chinese case, the lack of epistemological pessimism implies precisely the lack of a prior epistemological optimism. It is paradoxically this lack of epistemological optimism that has allowed the Chinese epistemological tradition to maintain a surface optimism. I call it surface optimism in the sense that it is not informed by an underlying quest for certainty as the hallmark of knowledge. As the trajectory of the Socratic tradition has repeatedly shown, the quest for certainty goes hand in hand with skepticism and has a uniquely powerful potential to lead to pessimistic conclusions about knowledge or at the very least to deflate overly confident claims regarding its possibility or scope.[8] In the absence of this quest, it is not surprising that the main tenets of the Chinese intellectual tradition have enjoyed remarkable stability. Nor is it hard to explain the longevity of the surface optimism, for it is precisely the quest for certainty that is ultimately corrosive of epistemological optimism.

In this light, the distinction between epistemological optimism and pessimism is not a fundamental dividing line but only a derivative of

---

[7] This line of thought belongs to Friedrich Nietzsche, who has the insight both to see in Socrates "the prototype of the theoretical optimist who, with his faith that the nature of things can be fathomed, ascribes to knowledge and insight the power of a panacea, while understanding error as the evil *par excellence*" and to uncover the logic whereby "science, spurred by its powerful illusion, speeds irresistibly toward its limits where its optimism...suffers shipwreck." See *The Birth of Tragedy* (and *The Case of Wagner*), trans. Walter Kaufmann (New York: Random House, 1967), sec. 15.

[8] For an account of the inner dynamic of the quest for certainty, see Martin Heidegger, "Metaphysics as History of Being," in *The End of Philosophy*, trans. Joan Stambaugh (New York: Harper and Row, 1973), pp. 1–54.

the deeper distinction between the presence and absence of the quest for certainty. Given that Metzger is well aware of the importance of the quest for certainty (41, 44–46), it is somewhat surprising that he should operate most of the time at the level of surface outcomes rather than underlying causes. What he calls Western epistemological pessimism is the outcome of the quest for certainty turning the tables on its own products, whereas there are no comparable tables to be turned in the case of so-called Chinese epistemological optimism, and this gives these two paradigms their radically different trajectories.

The absence of the standard of certainty does not, of course, prevent appeals from being made to nondisputables in discourse #1 and discourse #6, nor does this absence prevent nondisputables from being loosely referred to in objectivist-sounding terms. It is nevertheless quite obvious that we are dealing here with a distinct paradigm. In this paradigm, regular appeals are made to truth and knowledge as a basis for normative principles and normative authority, and yet, as we saw earlier, there is relatively little *politically* permitted room for informed epistemic challenge. What has just emerged from our discussion of the quest for certainty is that within the paradigm comprising discourses #1 and #6 there is also relatively little *epistemic* potential for Chinese society to negate its own ideas and convictions through the sheer operation of its members' will to truth (given appropriate social conditions) – the sort of potential that is the ultimate hallmark of epistemic seriousness.[9]

9

While I have called into question the appropriateness of describing the differences between discourse #1 (mainstream modern Chinese political thought) and discourse #2 (mainstream modern Western political thought) in terms of epistemological optimism and pessimism, I have also alluded to one sense in which it remains accurate for Metzger to speak of pessimism in the case of discourse #2, that is, pessimistic *conclusions*

---

[9] One example of such epistemic seriousness is atheism arrived at in a certain way. "Unconditional honest atheism (and *its* is the only air we breathe, we more spiritual men of this age!)," writes Friedrich Nietzsche, "is... *not* the antithesis of that ideal [the ascetic ideal], as it appears to be; it is rather only one of the latest phases of its evolution, one of its terminal forms and inner consequences – it is the awe-inspiring *catastrophe* of two thousand years of training in truthfulness that finally forbids itself the *lie involved in belief in God*" (*On the Genealogy of Morals* (and *Ecce Homo*), trans. Walter Kaufmann and R. J. Hollingdale [New York: Random House, 1967], third essay, sec. 27).

arrived at through the pursuit of an outlook and a standard that are not themselves pessimistic.

Metzger is quite right to link epistemological pessimism, thus construed, to the quest for certainty and the resultant distinction between knowledge and opinion (41, 44). This quest has led to paradigm shifts from, very roughly put, the premodern conception of knowledge to the modern and then the postmodern. With the term Great Modern Western Epistemological Revolution, Metzger designates essentially the second of these shifts, which has been recounted many times before.[10] In Metzger's version of the story,

> the GMWER revealed a so-far unresolved problem – does the subjective side of thought outweigh the objective, or vice versa? – and in an arbitrary, intuitive, vague, but highly suggestive way alleged that the subjective side should generally be given the benefit of the doubt. In other words, sympathizing with this allegation, many Western intellectuals "turned the corner," so to speak, putting the burden of proof on those claiming to state objective truths. (47; see also 258–59)

The GMWER's application of the standard of certainty can lead to "maximum epistemological pessimism" (41–42) – the radical conclusion that nothing is sufficiently objectively certain to count as knowledge. At some distance from this is a more moderate version of epistemological pessimism, which less radically increases the difficulty of access to truth and narrows the scope of what is good enough to count as knowledge. By epistemological pessimism Metzger means sometimes the former and sometimes the latter. But the important thing is that in either case epistemological pessimism has the distinct rational momentum to lead to the positing of the fact/value distinction and the rejection of normative objectivism – in other words, to "the epistemological demotion of normative ideas from the status of true propositions or knowledge to that of ideas to which the standard of truth is not applicable" (128). And once the fact/value distinction is drawn, the important question for political philosophy concerns not so much the status of knowledge as that of values.

As far as the latter is concerned, our interest in the epistemological conditions of freedom makes it essential to identify three distinct objects of

---

[10] For example, Jean-François Lyotard, *The Postmodern Condition*, trans. Geoff Bennington and Brian Massumi (Minneapolis: University of Minnesota Press, 1984); Richard Rorty, "Heidegger, Contingency, and Pragmatism," in *Essays on Heidegger and Others* (Cambridge: Cambridge University Press, 1991), pp. 27–49; and James C. Edwards, *The Plain Sense of Things: The Fate of Religion in an Age of Normal Nihilism* (University Park: Pennsylvania State University Press, 1997), chap. 1.

skepticism and hence of potential pessimism, namely: (a) the objectivity of values, (b) human epistemic powers to grasp values (whatever the status of values), and (c) human moral powers to act on values (whatever the status of values). It makes a big difference to ways of thinking about politics whether it is believed that there are objective values. Given a belief in the objectivity of values, it makes a big difference whether it is further believed that human beings have nearly perfect epistemic powers to comprehend such supposedly objective values, and given an affirmative answer to this question, whether it is yet further believed that they have nearly perfect moral powers to act on such supposedly objective values. Otherwise, in the absence of belief in the objectivity of values, the question still arises as to human moral powers in relation to whatever values happen to be considered worthy of implementation. At each point, there is room for a more or less optimistic answer and for a more or less pessimistic answer, and it does not necessarily take pessimism about the objectivity of values, still less a wholesale pessimism, to justify prudence in the design of political institutions. It may be sufficient that human epistemic or moral powers, or both, are believed to be limited or fallible.

John Stuart Mill, for example, whom Metzger cites as an example of epistemological pessimism (30), believed in the objectivity and even priority of the good and yet argued for liberty and tolerance on the grounds of human epistemic and moral fallibility in relation to what is objectively good. What differentiates Mill as an exemplar of discourse #2 from a proponent of discourse #1 is not whether values are regarded as objective but whether (at least some) human agents are presumed to have infallible or nearly infallible epistemic and moral powers in relation to values and what institutions are necessary in the light of the assessment of human epistemic and moral powers.[11] Likewise, John Rawls, another exemplar of epistemological pessimism in Metzger's account, is able to justify what he calls "reasonable pluralism" through recourse to the idea of "burdens of judgment," that is, the sources of disagreement among reasonable persons, without taking any position on the objectivity of values.[12] To take yet another example, also mentioned by Metzger (704), Lord Acton's dictum that power corrupts and absolute power corrupts absolutely, an idea the likes of which have significantly informed Western

---

[11] As John Skorupski rightly points out, "objectivism, fallibilism, and pluralism can go together, and this is essential in a proper appreciation of Mill" (*Ethical Explorations* [New York: Oxford University Press, 1999], p. 204n17).

[12] See John Rawls, *Political Liberalism* (New York: Columbia University Press, 1993), p. 55.

political institutions, consists of deep doubts about human moral powers quite irrespective of the ontological status of values and even of human epistemic powers in relation to values.

These examples suggest that in making sense of the pessimistic conclusions characteristic of discourse #2, it is necessary to distinguish carefully between recognition of human fallibility on the one hand and skepticism about the objectivity of values on the other, and, in the case of the former, further between epistemic and moral fallibility. Although elements of all three are found in discourse #2, they do not necessarily go together and often do not actually go together. Where human moral fallibility is used as the main argument for prudence in the design of political institutions, the pessimism in question is not exactly epistemological. The other two cases do involve epistemology, but skepticism about objectivity is much more radical than belief in human epistemic fallibility. It is arguable that of the three pessimistic conclusions that make up discourse #2, only skepticism about objectivity is quintessentially part of the GMWER.

We need to pin down the meaning of this radical skepticism in order to grasp its implications for freedom – and the implications of its absence for freedom. Skepticism about the objectivity of values undermines belief in any good that is independent of human desire or choice. It is no longer possible to speak of the good as such and in the singular, as an object of quest and discovery, as something worth aspiring to regardless of what one may happen to desire, and as the locus of the highest stakes for human life. The good is no longer conceived, that is, as the goal or end of freedom and hence as something that, while needing freedom for its true realization, is bound to exist in tension with the exercise of freedom and is in principle fit to provide the right kind of rationale for guiding and, if necessary, limiting freedom. The good has lost its priority in favor of freedom. Thus, thanks in part (for we must not forget that material conditions are just as important) to radical skepticism's destructive work on the good, freedom takes on the distinctively modern meaning of supposedly autonomous individuals no longer being bound by any singular, objective, independent good. In this sense, the freedom of the modern individual is, fundamentally, freedom *from the good*. Freedom thus unbound enjoys priority, with the right (in the so-called priority of the right) serving to provide a scheme of fair and mutually compatible freedoms for everyone. Accordingly, what used to be thought of as *the* good undergoes a profound semantic and psychological change – from the singular, prior end and determinant of freedom to a mere function of freedom and thus an output, as it were, that is as diverse and divergent

Freedom and Its Epistemological Conditions 83

as the desires and choices of free agents. In those societies where the GMWER has carried the day, the time-honored notion of the good with respect to which some may have more knowledge and therefore deserve to exercise more authority, even political, than others do has irrevocably lost its place in public culture.

If there is any nearly invincible epistemological condition for what Metzger calls thin parameters of freedom, then, it must be the radical skepticism unique to the GMWER. The opposite of thin parameters of freedom, what Metzger calls thick parameters of freedom, are nothing but the good as conceived in the ancient or premodern way, the "thickness" (as it were) coming from the "priority" of the good. It is also worth noting that the radical skepticism about the objectivity of values renders skepticism about human epistemic powers superfluous, for there are no longer objective values for such powers to work on. In skepticism about human moral powers, on the other hand, radical skepticism finds a natural ally. With radical skepticism's decisive removal of one crucial precondition of moral inequality, the old-fashioned skepticism about human moral powers receives a new lease of life as a distinctively modern belief in moral egalitarianism or moral populism – the belief that by and large people are made of the same stuff with regard to moral competence, or sufficiently so in relevant respects that they ought to be treated as if they are. This lends yet further inevitability to the establishment of thin parameters of freedom.

These conditions for freedom, for what Metzger calls thin parameters of freedom, do not quite exist in China even today. When I tried earlier to show the ideological and nonepistemic character of discourse #1, I may have given the impression that I was mounting a critique. In a way I was, but only in a small way, for my main objective was to prepare the ground for making the largely descriptive point, as I am ready to do now, that in China the traditional category of the good as something prior to and independent of human desire and choice has never been dealt the fatal blow that has been part of the story of morality in the modern West. This does not mean that this category of the good or the moral values that have instantiated it in the recent past have not been the object of strong negative reactions, such as cynicism and even the will to act contrary to morality. But such reactions are not epistemological in the way that the GMWER's rejection of the objectivity of values decidedly was. Whatever the state of morality in Chinese society today, we can say with some confidence that there has been no *epistemological* overthrow of the good and, by implication, no epistemologically based triumph of moral egalitarianism or moral populism. The nihilism and moral crisis I describe in earlier chapters are moral and political, not epistemological.

This does not necessarily mean that China today lacks conditions for freedom, that is, a strong need for freedom internal to Chinese society as we find it today and favorable circumstances for meeting this need. It means only that those conditions, strong or weak, do not include the epistemological ones that have played such an important role in the rise of thin parameters of freedom in Western societies. The challenge for China is to find a path to greater freedom or thinner parameters of freedom in the relative absence of these epistemological conditions. But precisely because these conditions are absent or weak, it is unlikely that when freedom finds its natural place in Chinese society through endogenous development it will do so under the (implicit) rationale that the good has lost its ground and priority so that freedom must mean, at the deepest level, freedom from the good. This may augur a more tortuous path to freedom, but there is no reason to assume that it will be a worse path. Above all, insofar as the epistemological factors we have considered make a difference, we should expect that China's path to freedom will be different and that therefore the shape of its future freedoms and their meaning are likely to be different as well.

10

I want to conclude this chapter on an altogether more speculative note. My speculation is prompted by a systematic ambivalence on the part of Metzger about discourse #2 and the GMWER and, by extension, about discourse #1, an ambivalence that seems to suggest some deep, unresolved problem.

Metzger shows an entirely positive attitude toward discourse #2's epistemic cautiousness and moral realism and yet evinces a deep uneasiness with its deflationary effects on collective political psychology. He sees discourse #1, on the other hand, as displaying a healthy dose of hopefulness and resoluteness necessary for motivating efforts to improve political life and yet lacking the sobriety and prudence to make such efforts successful. Metzger thus credits each of these two combinations for exhibiting something valuable that the other lacks while taking issue with each for missing something just as valuable that the other has in abundance. In other words, both discourse #1 and discourse #2 are "partly irrational" (121), in opposite ways. This state of affairs Metzger dubs "the seesaw effect" (115–21), and according to him, whether the seesaw effect can be avoided is "the key issue in the search today for a rational political theory" (558). This is a bold and thought-provoking claim.

I find it puzzling, however, that Metzger should conceive the problem of political rationality in terms of the distinction between the rationality of ends and instrumental rationality and characterize the seesaw effect in terms of discourse #1 scoring high with respect to the former and discourse #2 with respect to the latter. This way of viewing the matter does not do justice to the fact that each discourse is of an entire way of life comprising both kinds of rationality in its own way. What Metzger seems to be hoping for, rather, is some combination of epistemological pessimism (from discourse #2) and political optimism (from discourse #1). But this immediately raises the question whether such a combination is intellectually coherent and psychologically practicable.

Nor is it clear why Metzger considers it *irrational* to place no more "emphasis on hopeful, resolute political action" than, say, John Rawls and John Dunn do, both being Metzger's targets of criticism in this regard. If by hopefulness about politics Metzger means the a priori or transcendental kind of hope that treats belief in a minimal degree of human goodness and reasonableness as a precondition for human life, including human political life, to be at all worthwhile, then Rawls for one has it in abundance.[13] Otherwise, rational hopefulness about politics depends on a proper assessment of relevant facts of the matter. Here one can go some distance along with Metzger when he writes, "The heart of the problem... is how to combine an emphasis on hopeful, resolute political action with one on accuracy in depicting facts and caution in defining the scope of knowledge" (119). But if one takes "accuracy in depicting facts and caution in defining the scope of knowledge" seriously, one must leave open whether the exercise of such epistemological virtues in the context of experience will lead to pessimistic political conclusions. It will not do to rule out such conclusions by simply suggesting, with little argument, as Metzger does in his criticisms of Dunn (516–18, 537), that the standard of precision employed in reaching such conclusions is too high and inappropriate for the messy business of politics.

A further problem I have is with Metzger's argument for a "transcultural critical perspective" (121), which is supposedly needed to overcome the seesaw effect. Crucial to Metzger's argument is the idea, repeatedly stated throughout the book, that "a discourse is a paradoxical

---

[13] See, for example, Rawls's "Concluding Reflection," in *The Law of Peoples* (Cambridge, MA: Harvard University Press, 1999), pp. 127–28.

combination of culturally inherited premises with a reflexivity oriented to objective reality and universal issues" (77). Granted that human beings possess such reflexivity, the exercise of this capacity is still framed by premises whose historical givenness such reflexivity seems unable entirely to remove or transcend. If this is true of each and every discourse, the capacity for reflexivity in itself is not enough to support the belief that a transcultural critical perspective capable of overcoming the seesaw effect is possible. It seems that one must settle for something less ambitious than the discovery of such a unifying transcultural critical perspective.

Most baffling of all, because Metzger says nothing on this subject, is how Metzger's ambivalence about discourses #1 and 2 is to apply to thick and thin parameters of freedom, for, after all, Metzger sees the importance of the epistemological differences between the two discourses to lie chiefly in their bearing on freedoms. But it is precisely here that we can begin to make sense of the tension in Metzger's frustrated synthesis. Since Metzger does not tell us what to make of his ambivalence regarding epistemological optimism and pessimism in relation to thick and thin parameters of freedom, we are left free, because obliged, to do it ourselves.

We can take a helpful first step by simplifying "thin parameters of freedom" to "freedom" and translating "thick parameters of freedom" into "the good." With the benefit of this simple translation, whose rationale is implicit in what I have said about parameters of freedom and their relation to the good, we are led to see more directly what the tension in Metzger's thinking is really about. It is none other than the most important opposition in moral orientation between East and West, between the ancients and the moderns, namely, the opposition between (the old notion of) the good and (the modern notion of) freedom.

Against this background, we can appreciate immediately that Metzger, being a deeply thoughtful comparativist and synthesizer rather than an uncritical believer in the modern and in the West, has good reason to feel this tension and be moved to find a way out of it. Metzger has his own take on this tension, to be sure, and proceeds in his own vocabulary. But in view of his somewhat unfocused and diffuse treatment of the matter, one that belies the unity and depth of his best intuitions and insights, it may help clarify Metzger's undertaking if we set it in the broader context I have just sketched, translating what we reasonably can of it into the language of the good and freedom. Thus, when Metzger expresses concern for the deflationary effects of discourse #2 on collective political motivation, he may be taken to deplore the much too one-sided victory of freedom over unconditional belief in the good. When, conversely, he looks with envy to the store of hopefulness and resoluteness in discourse #1, he may be taken to hanker after the life-giving force of the good, in politics and much else. When, time and again, he finds discourse #1 wanting in the opposite way, he may be taken to show a keen awareness of the liabilities not only of freedom without the uplifting effect of the good but also of attraction to the good without freedom's containment of its endemic imprudence and excess, well beyond its possible lack of instrumental rationality. When Metzger later sets out in search of a way to overcome what he calls the seesaw effect, he may be taken to rest his hope in somehow combining the best of both moral universes, of the good as the heavenly source of hopefulness and of freedom as the earthly ground of prudence. When he thus seems to fall into wishful thinking or incoherence, it is because the good is part of *the priority of the good* just as freedom is part of *the priority of freedom*, and there is no way of accommodating two such priorities in a stable synthesis.

But what about the "transcultural critical perspective," as Metzger calls it? Why not think of it as a dual perspective that holds the good and freedom, in one society or between societies, in an ever-changing balance through healthy moral and political contestation? What will become of the transcultural critical perspective if one state of this balance is fixed once and for all in favor of the good or of freedom? Will there, in such an event, be any such perspective left that is worthy of its name? These questions suggest that the most generous response to the seesaw effect is not to try to overcome it but to see in it or behind it the life-giving tension between the good and freedom, the kind of tension that is impossible ever to remove without either impoverishing or endangering human life. Perhaps the best form for the "transcultural critical perspective" to take is some happy dialectic between freedom and the good.

5

Freedom and Identification

I

In Chapter 3, I proposed an understanding of freedom in terms of the deeper notion of agency, and then in Chapter 4, I reinforced this proposal with a brief critical discussion of the conventional approach to the matter as represented by Thomas Metzger. Unlike in the conventional approach, I am inclined to start with the hypothesis that freedom is but a configuration of agency, to proceed with an argument for treating agency as the fundamental common denominator of all human values and their forms of expression, and then to see freedom (modern West) as one configuration of agency alongside of identification (China) as another possible and actually realized configuration. This is a line of thought I want to complete in this chapter.

There are two reasons for pursuing this line of thought and hoping that it succeeds. The first has to do with the reasonable yet by no means straightforwardly accomplishable ambition of wanting to understand different, sometimes very different, moral cultures (and other social constructions) in such a way that they can be compared and even, where appropriate, ranked. This ambition is easily derailed by two tendencies common in attempts to address the old and familiar question of how to characterize differences between, say, Chinese and Western moral cultures. One tendency is to conclude too quickly that the objects of comparison are somehow incommensurable, that is, incapable of being described and appraised in terms of a significant common denominator, a precondition for meaningful comparison. The other tendency is to settle for a common denominator that is actually drawn from one of the objects compared, and as a result the comparison is skewed from the outset. To save the comparative enterprise, we must find a common denominator that is free of both tendencies.

The second reason for seeking such a common denominator is the need to account for what appears to be radical moral change – the kind of major shift in a society from one type of moral culture to another that China badly needs to bring about if it is to find a way out of its current moral crisis. The very idea of *radical* moral change invites explanations in terms of discontinuity: break, rupture, eruption, leap, revolution, and so on. But such occurrences are possible only if there is something in them or beneath them that allows the people involved in the change to remain, to themselves and to others, recognizably human after the change and despite the change. Not only does the very possibility of moral change, including radical moral change, rest upon some underlying continuity, our ability to comprehend such change also requires the postulation of this continuity in the form of one common denominator or another. Only in this way can we see a new moral culture as evolving from the old and serving the same basic functions as the old. Indeed, only in this way – by pointing to the breakdown of the same basic functions in the old moral culture – can we explain the need for a new moral culture in the first place and understand the new moral culture as emerging precisely in response to such a breakdown.

There is a sense in which the two reasons for seeking a common denominator among moral cultures (and other social constructions) are, in fact, one: after all, a shift can happen from one moral culture to another only if the two moral cultures are comparable, sharing deeper features and functions that make the shift, however seemingly radical, both possible and meaningful. It is for this convergence of reasons, then – or especially for the second reason insofar as the two reasons are conceptually distinct – that I want to put forward a notion of agency as a candidate common denominator. I hope to show, in a preliminary way, that this common denominator is sufficiently significant and freestanding to allow us to make sense of different ways of organizing human moral life as different strategies for giving cultural expression and institutional form to human agency while also meeting the need for social order.

2

Since agency is a wide-ranging subject in its own right, I can include in my all too brief account here only those elements of it that are particularly relevant to my comparative task at hand. I start with two such elements – simple building blocks, as it were – in this section, with further elaborations and new elements to be added as I proceed.

The first element is *power*, understood in a broad sense to cover all instances of human causal efficacy. It is worth emphasizing that power in this generic and neutral sense is not to be reduced to either specific instances of it such as political power or morally loaded instances of it such as domination. As such, power is any human causal efficacy whatsoever and can take any form, good or bad or indifferent.

Power matters essentially to human beings as agents. But why it matters, beyond self-preservation, is a question that must be answered with reference to a second element of agency, namely, *subjectivity*. By subjectivity we mean the formation and development of a self, along with its reflexive dimension in the shape of a sense of self, moral and otherwise. Power comes into the picture here because selfhood is a capacity that leads to the reality of a self only through experiences of power, of meaningful effort and success. It bears repeating (from Chapter 3) that only through such experiences, from the very beginning and continuously, can a self emerge and persist: a subject who forms so-called intentions and causes things to happen in accord with such intentions, registers such intentions and the effects of carrying them out as emanating from and belonging to a self, attaches value to this self and its activities – and, of course, who does all these things as a subject among subjects. Thus, power otherwise merely generic and neutral becomes truly human power only when it comes into relation with subjectivity, aiding or hindering it, helping give it one form or another, just as subjectivity otherwise merely a potential becomes actual and concrete only when it is allowed to emerge from experiences of power as their spirit and center. This indistinguishable amalgam is what we call human agency, and its dynamic can be succinctly captured, as we saw in Chapter 3, in terms of power organized as subjectivity, or subjectivity achieved through power.

3

The organization of power as subjectivity takes place through a mechanism of *attribution*, making the latter a further, crucial element of agency. No matter what power is organized into whose subjectivity, one condition must be met, and that is the successful attribution of causal efficacy, good or bad, to a subject or potential subject. One becomes a subject, whether one likes it or not, on the basis of such attributions. One becomes a "normal" subject by learning how to make and accept "normal" attributions. It is only to be expected that attributions from society, especially in the shape of various figures of authority, are prior to self-attributions, attributions of power by a self to oneself. Of special importance among such socially authoritative attributions are evaluative ones involving praise and blame, reward and punishment, and hence serving to make individuals responsible for what they do and creating a memory and conscience in support of such responsibility.[1] Even after one becomes routinely capable of self-attributions – that is, after one is properly formed as a self or subject – one continues to rely on society and others to confirm one's self-attributions.[2]

The important thing about attributions, no matter by whom and to whom, is that they are acts of interpretation, and, as such, are plausible or implausible rather than true or false. This does not make attributions any less indispensable or serviceable. Since causal efficacy is a tricky business and humans wisely conduct this business with the flexibility and room for change that signal interpretation, judgments in terms of the true or false are entirely out of place. This is not at all a cause for worry, however, since subjectivity alone is what is ultimately at stake and, given this stake, attributions are quite sufficient as long as they are plausible to the parties concerned. What all this means is that human agency has its basis not in facts but in interpretations of experience. And the most important implication of this understanding is that what matters for the organization of power into subjectivity is not power as such but the *feeling of power*, which we may therefore identify as an element of agency distinct from power. The feeling of power alone is *directly* necessary and sufficient for the constitution of subjectivity.[3]

The feeling of power is subjective in an obvious sense. As far as the constitution of subjectivity is concerned, there is no avoiding the part

---

[1] See e.g., Friedrich Nietzsche, *On the Genealogy of Morals* (and *Ecce Homo*), trans. Walter Kaufmann and R. J. Hollingdale (New York: Random House, 1967), second essay, secs. 1–3; *The Gay Science*, trans. Walter Kaufmann (New York: Random House, 1974), aphorism 354.
[2] Nietzsche speaks derogatorily of some human beings as herd animals. By herd animals Nietzsche is best taken to mean not those who rely on attributions by others as such, for all humans do so by virtue of the way in which subjectivity is formed and sustained, but only those who rely exclusively on *conventional* attributions or attributions by institutional authorities.
[3] For discussion of the distinction between power and feeling of power and their relation, see my "Evaluating Agency: A Fundamental Question for Social and Political Philosophy," *Metaphilosophy* 42 (2011): 261–81 esp. at 263–64.

played by this subjective factor. In the total absence of feeling of power, no subjectivity can be formed or maintained. By the same token, in order for subjectivity to be stable, the feeling of power must be stable. Not surprisingly, the required stability of feeling can be, and all too often is, produced by ideological manipulation. One antidote to this all too human liability is the insistence that the feeling of power be stable *under reflection*. For stability that can withstand reflection is not only the most worthy of endorsement but also, and for this very reason, the most durable, other things being equal. Reflection itself is of course open to ideological manipulation, to which the answer is yet more reflection, itself not immune from ideological manipulation, ad infinitum, forming a circle out of which there is no guaranteed exit.

But this is not a purely subjective affair. Even ideological manipulation must appear plausible to those for whom it is intended if it is to create and sustain a feeling of power. And the bar of plausibility can be raised by the insistence on – and under favorable circumstances the engrained practice of – subjecting de facto stability to critical reflection. Such plausibility, properly reflective or otherwise, requires not only a minimum of internal coherence regarding the employment of concepts but also, and no less crucially, a minimum of "objective" conditions that help give credence to attributions of power and sustain a corresponding feeling of power. For example, in a society that does not choose its rulers through universal suffrage, it would be difficult for the attribution of power to "the people" to acquire plausibility and engender a feeling of power necessary for a collective "democratic" subjectivity. In this case, the fact of universal suffrage may be thought of as an objective condition whose absence helps explain the implausibility of a certain attribution and hence the inability of that attribution to support a certain subjective experience. It does not follow that the presence of objective conditions, to one degree or another, means the absence of ideological manipulation.[4] For objective conditions in turn are unavoidably subject to interpretation, and where there is room for interpretation there is also the possibility of ideological manipulation. Still, attributions of power must be plausible to the intended party in order to create a feeling of power necessary for subjectivity, and such plausibility depends to a significant degree on objective conditions that must be interpreted, to be sure, but cannot be distorted at will.

---

[4] See my "Political Agency in Liberal Democracy," *Journal of Political Philosophy* 14 (2006): 144–62.

Given these complications, an inquiry such as mine that is centered on subjectivity needs to give special attention to the plausibility of attributions of power, as viewed especially by those whose subjectivity is on the line, while it must also take account of other factors, including objective ones, via the impact they have on the plausibility of attributions.

4

Agency thus understood – power organized as subjectivity through stably plausible attributions requiring objective conditions – is, I would claim, a fundamental common denominator shared by all moral cultures. As I understand it, a moral culture is a stable though arbitrary set of power-attributing and subjectivity-constituting values and practices. All humans, qua agents, perform attributions of power, and all moral cultures contain values that allow such attributions to take place in the interest of subjectivity. This does not mean, of course, that all moral cultures resort to the same set of values. Only some moral cultures, for example, make prominent use of such values as freedom and autonomy, while other moral cultures do not subscribe to such individual-centered values at all. In trying to make sense of differences between apparently incommensurable moral cultures, such as that of Chinese society and that of a modern Western society, it is crucial to bear in mind the common denominator in terms of which they can be characterized and assessed. It is true of all moral cultures, or so I claim, that what is at stake is power organized as subjectivity, and that this organization is in turn a matter of attributions whose plausibility as interpretations depends significantly on objective conditions.

5

The broad notion of agency I am working with does not reduce individual agency to individualism. Since the need and potential for agency is characteristic of human being as such, not just of human being in modern liberal societies, we must treat individualism as but one strategy for the attribution of power and the constitution of subjectivity. Call this strategy *agency-through-freedom*: at work here is the attribution of power to the individual under such familiar modern descriptions as freedom and autonomy and the formation of a corresponding type of subjectivity. We may think of this strategy as an ideal type, one that captures what is broadly characteristic of modern liberal societies.

Unlike such societies, a society such as (traditional and, to some extent, Mao's) China calls for explanation in terms of another ideal type, which consists of power-attributing and subjectivity-constituting values and practices that do not revolve around the supposedly free individual. Rather, the source of whatever is valued, or at least the means of access to it, is some authority or exemplar with whom ordinary people identify, and only through such identification are ordinary people supposedly able to stand in a proper relationship to the good or the correct and acquire the full-fledged motivation to act accordingly. Such identification always goes together with the attribution of power, indeed special power, to the authority or exemplar in question. Often, the power thus attributed involves knowledge of especially important truths, in which case identification with the authority or exemplar takes the form of belief or faith. Whatever the power may happen to consist in, the important thing is that when one identifies with an authority or exemplar, one simultaneously denies power to oneself and recuperates it, to one degree or another, through identification with those to whom power has been lopsidedly attributed. Thus, identification does not preclude but rather presupposes attribution of power (to someone other than oneself) and effective participation in that power (through identification). The need for agency, for power organized as subjectivity, is always expressed, however obliquely, in what may appear to be acts of pure identification, and accordingly such acts are better characterized in terms of *agency-through-identification*.

In a society informed by principles of agency-through-identification, then, such as traditional or Maoist Chinese society, power does not evaporate. Nor does power somehow belong to the collective, in the shape of a tradition or community or movement. Rather, power is attributed to, and hence is allowed to be wielded by, specific individuals who diffuse it – or, as it were, collectivize it – by making themselves appear as qualified mediators of a tradition or true representatives of a movement and hence as suitable loci of identification. Ordinary people identify with a tradition or community or movement through the more direct and tangible identification with its messengers or representatives. It is only in this light that we are able to appreciate the inner logic, the attractions and liabilities, and the typical socializing devices of so-called collectivistic societies.

This is only half of what is involved in identification, however, and the other half is scarcely less important. In agency-through-identification, although the attribution of power is not made directly to the individual, it is nevertheless the individual who must undertake the identification. Moreover, given the role of identification in the formation of subjectivity in this type of moral culture, the individual must perform such identification with a significant measure of willingness: the individual must *will* such identification. Thus the existence of individual free will is presupposed, indeed honored, in the very act of self-denial (it is *self*-denial, after all), whether such self-denial takes the form of submission to the Mandate of Heaven or unquestioning belief in a supposedly objective teleology. In this sense, there is a moment of freedom to identification, even if such freedom involves little more than the capacity for willing identification. Thus, the key to understanding so-called collectivistic societies is not to avoid explanations in terms of agency but to figure out how attributions of power are possible, even if not made through such values as freedom and autonomy, and how subjectivity is possible, even if not constituted through attributions of power to the individual.

6

I have drawn a sharp line between freedom and identification in order to indicate in a rough and ready fashion the two general forms that the attribution of power and the constitution of subjectivity can take. In doing so, I have emphasized that identification involves not only an attribution of power, albeit to someone other than oneself, but also an exercise of freedom. It is worth noting that the converse is also true, namely, that the exercise of freedom, even in agency-through-freedom, always involves identification.

Power, as I have noted, finds its meaning or point only in the province of a subject. But the subject that acts and maintains its subjectivity in the process is not some generic subject but a subject with a specific *identity*. A subject values power primarily in those domains of activity that bear on its identity. These identity-forming domains of activity, in turn, presuppose a *horizon*. A horizon is that which serves to distinguish those things that matter from the potentially infinite number of things that do not – forming, in Nietzsche's words, "a line dividing the bright and discernible from the unilluminable and dark."[5] It narrows the field of vision so that one is able to focus on seeing and doing a limited number of things and thereby to acquire and maintain one's subjectivity.

---

[5] Friedrich Nietzsche, "On the Uses and Disadvantages of History for Life," in *Untimely Meditations*, trans. R. J. Hollingdale (Cambridge: Cambridge University Press, 1983), pp. 57–123 at p. 63.

It is a commonplace that such a horizon is socially rather than individually constituted. Thus, when people act as so-called free individuals they actually choose their projects from among those that are endowed with value and meaning by their society, or a segment of their society, and only by identifying with and carrying out such *socially* valued projects are they able to express their freedom as *individuals*. If the exercise of freedom is channeled by identity, identity in turn is formed through *identification*.

Now, given that agency-through-freedom and agency-through-identification both contain an element of identification (just as both contain an element of freedom), how can we properly distinguish the former from the latter? Above all else, this is a matter of a society's shared self-understanding. In agency-through-freedom, although identification unavoidably plays a part, indeed an important part, this part is conceptually minimized, sometimes even denied, in favor of the part played by individual freedom. This is how agents-through-freedom understand their power in the moral scheme of things: they value and justify what they do under the shared description of freedom.[6] As long as this description is plausible to these agents themselves, whether or not it is valid otherwise, it is constitutive of the kind of moral agents that they are. There is something subjective about this description, to be sure, in the sense that what is required is its plausibility to those whose agency is informed by it. Still, this subjective requirement depends for its satisfaction on more or less objective conditions. Thus, the kind of identification that is present in agency-through-freedom must have something permissive about it. While the various domains of human activity are socially constituted, in both range and substance, the individual must, up to a significant point, be legally (objectively, if you will) in a position to choose from among them in the absence of obtrusive state interference or the compulsory mediation of exemplars. The fact of this permissiveness helps make plausible the attribution of power to individuals under the description of freedom and helps make possible the constitution of a corresponding type of subjectivity. To the extent that this state of affairs obtains, the individual is able to experience what he or she does as free, and it is this experience, including the subjective (however objectively mistaken) downplaying of identification, that is picked out by the notion of agency-through-freedom.

It cannot be taken for granted that this state of affairs will obtain. There is always the risk that the attribution of power to the individual,

---

[6] There is perhaps no better philosophical statement of this description than Immanuel Kant's essay "An Answer to the Question 'What Is Enlightenment?'"

an interpretative exercise seldom free from ideological exaggeration, may lose its conditions of plausibility, not least objective ones. The weakening of such conditions gives rise to attribution problems. At their most serious, attribution problems can amount to a crisis of subjectivity, as when members of a supposedly free society no longer find plausible the attribution of power to themselves as individuals under the description of freedom, or when members of a supposedly democratic society no longer find plausible the attribution of power to themselves as citizens under the description of democracy.

Even when this kind of risk is kept at bay, it does not follow that the notion of freedom is an unproblematic one. After all, the individual has to be socialized into becoming a free chooser in the first place, and socialization is itself a value-laden process whose outcome is determined by ceaseless political contestation. Such contestation may well result in the reification of the range and substance of socially delineated freedoms, and such reification may in turn bespeak relations of domination. The fact that freedoms can be framed by relations of domination, along with the fact that people can be ideologically induced to turn a blind eye to such framing, is the Achilles heel of a society marked by agency-through-freedom. Correspondingly, how to prevent or minimize this danger is its main moral and political challenge.

7

What gives agency-through-identification its distinctive character, setting it apart from agency-through-freedom, is no less a matter of a society's shared self-understanding. Agency-through-identification does not uniquely resort to identification in the construction of subjectivity but rather foregrounds and valorizes the identificatory dimension of subjectivity under one description or another. The phenomenon of identification, as I have noted, is common to all moral cultures. The important thing for our purposes is that, however identification is to be understood as a phenomenon, it is given much greater importance in some moral cultures than in others. It is the valorization of identification as a fact of moral culture, rather than the mere presence of identification as a general phenomenon, that characterizes agency-through-identification. As far as subjectivity is concerned, the description under which people conduct themselves matters decisively. What happens in the case of agency-through-identification is that people conduct themselves morally under some description of identification.

The plausibility of this description, as of the description of freedom, rests upon objective conditions, among others. Unlike its counterpart in agency-through-freedom, the identification that figures in agency-through-identification has something rather obligatory about it, both in the sense that there is only one kind of path that one is expected to follow, in the shape of *the* good,[7] and in the sense that one's relation to the good is overtly mediated by an authority or exemplar. The important question here is not whether one is constrained by social categories of human being but whether one is permitted, and treated as having the ability, to choose from such socially given possibilities without obtrusive interference or compulsory mediation. In the case of what I am calling agency-through-identification, the lack of permissiveness sets an objective limit to, and is in turn informed by, a shared understanding that attributes little power to individuals except the capacity to follow. It is this combination of subjective and objective elements that defines agency-through-identification and distinguishes it from agency-through-freedom.

In a moral culture marked by agency-through-identification, such as the moral culture of traditional China and of what is loosely called communist China, an exemplar acts as some sort of intermediary between moral standards and the followers of those standards. These standards may be treated as forming part of a tradition and community, as in the case of Confucianism, or as belonging to a theory-informed movement, as in the case of Chinese communism. To follow the exemplar is to follow the standards as embodied in his knowledge and conduct and, especially in traditional, largely Confucian China, as concretely manifest in an elaborate web of ritual and ceremonial practices.[8] To be sure, a proper exemplar supposedly does no more, and no less, than exemplify the values of a tradition or community or movement. But the important thing is that the exemplar alone supposedly stands in a direct relation to that which he exemplifies, such that ordinary people have no access to the real meaning of the tradition or community or movement except through such exemplification or mediation. By the same token, conformity to that which is exemplified takes the form of identification with the exemplar.

---

[7] See Hsieh Yu-wei, "The Status of the Individual in Chinese Ethics," in Charles A. Moore, ed., *The Chinese Mind: Essentials of Chinese Philosophy and Culture* (Honolulu: University of Hawaii Press, 1967), pp. 307–22.

[8] For an example of the ritual dimension of exemplification, see Monika Übelhör, "The Community Compact (*Hsiang-yüeh*) of the Sung and Its Educational Significance," in Wm. Theodore de Bary and John W. Chaffee, eds., *Neo-Confucian Education: The Formative Stage* (Berkeley: University of California Press, 1989), pp. 371–88.

Any particular exemplar can be challenged or replaced, but the *category* of the exemplar is part and parcel of this kind of moral culture and psychology.

Identification with an exemplar must involve my active participation, however, if I am to internalize the standards exemplified to the point of making them my own.[9] And I must make them my own in order to become or remain a moral subject: internalization is a requirement of subjectivity. Hence the pivotal role of self-cultivation in Confucian moral psychology. Because of this reliance on self-cultivation, however, identification presupposes a certain free will, and this gives rise to a problem at the core of Confucian moral psychology. In cultivating oneself, one must be presumed an agent, and yet with respect to the standards that one is supposed to internalize by means of self-cultivation, one must defer to an exemplar. That is to say that one is regarded as an agent – as free and reasonably discerning – in one respect but not in the other.

Thus, two apparently contradictory activities are held in a delicate balance, with the required kind of identification depending on a degree of individual initiative that cannot but threaten to destabilize or even undermine it. Each of these activities has received emphatic treatment in canonical Confucian texts. On the one hand, these texts abound in unambiguous references to the indispensable role of exemplars. In one famous passage in the *Analects* Confucius is reported to have said, "A ruler who governs his state by virtue is like the north pole star, which remains in its place while all other stars revolve around it" (*Analects*, 2:1). In another, oft-quoted saying credited to Confucius, we are told, "If you desire what is good, the people will be good. The character of a ruler is like wind and that of the people is like grass. In whatever direction the wind

---

[9] Strictly speaking, natural feelings are prior to standards according to Confucianism. Accordingly, moral identity is formed through the actualization of inborn moral potential rather than the internalization of externally supplied standards. That which on other views requires internalization is, according to Confucianism, already there, from the very beginning, and it needs only to be actualized or awakened. This idea finds classic expression in the *Mencius* (e.g., 6A: 6, 2A: 6, 7A: 4). For example: "Humanity, righteousness, propriety, and wisdom are not drilled into us from outside. We originally have them with us. Only we do not think [to find them]. Therefore it is said, 'Seek and you will find it, neglect and you will lose it'" (*Mencius*, 6A: 6). If we grant, for the sake of argument, that morality consists in the actualization of inborn potential, we can still ask how that potential, whatever it may be, can be actualized. Answers to this question can then be taken, with some adjustment, to be answers to the alternatively conceived question of how standards are internalized. Translations of quotations from classical texts throughout this chapter are taken from Wing-tsit Chan, *A Source Book in Chinese Philosophy* (Princeton: Princeton University Press, 1963) and cited parenthetically.

blows, the grass always bends" (*Analects*, 12:19). The idea contained in these paradigmatic formulations is one that runs through the entire Confucian tradition of moral and political thought and, as these sayings clearly show, what is at issue goes far beyond the pedagogic function of exemplars for the young.[10]

Yet on the other hand, classical Confucian texts set great store by self-cultivation, not even sparing ordinary people the need to practice it. "From the Son of Heaven down to the common people," reportedly says Confucius in *The Great Learning*, the central text in this regard, "all must regard cultivation of the personal life as the root or foundation. There is never a case when the root is in disorder and yet the branches are in order." A crucial virtue that informs such cultivation is sincerity, and we are told, in a commentary by Zeng Zi that forms part of this text, that sincerity means that "the superior man will always be watchful over himself when alone" (*Chapters of Commentary*, 6). In this context Zeng Zi stresses the need to avoid *self*-deception, just as, in another canonical Confucian text, the emphasis is placed on avoiding *self*-dissatisfaction. "The superior man," we read in *The Doctrine of the Mean*, "examines his own heart and sees that there is nothing wrong there, and that he is not dissatisfied with himself. The superior man is unequalled in the fact that he [is cautious] in those things which people do not see."

These two imperatives, identification with exemplar and cultivation of self, make up the inner logic of Confucianism. It is a mistake to regard the hierarchical elements of Confucianism as somehow less fundamental than or subordinate to the idea that every person has the capacity for reflective self-direction.[11] If anything, the hierarchical dimension of Confucianism is even more basic, in that it is a direct expression of the identificatory character of agency in Confucianism whereas individual initiative comes into play only as a presupposition and enabling condition of wholehearted identification. I do not want to emphasize this

---

[10] According to Joel J. Kupperman, "The chief difference between Aristotle's and Confucius' moral psychology, as it pertains to young children, is ... the latter's emphasis on the educational use of role-modeling." See his "Tradition and Community in the Formation of Character and Self," in Kwong-loi Shun and David B. Wong, eds., *Confucian Ethics: A Comparative Study of Self, Autonomy, and Community* (Cambridge: Cambridge University Press, 2004), pp. 103–23 at p. 108. Although Kupperman is correct on this point, the difference identified by him applies beyond education of the young, for an essential role of exemplars is integral to the entire Confucian moral culture and psychology.

[11] For an example of this mistake, see Alasdair MacIntyre, "Questions for Confucians," in Shun and Wong, eds., *Confucian Ethics*, pp. 203–18 at p. 210.

hierarchical dimension, however, since the inner logic of Confucianism is dialectical rather than either straightforwardly hierarchical or straightforwardly centered on self-direction, in that identification with exemplar and cultivation of self are both crucial components of Confucianism, and yet they are also opposed, even as the former presupposes the latter, without either being capable of total assimilation to the other.

The central challenge, then, is to align, on the levels of moral culture and of individual moral psychology, these two imperatives or components – the complete denial of power to oneself with regard to the setting of standards on the one hand and the indispensable role of individual initiative in cultivating oneself in accordance with these standards on the other.[12] It is noteworthy that while these two components are treated separately in the Confucian canon, their dialectical relationship has not been noticed, let alone resolved. Thus, the presumed capacity for willing and discerning identification is always on the verge of exceeding itself and dispensing with the need for compulsory identification in the first place and yet this logic has not been allowed to run its course. What we find, again and again, are unconvincing half measures – the recognition of just enough individual initiative for purposes of identification and no more.[13]

One may be tempted to point to exceptions, especially the Ming-dynasty scholar-official Wang Yangming. Wang sees the mind as encompassing all things and principles and proposes a fundamental shift of attention from the investigation of things to the rectification of mind.

[12] The degree of individual initiative is somewhere between the two poles described by Kupperman when he writes that "passive absorption of an ethics does not guarantee reliable goodness, and it is plausible that only someone who comes of herself or himself to certain conclusions is likely to internalize them" ("Tradition," p. 110). What the individual needs to do in Confucian moral psychology stops short of reaching conclusions for oneself, and yet the individual must somehow willingly come to accept the conclusions presented to him or her by exemplars.

[13] For a different view, see Kwong-loi Shun, "Conception of the Person in Early Confucian Thought," in Shun and Wong, eds., *Confucian Ethics*, pp. 183–99 at pp. 185–86. Shun speaks here of self-direction as part of a Confucian conception without qualification. On a related issue, if one speaks of "autonomy" in the Confucian context, as Shun does (p. 193), it is important to stress that the autonomy in question is internal rather than external. Belonging to the internal kind, the "autonomy" in the Confucian conception of the self is quite compatible with identification with an exemplar, especially when the exemplar supposedly exemplifies precisely internal autonomy. As Shun remarks, Confucians "do not view this capacity as one of freely choosing one's own ends subject only to certain constraints, whether rational constraints or the constraint that one does not thereby interfere with the exercise of a similar capacity by others" (p. 194). On the conceptual distinction between internal and external autonomy, see John Skorupski, *Ethical Explorations* (New York: Oxford University Press, 1999), p. 225.

Important as this innovation is within the Confucian tradition, it has to do chiefly with the ontological status – the locus, if you like – of moral imperatives, among other things, rather than with the content of those imperatives. As far as the latter is concerned, Wang remains essentially in agreement with other Confucians, including Zhu Xi of the Song dynasty, who was one of the main targets of Wang's criticism. Wang, too, speaks of filial piety and loyalty to ruler, taking for granted that these are correct moral imperatives and insisting only that their status as moral imperatives derives from their presence in the mind. Given this, there is little room for the ordinary moral agent to put his mind to active use in the shaping of his moral life beyond the cultivation of willingness to follow existing principles.

This is not to deny that the inward turn to the mind has far-reaching implications for how one should go about self-cultivation. Instead of trying to see things in their true light, one is now supposed to rid one's mind of distorting influences so as to gain access to the wellspring of all knowledge and good conduct. It seems natural to conclude from this that self-cultivation is best carried out by relying on oneself, as turning inward and relying on oneself seem two sides of the same coin. And Wang Yangming sometimes reaches precisely this conclusion. But then, in a way reminiscent of Confucius and other major Confucian figures, Wang observes that those who are capable of bringing this off all by themselves are few and far between and that therefore most people need to be enlightened and instructed. If Wang famously sees sages everywhere, he is no less adamant that some are vastly more sagely than others – more intelligent and less dominated by mind-obscuring habits. Via this time-honored logic, moral teachers and exemplars make their predictable appearance, despite the fact that Wang has put a big potential obstacle in their way.

Thus, even in as radical a figure as Wang Yangming, the tension between identification and self-cultivation is left unresolved. If anything, this tension is raised to the highest level of intensity in Confucianism: one is supposed to turn entirely inward for that which makes insight and good conduct possible, and yet even in turning inward most people have to receive external help from moral teachers and exemplars. Will the need for such help always be necessary for at least some people? Are these people not intrinsically inferior beings, if only quantitatively, if they necessarily need external help? Or, is there rather a point at which even they can dispense with such help, having been set on the right path, and turn truly inward? Wang does not say precisely. What he does say with considerable lucidity is enough to suggest that he goes further than most Confucians in following through the logic of moral agency, but even he does not take the decisive final step of dispensing with external moral authority and exemplar in principle and attributing moral power directly to the individual moral agent. In the end, what might have been the Chinese equivalent, as it were, of the Protestant Reformation never took place in the Confucian tradition – even in thought.

Even today, the difficulties and challenges posed by the dialectical relationship between identification and free will retain their full force. Why should one attribute power to an exemplar and then identify with the exemplar if one is presumed, as one must be, to possess the ability to make the correct attribution in the first place? Given this presumption, what rationale can there be for self-effacing deference to authority or exemplar? How can such self-effacing deference be squared with the fundamental idea, as expressed by Mencius and taken further by Wang Yangming, that "The sage and I are the same in kind" (*Mencius*, 6A:7)? The painstaking, often ingenious but never wholly plausible ways of preempting questions such as these make up the staple of Chinese moral thought, and the unresolved contradiction is still with us.

In the absence of plausible answers, it is almost predictable that the result will be at best superficial identification unsupported by probing self-cultivation and at worst feigned identification performed for opportunistic reasons. In both cases, the values that are meant to be taken up through identification and self-cultivation are not deeply internalized or not internalized at all. As a result, compliance with the norms informed by these values will have to be motivated by considerations of interest or prudence, and when such considerations happen to be weak and enforcement ineffective, compliance is unsurprisingly sporadic. Less visibly, this more or less external and opportunistic relation to the dominant moral values of society will help form a kind of subjectivity only the surface of which is touched by these values, even though this surface can harden into habit and dogma.

8

The logic of agency-through-identification that I have tried to spell out is one that applies to what is loosely called communist China no less than it does Confucian China. That this is so can be seen from the character of the moral crisis in post-Mao China. Of the multiple causes of this crisis, one especially important one is a certain breakdown of identification with moral authority or exemplar. Now, by the moral crisis in post-Mao China I mean in part an unusually serious lack of willingness to comply with moral norms, for the most part norms that are themselves regarded as more or less acceptable even by those who violate them. The question thus arises as to what are the necessary conditions for the production of willingness to comply with moral norms. I want to suggest that one extremely important condition in the case of communist China, given its configuration of agency, has to do with identification.

This condition has two sub-conditions, and a brief account of them gives me the chance to introduce a distinction that I did not clearly draw in discussing identification in the context of Confucian China.[14] The first sub-condition, *the authority condition*, is the willing submission to the authority that is responsible for the establishment and enforcement of moral norms. This condition, though by no means unique to communist China, finds an especially pure expression in it, for the Party-Government is to this day the only institutional initiator and authorizer of moral norms. The second sub-condition, *the exemplar condition*, assigns a prominent role to exemplars and relies on the general belief that the exemplars are playing their role properly and are worthy of imitation. Moral authority and moral exemplars are conceptually distinct roles, but these roles need not be performed by distinct agents. In the Chinese case at hand, those who play the part of moral authority, that is, the Party-Government in the persons of officials at various levels, happen to be the same people who must act as moral exemplars and whose deeds are most closely watched as society's moral barometer and as cues for how ordinary people ought to behave or can reasonably be expected to behave.

There is one important property shared by the authority condition and the exemplar condition, and that is the fact that the access of ordinary moral agents to the moral universe of norms and motivations is taken to require mediation by those who are supposed to know better and act better. This common property gives us reason to subsume these two conditions under one larger condition called *the identification condition*. The idea is that it is only through identification with moral authority and moral exemplars that ordinary moral agents, in a moral culture such as China's, are able to become moral – to acquire the correct understanding of morality and a sufficiently strong motivation to act accordingly. Put

---

[14] The same distinction is first drawn in Chapter 1, but revisiting it in the present context allows me to make certain points clearer and to bring out some different nuances.

another way, the relation in which ordinary moral agents stand to morality is treated as dependent or even parasitic on the relation in which they stand first to moral authority and moral exemplars.

In this light, the moral crisis in post-Mao China is in large part a crisis of identification comprising a crisis of authority and a crisis of exemplification. There is no denying a crisis of authority when the Party-Government, to this day the only moral authority in China, never tires of moral exhortation only to see it fall on progressively deaf and cynical ears. Considering the thoroughly political character of this moral authority, one shudders to reflect on the political implications of the moral crisis – and the other way around.

No less undeniable is a crisis of exemplification as manifest in a sweeping distrust not only of exemplars but increasingly of the very category of the exemplar. This is the true crime of official corruption in a moral culture like ours. We have well passed the point where so many cases of proven corruption created an irresistible temptation to suspect the worst about the entire officialdom. The moral consequences of corruption *as exemplification* are all too visible in the unraveling of the moral fabric of the entire society. It sometimes looks as if the corruption of officials is enough to give ordinary people the license to behave as they damn well please, especially if they think they can get away with it.

The cognitive value of the moral crisis involving authority and exemplification, then, is that it allows us to extrapolate something of fundamental importance about Chinese communist moral culture, and that is the crucial role of identification in the formation of the moral self. A moral crisis is nothing but a crisis of the moral self on a society-wide scale, a crisis of the self's willingness to think, feel, and act in a certain way. Where such willingness is undermined by a blocking of identification, it can be inferred that the very formation of the moral self in question rests upon what I have called the identification condition.

I do not mean to suggest, of course, that Chinese communist moral culture and Confucian moral culture are the same; far from it. Yet, and this is what I have tried to show, they do have one important feature in common, that is, an affirmed reliance on mechanisms of identification in giving cultural expression and institutional form to human moral agency. This kind of reliance is a central component in the self-understanding of these two moral cultures alike. At the level of structure rather than substance, this self-understanding constitutes an ideal type – agency-through-identification – to which belong both the Confucian and the Chinese communist conceptions of moral culture and moral self.

9

I have said that a moral culture is a set of values and practices that serve to foster agency. This characterization is incomplete, for it leaves out the preservation of social order, to which I made only passing reference at the beginning. The preservation of social order is not only a matter of first importance in its own right but also a precondition for agency, and, as such, is a cultural task on a par with the promotion of agency. The complexities of culture derive in large part from the duality of its functions and cannot be grasped in terms of either its agency-enabling function or its order-promoting function alone.[15]

Thus the principal values of individualism, such as freedom and autonomy, must be understood in terms of the *combination* of these functions of culture rather than solely in terms of the agency-fostering function. The same duality of explanation applies to the principal values of collectivism. The premium placed on deference to and identification with authority that is characteristic of collectivism tends, unsurprisingly, to invite explanation in terms of the strengthening of social cohesion in the interest of order. But even in a society informed by collectivism, culture cannot brush aside the human need for agency. Even as the values and practices of identification serve to secure social cohesion, they must do so *in a way that simultaneously takes care of the need for agency.*

Adding the need for social order to our account of agency, we arrive at a common denominator that comprises the promotion of agency and the securing of social order. With this expanded common denominator, we can understand and appraise different ways of organizing human moral life, such as the Chinese and the modern Western, as different strategies for giving cultural shape to human agency in a way that is compatible with meeting the need for social order.

Some such broad common denominator is to be preferred to the conventional, narrower one conceived in terms of freedom. In this connection, it may be recalled that in Chapter 4 I discuss two instructive mistakes made by Thomas Metzger, the first being that of comparing China and the West in terms of the concept of freedom, the second that of misconceiving the relation between freedom and order. With regard to the first mistake, we have seen that any reasonably neutral question for the comparison of moral cultures must be conceived not in terms of more

---

[15] See Mark Warren, *Nietzsche and Political Thought* (Cambridge, MA: MIT Press, 1988), pp. 46–47, 238.

freedom or less freedom but in terms of how well the two tasks of every moral culture are articulated, that is, how well it is brought about that a society meets its members' need for agency in a manner that is compatible with maintaining a stable order over time. With regard to the second mistake, we have seen that agency-through-freedom, or what Metzger calls thin parameters of freedom, serves order as much as it does agency, just as agency-through-identification, or what Metzger calls thick parameters of freedom, promotes agency as much as it does order. Both agency-through-freedom and agency-though-identification, then, represent ways of *simultaneously* catering to the need for individual agency and the need for social order.

It is with reference to meeting these twin needs – a common denominator underlying all moral cultures – that unbiased and significant comparisons between moral cultures can be made and that moral change, including radical moral change, can be explained. A satisfactory execution of this twofold cultural task requires, of all moral cultures, that the attribution of power as a basis of subjectivity be plausible to those whose subjectivity depends on it (and hence sufficient for the constitution of subjectivity), stable under reflection (and hence conducive to the continuation of subjectivity), feasible under given material conditions, and compatible with securing and maintaining social order, itself a precondition for individual agency. All four requirements are dictated by the nature of the tasks that every moral culture has to carry out, and yet none of them refers to the actual content or even type of any of the moral cultures being compared. This ensures that the framework for comparison or explanation rests upon a common denominator that is both significant and freestanding. Only in some such way, in my view, can the comparison of moral cultures or the explanation of change from one moral culture to another properly get off the ground.

6

Neither Devotion Nor Introjection

I

This chapter is in some ways a summation of everything that has gone before in this book. If Chapters 1 and 2 provide a diagnostic account of the moral crisis in post-Mao China without yet drawing on the apparatus comprising the notion of agency and the distinction between freedom and identification as different configurations of agency, and if Chapters 3–5 supply that apparatus, then this chapter attempts an analysis of the moral crisis against the conceptual backdrop of the distinction between freedom and identification. Instead of directly employing the terms of this distinction, however, I will work with variations upon them, that is, in terms of the contrast between devotion and introjection, between a leader-centered and a superego-centered morality.

This terminological shift is due to the fact that in this chapter I draw heavily on Freud, and the main reason I draw on Freud at this point in my inquiry is that his way of looking at certain things allows me to take a natural next step on the basis of my preceding ones. In particular, Freud's ideas of the superego and group psychology make it possible for me not only to cast my preceding analysis of the moral crisis in a comparable yet different and enriching framework but also to bring an otherwise largely typological distinction (between freedom and identification) to bear, in a natural way, on what is involved in a possible transition in China today from one type of moral culture to another.

Given the specific purposes of my inquiry, it should come as no surprise that I am positive about Freud for the most part, if only implicitly, and only occasionally critical. I have no interest, however, in either challenging or defending Freud's main ideas in their own right, even those I have seen fit to draw upon in one way or another. Nor am I in the business of applying Freud to China, for that would be to assume that Freud's ideas are in principle of cross-cultural, even universal, scope and are valid as such, and I do not make such assumptions. The reason I go to Freud for illumination as I try to make sense of China's moral crisis is that I find his way of thinking and some of his ideas suggestive in a way that allows me to be free and precise at the same time – free with regard to Freud as a source of insights and precise in formulating my own hypotheses about China's moral crisis as the problem at hand. Whether or not I have actually achieved the precision that this approach makes possible, the more important thing is that the hypotheses are my own and are about China, not Freud. I take certain ideas from Freud and put them to work for my own purposes. Freud's ideas themselves may or may not be correct, my understanding of them may or may not be accurate, and my uses of those ideas, even if assuredly of Freud, may or may not be appropriate or fruitful. In the end, my hypotheses as I try to make them plausible must stand or fall on their own merit, on their adequacy and power as an explanation of the moral crisis in post-Mao China. Whether, and to what degree, they can properly be considered Freudian – and hence be taken to reflect in one way or another on Freud – is of decidedly secondary significance.

2

A moral crisis being the failure of a morality, the fundamental diagnostic question is *what* morality has failed, and this question is essentially about how that morality is meant to work. Conversely, there is no better way of figuring out how a morality is meant to work than by examining the mode of its failure. The guiding idea here is that we speak of a moral crisis when a morality fails *in its own terms*, that is, when it fails to work in the way it is meant to work, rather than in the sense that it fails to work as, or as well as, some other, supposedly superior morality does.

What, then, is the morality that has failed in post-Mao China? How is this morality meant to work in the first place? For anyone who approaches these questions from a Freudian perspective, the default explanatory strategy has to place the superego at the center of it all: when one's superego is in good working order, one will generally comply with the moral norms that prevail in one's society; otherwise, not.¹ This line of explanation is unsuited to the Chinese case, or so I hypothesize, and thus it is worth taking a close look at the possibility that, in what is loosely called communist China, both under Mao and after Mao, group psychology in good working order, rather than the superego in good working order, is how morality is meant to work and, correspondingly, is what becomes problematic in the case of a crisis.

As is well known, Freud explains the workings of group psychology through comparison with "love that is unhappy and cannot be satisfied." As far as such love is concerned, Freud observes,

> the functions allotted to the ego ideal entirely cease to operate. The criticism exercised by that agency is silent; everything that the object does and asks for is right and blameless. Conscience has no application to anything that is done for the sake of the object; in the blindness of love remorselessness is carried to the pitch of crime. The whole situation can be completely summarized in a formula: *The object has been put in the place of the ego ideal.*²

The same formula (where the ego ideal is the earlier term for the superego), Freud tells us, applies to hypnosis: "No one can doubt that the hypnotist has stepped into the place of the ego ideal.... The hypnotic relation is the unlimited devotion of someone in love, but with sexual satisfaction excluded."³ This goes to the heart of group psychology, for group psychology is nothing but the hypnotic relation writ large. As Freud writes,

> Hypnosis is not a good object for comparison with a group formation, because it is truer to say that it is identical with it. Out of the complicated fabric of the group it isolates one element for us – *the behavior of the individual to the leader.* Hypnosis is distinguished from a group formation by this limitation of number, just as it is distinguished from being in love by the absence of directly sexual trends.⁴

Think of members of such a group with regard to moral behavior. The members' willingness to follow the moral norms that regulate their interaction in the group depends above all on their relation to the leader. Things go well, morally, when their *relation to the leader is in good working order.* Call this type of morality a *leader-centered*

---

¹ See, e.g., Sigmund Freud, *The Future of an Illusion*, trans. and ed. James Strachey (New York: W. W. Norton, 1961), p. 14.
² Sigmund Freud, *Group Psychology and the Analysis of the Ego*, in *The Standard Edition of the Complete Psychological Works of Sigmund Freud*, ed. James Strachey, vol. 18 (London: Hogarth Press, 1955), p. 113.
³ Ibid., pp. 114–15.
⁴ Ibid., p. 115, emphasis added.

morality – leader-centered in the sense that when people comply with moral norms it is the ego's relation to the leader that does the work. By contrast, call a morality *superego-centered* if it is the ego's relation to the superego that determines moral behavior. This is not a distinction between individual and group morality but one that pertains to how individuals behave morally. What characterizes a leader-centered morality is that *individual* moral behavior rests on a central fact of *group* psychology.

This central fact, to repeat, is the ego's relation to the leader. In the relevantly similar hypnotic relation, Freud remarks, we find the kind of unlimited devotion that is displayed by someone in love except for the exclusion of sexual satisfaction. Given the structural identity of hypnosis and group psychology, the same devotion must be true of the relation to the leader. And the unlimited extent of this devotion, as Freud says of unrequited love, is a matter of the "hypercathexis of [the loved object] by the ego and *at the ego's expense*."[5] Thus it can be inferred what it means for the relation to the leader to be in good working order: the presence of unlimited devotion to the leader, or the ego's hypercathexis of the leader to the point of self-effacement.

It follows that when individuals who are subject to this kind of morality fail regularly and seriously to comply with the moral norms of their group, something must be amiss with their relation to the leader. The ego's hypercathexis of the leader, we may surmise, has become weak or even absent. To the extent that this happens, the individual, in this kind of morality, loses the motivational basis for voluntarily complying with the moral norms of his group. The crucial relation that is meant to do the work of motivating moral behavior is no longer strong enough, and a moral crisis ensues.

Not surprisingly, a leader-centered morality will treat as its first order of business the promotion of the relation that lies at its center. With regard to the normal functioning of the group, including the normal moral behavior of its members, nothing is more crucial than keeping the ego's relation to the leader in good working order. In the case of China, myriad discourses, often supported by rituals, are developed to this end. We can take note of such discourses and of the close relation between how well they succeed and how well members of the group behave morally. It is on the basis of such observation that I am led to the hypothesis that Chinese morality, both under Mao and after Mao, is of the leader-centered variety par excellence. To the extent that this morality was effective under Mao,

---

[5] Ibid., p. 114, emphasis added.

so the hypothesis goes, it was not a robust superego that did the work but a strong relation to the leader,[6] and if the same form of morality has been less effective since, it is because the ego's relation to the leader has come under increasing strain. To call the latter situation a crisis is to regard that strain as so severe that a leader-centered morality is no longer supportable.[7]

3

The example of Mao's China affords an unusually clear view of the underlying logic that informs the organization of a society based on devotion to the leader – a logic that has been pursued with less conviction and fanfare since but, *as far as the form of morality is concerned*, not fundamentally abandoned. Then, as now, the relationship between the leader (or leadership) and the people in the domain of morality is one of undisguised paternalism and, discursively, one of exhortation. The leadership stands in a relation of "guidance and instruction" (*yindao*) to the masses, plays the self-appointed role of educating the latter in correct thought and morally acceptable conduct (*sixiang daode jiaoyu*), and adopts the discourse of "must..." (*yao*...) as if from a birthright. Party members, including the rank and file, are supposed to set an example for the rest

---

[6] It was part and parcel of this strong relation to the leader that, in the name of public ownership, the leader controlled virtually all the means of production and was the sole provider of livelihood for everyone. It should not be surprising that the leader's total control over morality went hand in hand with his equally total monopoly regarding the possession and distribution of resources. These were inseparable dimensions of the strong relation to the leader.

[7] The devotion to the leader that is constitutive of a leader-centered morality need not be anything remotely based on natural bonds and may well be something thoroughly politically contrived, with all the characteristics and liabilities of such contrivance. In the case of China, the devotion to the leader, in the shape of Mao and more generally the Party, was manufactured as an integral part of a heavy-handed political organization of all aspects of life, without which such devotion would have been neither necessary nor possible. To be socialized into normal membership of such a society was to acquire a proper measure of devotion to the leader, as embodied in everyday practices of allegiance and obedience and interpreted through corresponding discourses. There is thus a sense in which the values and dispositions that make up such devotion to the leader belong to the phenomenon of adaptive preference formation. Indeed, we can appropriately speak of devotion to the leader, as distinct from enforced submission, only to the extent that adaptive preference formation has taken place. There is little doubt that such formation happened on a massive scale in Mao's China, although it obviously went together with enforced submission on the part of significant numbers of people. On adaptive preference formation, see Jon Elster, *Sour Grapes: Studies in the Subversion of Rationality* (Cambridge: Cambridge University Press, 1983), chap. 3.

of society (*xianfeng mofan daitou zuoyong*). All this, even today, presupposes a collective cause and a corresponding leader(ship) and requires devotion as the chief political virtue and the chief psychological basis of morality.

An organization of society based on such devotion must have made perfectly good sense at its inception: it must have originated under circumstances that inhibited manifestation of power except through a group formation. Under such circumstances – circumstances that endanger members of a society with respect to livelihood and even identity – devotion to the leader does not suppress individual power but serves to overcome individual powerlessness. Through devotion to the leader, individual powerlessness is turned into a form of collective power in which all individuals partake and which gives each powerless individual a feeling of power as part of a whole.[8]

Powerlessness does not mean lack of *will* to power. It consists rather in the lack of opportunities for the expression of will to power, that is, for its expression by individuals as the smallest integral units of power. Thus a condition of powerlessness contains within it a will to power that seeks an outlet, an opportunity for expression. This thwarted will to power – power within powerlessness – finds expression in unquestioning devotion to a collective cause and its leader. When I say that individual powerlessness is turned into collective power through such devotion, then, what I mean is that the will to power that cannot find expression in the form of individual power is given an outlet in the form of collective power – power under a leader, and, via the shared relation to the leader, power in solidarity with fellow members of the group.

The conversion of the thwarted power of individuals into collective power can take place only through a set of valorizing interpretations (i.e., what are usually called values) that inform the collective enterprise. These interpretations work by making a virtue of necessity – the necessity of directing power into collective channels, of power through devotion. But this necessity must already be present to a significant degree: the powerlessness of individuals must be part of lived experience if the interpretations are to make sense. The interpretations must be interpretations *of* experience, not just interpretations arbitrarily imposed upon experience. It is only when interpretations speak to the experience of those involved that they can acquire plausibility, and only plausible

---

[8] See my *Dialectic of the Chinese Revolution: From Utopianism to Hedonism* (Stanford: Stanford University Press, 1994), pp. 187–92.

interpretations – interpretations plausible to those involved – can be internalized and make the conversion of power possible.

Four sets of such interpretations, or discourses, have played a significant part in making a virtue of the necessity of collective power in Mao's China. The expression of the will to power in the form of collective power requires, above all, a collective cause. The *discourse of collective enterprise*, specifically of communism, identifies such a cause, thereby making a *virtue* of the necessity of directing power into collective channels and providing a *positive* rationale for it. It is the job of official theoreticians and propagandists to churn out version after version of this discourse.

The discourse of communism is a discourse on the nature and substance of the collective enterprise, and as such this discourse supplies a set of reasons for a particular, collective expression of power. Proof is needed that this expression of power is possible and indeed has been successful, that the initial powerlessness of individuals has been transcended through feats of collective power. To provide such proof is the function of the *discourse of collective achievement*. Through this discourse, the collective expression of power is given the reality of concrete deeds so that people are spurred on to ever new heights of collective power. This is why so much of the official media is devoted to recounting (sometimes inventing) collective achievements.

In such achievements the leader plays a crucial role. It is through the leader that quantities of thwarted power are organized into collective power in the first place. The leader, in turn, converts collective power into a form of individual power he alone possesses, and he does so in the name of the collective. This individual power is none other than the leader's ability to bring about and maintain the conversion of the thwarted power of individuals into effective collective power. Members of the collective, for their part, keep a relation of devotion to the leader and thereby partake of the collective power the leader helps make possible and embodies in his own person.

But there is something intrinsically unsettling about devotion to the leader. For this kind of relation is meant to hold between two parties that are not merely unequal but extremely unequal, and this presupposition of *extreme* inequality prompts questions. Are the two parties really so unequal in their cognitive, moral, and other powers as to justify devotion? Is there good reason for people to forego the exercise of their own agency except for the will to devotion to the leader? Answers to such questions are provided, or the very questions preempted, by a *discourse of the infallibility of the leader(ship)*. Such a discourse, at its most conspicuous, takes the form of the personality cult surrounding Mao, which accompanied the entire career of Mao as leader and reached its apex during the Cultural Revolution.

As the personality cult of Mao demonstrates, the discourse of infallibility cannot stand alone and needs to be backed up with hagiography. Conversely, the very need for hagiography shows the discourse of infallibility to be a form of distorted communication. There is an implicitly acknowledged gap between the reality of the leader and the discourse of his supposed infallibility. The need thus arises for hagiography, for distorted narrative of the powers and achievements of the leader, and of the larger history of which he is a part, in the interest of preserving an appearance of infallibility. If the discourse of infallibility is an abstract discourse designed to show that a class of infallible leaders can exist, hagiography serves to create the appearance that a particular leader belongs to that class.

What all three discourses have in common is that they make a virtue of necessity – the necessity of power through devotion to a leader and a cause. But they implicitly do more than this: they make a *permanent* virtue out of what otherwise may well be a temporary necessity. This is made explicit in a fourth discourse, a *discourse of the permanent need for a leader(ship) and for a corresponding group formation*. If this discourse succeeds, the virtue it makes of the necessity will outlast the necessity itself and help prolong a situation when it is otherwise no longer necessary.

4

That such discourses are necessary at all suggests that identification is not meant to figure in the ego's relation to the leader. Comparing the army and the Christian Church, Freud has this to say about the former, which he means to be taken as an example of the typical group and of the typical relation to the leader:

It is obvious that a soldier takes his superior, that is, in fact, the leader of the army, as his ideal, while he identifies himself with his equals, and derives from this community of their egos the obligations for giving mutual help and for sharing possessions which comradeship implies. But *he becomes ridiculous if he tries to identify himself with the general*.[9]

[9] Freud, *Group Psychology*, p. 134, emphasis added.

For Freud, then, a relationship of devotion is definitely not one of identification. And yet we may recall that Freud also holds that in this kind of relationship the object – be it the leader, the loved one, or the hypnotist – "has been put in the place of the ego ideal."[10] Does this very formulation – "has been put in the place of the ego ideal" – not mean that somehow the object is internalized or introjected? Richard Wollheim seems to think so when he interprets Freud's remarks on the difference between normal individual psychology and group psychology in terms of "a distinction, implicit in what Freud said, between the *internalized* object being set up as the superego and the *internalized* object being set up in the place of the superego."[11]

This raises the question – what exactly does it mean for something to be internalized? – along with the further question – what is the connection between internalization and identification? To consider these questions, I will draw on a distinction that Wollheim makes in a later work, where he identifies two degrees of internalization.[12] In this later account of introjection, we have, first, an occurrent fantasy of incorporation and, then, the turning of this fantasy into a disposition to fantasize about the figure thus incorporated. Wollheim calls the second step internalization. It is possible, according to Wollheim, for this to be followed by a further development, a process whereby the child will "imagine the figure from the inside or centrally, and, when this comes about not haphazardly but as the manifestation, indeed as the expression, of the disposition, mere internalization has graduated to identification. In introjecting a figure the child has identified with it."[13] It is the completion of the entire trajectory, from the initial incorporation fantasy through internalization to the final identification, that makes up introjection in the fullest sense.[14] Now, in terms of this way of looking at the matter, the phenomenon of the leader taking the place of the ego ideal does not seem to qualify as internalization, still less as identification, as these are precisely defined by Wollheim.

---

[10] Ibid., p. 113.

[11] Richard Wollheim, *Freud* (Glasgow: Fontana/Collins, 1971), p. 230, emphasis added.

[12] See Richard Wollheim, *The Thread of Life* (Cambridge: Cambridge University Press, 1984), pp. 121–24.

[13] Ibid., p. 123.

[14] Charles Rycroft draws a similar tripartite distinction – between internalization, introjection, and (secondary or introjective) identification. These correspond, roughly, to what Wollheim terms incorporation, internalization, and identification, respectively. See the entries on "Introjection" and "Identification" in Charles Rycroft, *A Critical Dictionary of Psychoanalysis*, 2nd ed. (Harmondsworth: Penguin, 1995), pp. 87 and 76, respectively.

I am therefore inclined to interpret "has been put in the place of the ego ideal" functionally rather than spatially. Thus, to say that the leader has taken the place of the ego ideal is not to say that the leader has come to be *where* the superego would otherwise be but only to say that the functions of the superego are taken over by the leader, with all that this functional replacement entails.

This functional replacement entails, above all, that the leader and his commands must remain external, or, put another way, that the leader must not be internalized, still less identified with. If the leader is to take the place of the ego ideal instead of becoming it, it is essential that he not be made an object of internalization in either of Wollheim's senses.[15] If, from one point of view, there is no greater triumph for the leader than the introjection of him as a figure of authority, then, from another point of view, there is no deadlier enemy to the leader than precisely such introjection. For the introjection of the leader can come about only at the expense of the leader as *external* authority. To the extent that introjection takes place, the commands of the leader will no longer be perceived as (just) the commands of the leader. Indeed, for the leader to be introjected *is* for his commands to become independent of their original, external source, to function independently of their being perceived as emanating from that external source.

This independence is, in part, a matter of the description under which moral imperatives are comprehended. An internalized moral imperative is a command that has become independent of its original, external source or, more precisely, a command that one follows under the description of a command which one somehow issues to oneself, typically in the name of what is called one's conscience.

A mere change of descriptions – from external to internal source – is, needless to say, just a misdescription. The important thing is that under appropriate conditions the misdescription will be accompanied by misrecognition. The appropriate conditions are the internalization of some figure of authority and possible identification with the internalized figure. It is through such internalization and identification that misrecognition is accomplished, such that one not only places moral imperatives under

---

[15] The most important thing, for my purposes, is whether the leader is internalized at all or remains external, and the question, in the case of the former, of whether the leader is merely internalized, as Wollheim puts it (*Thread of Life*, p. 218), or is also identified with is of lesser importance. In what follows, therefore, I shall only occasionally find it necessary to attend to the distinction between mere internalization and identification. And I will use "internalization" and "introjection" interchangeably.

a particular misdescription but positively believes this misdescription. To the extent that misdescription is thus completed by misrecognition, one perceives moral imperatives as issued by an internal figure, in the case of internalization, or even by oneself, in the case of identification with that internal figure.

But no sooner is misrecognition accomplished in this way than it ceases to be misrecognition pure and simple. Thanks to the internalization of some figure of moral authority and, especially, to the identification with the internalized figure, if the latter happens, the possibility emerges that one can revise one's conscience in ways not fully determined by its original, external source, and that one's conscience thus revised can even come into conflict with that original, external source. To the extent that one makes use of this possibility, misrecognition turns into autonomy.[16]

Misrecognition of the leader through internalization and possible identification thus spells the end of the leader as such, that is, the leader as external authority. From this we can draw a crucial inference regarding what it takes to preserve the integrity of a leader-centered morality. In such a morality, people must *not* internalize, still less identify with, the leader. They must understand and follow moral imperatives under their *true* description: the commands of the leader. Everything must be done to prevent the misrecognition of commands issued by the leader as commands issued by oneself and thus to make sure that moral imperatives remain external. If all this is accomplished, then people will relate to moral imperatives by relating first and directly to their source, the leader, and they will act on such imperatives only if, or only to the extent that, this latter relation, with its characteristic hypercathexis and devotion, is in good working order.

This does not mean that there is no place in a leader-centered morality for internalization or identification of any kind. While a leader-centered morality precludes identification with the leader, it need not discourage identification with a different if related figure: the moral exemplar. What distinguishes exemplars from leaders, however, is that they do not issue moral commands. They act on moral commands issued by the leader, and they are moral exemplars in that they do so with a devotion to the leader that is deemed worthy of emulation – indeed of identification. The

---

[16] Wollheim speaks of "formal marks of internality," that is, "characteristics that qualify not so much the internal object itself as the mode in which it is represented" (*Thread of Life*, p. 128). Nothing is more characteristic of the internal mode of representation than its relative freedom from the external counterpart of the internal object – that is, potential autonomy.

important thing about moral exemplars is that they are like us, standing in the same relation to the leader as we do, and thus it is possible for us to identify with them. When we succeed in such identification, we shall be doing as well what they do so well – and for the same reason: devotion to the leader. We will not, however, have thereby internalized the leader. Even the exemplars have not internalized the leader, and they are not supposed to. They act on the leader's moral commands out of exemplary devotion, and in following in their footsteps, we can be doing no more. Thus, even with exemplars and the possibility of identification with them, the leader remains as external to us as ever. And only this externality can support a leader-centered morality.

5

One should not be surprised if the leader-centered morality in Mao's China does not assume anything like a pure form. As an ideal type, a leader-centered morality rests entirely on devotion to the leader and on the prevention of significant shortfall in such devotion. In reality, no matter how much is done to prevent such shortfall, there will always be some remainder, and the specter of this remainder makes tempting countermeasures that smack of internalization. One such countermeasure is what is called the raising of consciousness (*juewu*) or conscientiousness (*zijuexing*) – a constant motif of moral education in Mao's China. This is part of an elaborate discourse of individual moral initiative, and what makes this discourse special is its self-contradictory reliance on internalization. One is supposed to take moral commands from the leader in an ongoing fashion, and this means that one should never internalize the leader's moral authority and make the leader superfluous. Yet, simultaneously, one is supposed to act on the leader's moral commands with a conscientiousness that is possible only through internalization. The required internalization cannot be accomplished, however, unless the heightening of conscientiousness is inwardly directed and, as such, is distinct from the outward display of devotion to the leader, but then inward direction poses a deadly threat to such devotion even as it takes its original motivation from the latter. For this very reason, internalization cannot be allowed to run its natural course, and the inwardly directed conscientiousness must always yield to the outwardly directed devotion to the leader. Small wonder that this contorted attempt at having things both ways never really worked. When Mao's spell and power lasted, this failure was disguised by an abundance of devotion that passed for conscientiousness. But the seeming conscientiousness never took on a life of its own, with the result that when devotion to the leader waned, the semblance of conscientiousness lost its basis, evaporating along with the devotion instead of filling the vacuum left by it. If we reflect on the causes of this failure, we will learn further lessons about the nature and consequences of internalization.

The discourse of individual moral initiative speaks to the superego, indeed presupposes it. The superego issues commands to the ego under the description not of some external authority but of an independent moral center located in oneself. That the superego is able to do this is a double-edged sword, relieving the leader at once of the burden of moral supervision and of the very rationale for his continued existence as external authority. With his commands internalized by members of the group, the leader no longer needs to demand and enforce compliance with his commands: the superego will see to it that these commands, in their internalized form, are followed. Each member of the group, having internalized the leader, has become his or her own leader. The leader *of the group* is no longer needed. Herein lies the problem, for nothing is more important for a leader-centered morality than that the leader will always be needed. The idea that informs the discourse of individual moral initiative in Mao's China, to some extent even beyond, is that a state of affairs should be brought about in which members of the group have a significant degree of individual moral initiative as distinct from devotion to the leader and yet such initiative itself is firmly under the control of the leader and does not dispense with the need for the leader as an ongoing source of moral commands. Our reflection on the nature and consequences of internalization shows this to be an impossible task, because its two constituent objectives – an ongoing devotion to the leader and a strong superego capable of moral initiative – cannot be brought off except at the expense of each other. As long as the leader remains external, the moral behavior of members of the group will hinge on their devotion to the leader. Their moral behavior cannot simultaneously rest on a robust superego, for a robust superego can emerge and endure only through internalization of the leader, and once internalized the leader in its capacity as external authority will become dispensable and superfluous. There is no room for a robust superego in a leader-centered morality, just as there is no room for the leader inside the superego or a superego-centered morality except under another description.

This is not to say that because the dominant morality in Mao's China, and to some extent even in China today, is marked by a leader-centered structure, we Chinese must be devoid of the superego. The defining feature of a leader-centered morality is, rather, that the superego is not what is meant to do the heavy-duty work in motivating moral behavior; in other words, the crucial relation that motivates moral behavior is not ego's relation to superego or one's relation to oneself. Of far greater importance in this type of morality is ego's relation to external authority. It is a precondition, and, if the precondition is well fulfilled, also an ever stronger consequence, of maintaining the external authority that such superego as must continue to exist is not allowed to develop a strength that could pose a serious threat to the leader as external authority. Thus, the superego is kept weak even as it is drawn upon to make up for any attenuation in the ego's relation to external authority. And because the superego has been denied the room to become a robust moral force in its own right, we may surmise that it will be incapable of immediately taking up the slack if and when the ego's relation to external authority becomes dysfunctional, as has increasingly happened in the past three decades.

6

This has been the story of morality in Mao's China and, up to a point, of the descent to the moral no-man's-land today. Up to a point, but not entirely. There is little doubt that the ego's relation to external moral authority has weakened greatly, but, strictly speaking, it is not so much that the superego is unable to step into the gap left by a weakened external authority as that the superego is still not given sufficient room to progress beyond the early internalization of parental authority and become the independent moral force it needs to be if it is to play this role. That room is freedom.

What this story shows is that the transition in the superego from the internalization of parental authority early in childhood to the internalization of other, social forms of authority later throughout adulthood is more laden with problems, not least the possibility of stunted growth affecting an entire society, than often seems to be assumed. It is on the matter of this transition that the Chinese case becomes instructive – instructive, especially, regarding the place of freedom in morality. Now, the emergence of the superego through the introjection of parents provides the prototype for the continuation and expansion of the superego later in life. The child introjects parental authority and, in so doing, becomes at once identical with it and free from it. This can happen, however, only insofar as the child is able to misdescribe and misrecognize parental figures by imaginatively constructing internal figures corresponding to and yet distinct from them. Such misdescription and misrecognition require room: parental authority looms large, of course, but must not loom too large or too obtrusively, or else it will block the child's imagination and make internalization next to impossible. Thus, even in the face of overwhelming parental authority and the child's irresistible urge to introject it as a defense, the child will need considerable freedom to accomplish the introjection. In what may be considered normal circumstances, this freedom comes in no small part from the accommodation, or at least the counteracting of sheer fear, made possible by the unmistakable presence of parental love. As far as the superego is concerned, parental love translates into, and is to be measured by, the child's freedom to accomplish the task of introjection. Even the first emergence of the superego presupposes freedom.[17]

In this regard, the superego, it may be said, reveals a fundamental characteristic of morality. There is something unavoidably self-regarding, as distinct from selfish, about being or becoming a moral subject. Morality enters the life of a person, or comes to constitute a person, only when she herself thinks she ought to do, and is motivated to do, what morality requires. It must become *her* morality; only thus does she become a moral *subject*. Whatever its liabilities, the superego is the first mechanism that allows this to happen – by allowing some external morality to become one's own through internalization and identification. At the same time, this very process stands as a reminder of the partly illusory character

---

[17] This is my claim, not a claim that can be attributed to Freud. Still, there is nothing in this claim that need be incompatible with what Freud has to say about the superego. To be sure, "The super-ego," as Freud famously remarks, "seems to have made a one-sided choice and to have picked out only the parents' strictness and severity, their prohibiting and punitive function, whereas their loving care seems not to have been taken over and maintained" (*New Introductory Lectures on Psycho*-Analysis, in *The Standard Edition of the Complete Psychological Works of Sigmund Freud*, ed. James Strachey, vol. 22 [London: Hogarth Press, 1960], p. 62). But this has to do with the superego's character, as distinct from its formation. As far as the latter is concerned, Freud clearly assigns a significant role to love. Thus he writes, of the killing of the primal father:

His sons hated him, but they loved him, too. After their hatred had been satisfied by their act of aggression, their love came to the fore in their remorse for the deed. It set up the super-ego by identification with the father; it gave that agency the father's power, as though as a punishment for the deed of aggression they had carried out against him. (*Civilization and Its Discontents*, trans. and ed. James Strachey [New York: W. W. Norton, 1961], p. 79)

While Freud here picks out one role of love in the formation of the superego, I am suggesting another, that which affords a child the room – or freedom – to accomplish the introjection of parental authority.

of moral subjectivity: moral authority does not begin as one's own, and thus individual moral autonomy cannot do without misdescription and misrecognition. Nevertheless, this illusion has a kernel of truth which one makes good whenever one avails oneself of the considerable freedom that attaches to one's relation to internalized objects – if one is not prevented from doing so. It is this *continuing* freedom that makes possible the development of the early superego into a mature moral subject.

It is easy to forget that this precondition for misdescription and misrecognition, and hence for the expansion of the superego beyond the introjection of parental authority, cannot be taken for granted. When Freud writes, "As a child grows up, the role of father is carried on by teachers and by others in authority; their injunctions and prohibitions remain powerful in the ego-ideal and continue, in the form of conscience, to exercise the moral censorship,"[18] he sounds almost as if this transition would happen as a matter of course. In fact, it may well turn out that, as the child grows into an adult and beyond, he is prevented from introjecting further forms of authority. He is prevented because the leader, with all the power at his disposal and without any remote equivalent of parental love, looms too large and too obtrusively for introjection.[19] The leader, not wanting to be dispensed with, sees to it that the emerging adult obeys moral imperatives that will remain external, imperatives that are to be understood and followed under their true description, that is, as commands issued by the leader and not, through misdescription and misrecognition, as if by the emerging adult himself.[20] Thus, the superego is left confronting a huge obstacle in its struggle to grow beyond its infantile form, and, quite predictably, indeed by design, all too many people never quite become full-fledged adults, morally speaking. It is this failure

---

[18] Sigmund Freud, *The Ego and the Id*, in *The Standard Edition of the Complete Psychological Works of Sigmund Freud*, ed. James Strachey, vol. 19 (London: Hogarth Press, 1961), p. 37.

[19] As Wollheim says, "Freud was thinking of hypnosis and unhappy love as phenomena superimposed on, and to some degree effacing, the results of normal development: although, of course, the fact that such effacement can happen shows that the development was not robust" (*Freud*, p. 230). We can place the dominance of the leader in the same category of phenomena that are "superimposed on, and to some degree effacing, the results of normal development." The difference is that the impact of the leader, both comprehensive and long-lasting, is likely to stunt the growth of the superego for every member of the group. Under such impact, no one, whatever the strength of his or her normal development, is likely to escape unscathed.

[20] This extraordinary role of the leader needs to be understood in the context of the almost total, and totally overt, assimilation of morality to politics that marked Mao's China, especially during the Cultural Revolution. See my *Dialectic*, chap. 3.

to move decisively beyond the infantile form of the superego and thus to grow into morally reasonably independent adulthood, rather than the arresting of the earlier process of the interjection of parental authority, that marks Chinese moral culture in Mao's time.

From this *systemic* lack of a precondition for a mature and robust superego, we can infer that the leader rather than the superego is the linchpin of morality in Mao's China. And from the continuing absence of this precondition, we may surmise that the leader-centered morality is still with us, despite appearances to the contrary. When we speak of a moral crisis in post-Mao China, it is this morality that is in crisis. A crisis of *this* morality signifies that what is meant to produce moral behavior within it – devotion to the leader – is no longer in good working order. It also signifies that those forces that militated against a superego-centered morality in Mao's China remain in effect today.[21] The upshot is that the leader, as the original, external source of moral imperatives, is neither any longer an unquestioned object of devotion nor a permissible object of introjection. Put another way, a leader-centered morality has lost its foundation and yet an alternative, superego-centered morality is not there to take its place. Morally, we are between two worlds, one dysfunctional, the other yet to be (allowed to be) created.

---

[21] For discussion of these forces, see Chapters 2, 3, and 10 of this book.

7

The Insult of Poverty

I

It will have become obvious by now that my concern with freedom is informed by a larger and deeper concern with agency. Viewed from within this larger and deeper concern, freedom conceived and codified in one way or another is so important because it serves as the only plausible paradigm for giving moral and institutional form to the human need for agency under modern conditions of life. Also thus viewed, China's current moral crisis is a crisis of agency at the levels of the individual and of society as a whole, and it is only because of freedom's indispensable role for agency under modern conditions that China's route of escape from its moral crisis must be paved with freedom – freedom with Chinese characteristics, if you like – as one essential element among others. With agency thus serving as its framework and constant point of reference, an inquiry into freedom such as mine is naturally porous. For once we think of freedom, of China's moral crisis, and of the nature of China's need for freedom in this way, that is, at the deeper level of agency, there is no avoiding the need to confront other problems that have an equally weighty bearing on agency.

One such problem is that of poverty, and if in a book focused on freedom I cannot broach all significant problems that register on the horizon of agency, the problem of poverty is so important and is so much part of the moral crisis that I must devote at least a chapter to it. Doing so will allow me also to give some attention, if somewhat indirect, to the problem of equality. More importantly, it will help produce a better balance for the book as a whole, especially normatively, and thus a more precise impression of the moral impulses that drive my entire undertaking.

2

The nature of poverty resides in the character of those basic human needs that require material resources for their satisfaction. The needs in question are various and point to what I shall call "the stakes of poverty." It is these stakes that make poverty the evil that it is and give the task of preventing or removing poverty its importance. Every investigation of poverty, whether normative or empirical, expresses or implies some view of the stakes of poverty. In this chapter I place the stakes of poverty in the foreground and intersperse my theoretical discussion of them with brief, concept-guided narratives of the changing modes of poverty and reaction to it in Mao's China and after.

In particular, I shall distinguish three stakes, and three corresponding types, of poverty – which bear on subsistence, status, and agency, respectively – and examine the relations in which the three types of poverty stand to one another. This will allow me to present a reasonably comprehensive view of what significant forms poverty can take in China (and in the world at large), what is bad about each of them and about their combination, and how one might begin to think constructively and with some hope, at least in theory, about removing or reducing arguably the most damaging aspect of poverty without unrealistic expectations regarding the plenitude of material resources. The picture of poverty that will emerge in this way is one in which, to put it bluntly and perhaps simplistically, the problem of sheer material deprivation (what I call subsistence poverty) is, symptomatically and sadly, at once the most urgent and, in principle, the least important.

3

It is something of a commonplace that poverty can affect both subsistence and status. To be poor is to suffer a shortfall in one or both of these goods, which correspond to two different dimensions of a human being – as a biological being with subsistence needs, and as a social being with an equally irrepressible need for respect or recognition.[1] This commonplace distinction is worth pursuing.

---

[1] For the most part, I use the term "respect" in a broad sense, without distinguishing between respect and esteem, and interchangeably with "recognition." I will have occasion to consider the respect/esteem distinction in the final section of this chapter.

The Insult of Poverty

As a matter of subsistence, poverty is a simple and straightforward condition, however complex its causal story and controversial the assignment of responsibility for eradicating it.[2] It is a species of physical neediness and, as such, has nothing intrinsically and directly demeaning about it. What can make subsistence poverty demeaning is the character of those social relations that systematically cause and maintain it. In themselves subsistence needs are purely physical needs, and being unable to meet them adequately is a condition that is obviously fraught with bad or even life-threatening consequences for those who suffer from it. But material poverty need not cast any intrinsically negative social meaning on those who happen to be in this condition.

As a matter of status, on the other hand, poverty does carry an intrinsically negative meaning: the poor here are those who have the lowest social status, by virtue of, or as reflected in, their having the lowest income. Call it status poverty – not lack of status as such (for one can lack status, be poor *in* status, in many ways) but a special kind of lack of status that is characteristic of a society in which money is an all-important marker of social standing. Such poverty represents a shortfall with reference not to subsistence needs but to the need for respect. It is still income that is lacking, yet the needs for which income is lacking are not physical but social. In status poverty, what a very low income makes difficult or impossible is not subsistence but rather participation in a range of social activities that form the basis of respectable status.[3]

Now, subsistence poverty has a more or less fixed point of reference in human biology. Basic physical needs can go unsatisfied because of extreme scarcity or extremely inequitable distribution. But such needs are not themselves competitive or comparative and therefore are in principle capable of being satisfied for each and all. Status poverty is different. It is found in societies in which social status is closely linked to things that only money allows one to do, so that the lower one's economic position, the fewer such things one is able to do, and the greater one's

---

[2] The question of the causes of poverty, of whatever variety, and of responsibility for relieving it is not my focus in this chapter. Insofar as I touch on the question, I do so in the simplified context of a domestic society. For insights into this question, especially in the global context, see Thomas Pogge, *World Poverty and Human Rights* (Cambridge: Polity Press, 2002).

[3] André Gorz distinguishes between destitution and poverty, which correspond roughly to what I call subsistence poverty and status poverty. See his illuminating discussion in *Ecology as Politics*, trans. Patsy Vigderman and Jonathan Cloud (Montréal: Black Rose Press, 1980), pp. 28–29, 58. For the effects of poverty on participation in normal social activities, see Amartya Sen, *Development as Freedom* (New York: Anchor Books, 2000), pp. 89–90.

social exclusion will be. In such societies the economically worst-off will make up the status poor, whatever their absolute level of income. Status poverty is thus a strictly relative condition that derives from a society's hierarchical distribution of recognition on the basis of material wealth as a necessary means of participation in status-conferring social activities. For this reason, status poverty cannot be alleviated by improving material conditions alone, or by any other means that stop short of removing or at least weakening the link between status and income.[4]

4

Given that subsistence poverty and status poverty are conceptually distinct, three scenarios are possible. First, although those who suffer from status poverty have the least resources overall relative to others, they may have enough resources to meet their basic subsistence needs. This scenario is typical of the poor in so-called developed societies, although subsistence poverty is far from unknown in such societies. Second, it is possible for those who suffer from subsistence poverty to be free from status poverty, as when they happen to be members of a society in which income is not a significant marker of status. This was largely true, for example, of Mao's China, as we shall see.

Finally, although strictly speaking status poverty is a function of a lack of material resources for participation rather than for subsistence, in practice it is almost inevitable that in a society that permits status poverty, those who lack material resources for subsistence will also lack material resources for those activities that form the basis of respectable status. Thus, people can suffer simultaneously from subsistence poverty and status poverty, a possibility that is commonly realized in societies that are both underdeveloped and marked by a hierarchical structure of recognition based substantially on a certain level of income as a necessary means of participation. This is the form that much of the poverty in the world takes today.[5]

---

[4] This is especially true of modern, industrial societies, with their distinctive ways of perpetuating status poverty through such mechanisms as "polarization" and "obsolescence." See Ivan Illich, *Tools for Conviviality* (New York: Harper & Row, 1973), pp. 67–76.

[5] For poignant descriptions of poverty in present-day China that often involves hardship and low status at the same time, see Zhou Yongping et al., eds., *Kankan tamen* (Spare a Look at Them) (Beijing: Zhongguo qingnian chubanshe, 2004); and Xu Xiao and Liang Xiaoyan, eds., *Xiang tong, zai chengshi de shenchu* (The Rural Soul in Pain: In the Depths of the City) (Haikou: Hainan chubanshe, 2006).

It should not be surprising if the combination of status poverty and subsistence poverty causes the negative social meaning associated with the former to be attached to the latter as well. After all, the low level of income that makes subsistence difficult is also what prevents participation in normal social activities, and thus a low level of income per se will generally carry negative social meaning, irrespective of its effects on subsistence or status. There is nevertheless a sense in which this negative meaning belongs directly to status poverty rather than subsistence poverty.[6] We may think of the process involved as the inevitable superimposition of negative social meaning onto subsistence poverty via status poverty, indeed the assimilation of subsistence poverty to status poverty.[7]

As a result, a simple case of subsistence poverty that is otherwise free of social meaning receives a stigma whose effect can only be described as adding insult to injury.[8] This is not in itself an indictment of status

---

[6] It is indicative of this that low-income earners, even in rich societies, are often tempted to sacrifice subsistence for participation. See Amartya Sen, *Inequality Reexamined* (Cambridge, MA: Harvard University Press, 1992), chap. 7.

[7] Such superimposition of negative meaning onto subsistence poverty is aided by a powerful social mechanism. Insofar as people are called poor solely on account of their condition, without any explanation of this condition, the superimposition is blocked. If poverty is explained by tracing its causes to factors other than the poor themselves, say to social injustice or even to bad luck, then again the superimposition is blocked. But a predominant explanation involves attribution of a special kind of responsibility to the poor themselves for their own condition. The poor are poor, according to this explanation, because they lack either the willingness (moral virtues) or the ability (instrumental virtues) to be otherwise. Where some such explanation is accepted, subsistence poverty takes on a negative meaning that is not intrinsic to it, and status poverty takes on an *extra* negative meaning that reinforces its intrinsically negative meaning. In either case, poverty, which does not attract blame by itself, is turned into a proxy for things that do. Distinct from, and even more important than, whether one is responsible for one's condition of poverty in this sense is whether one has chosen this condition. The crucial role of choice is evident in a comparison of poverty and asceticism, which I will pursue shortly. The sting of the blame for poverty is the idea that the poor, in being responsible for their own condition, nevertheless are responsible in a way that does not bespeak autonomy. The poor do not choose poverty: they prefer not to be in their condition but supposedly lack the moral or instrumental virtues to avoid it. This combination of being responsible for one's poverty and yet not properly choosing it helps make possible the negative social meaning that poverty often has.

[8] In the context of discussing Nietzsche, Arthur C. Danto introduces a useful distinction between "extensional suffering and intensional suffering, where the latter consists in an interpretation of the former." See his "Some Remarks on *The Genealogy of Morals*," in Robert C. Solomon and Kathleen M. Higgins, eds., *Reading Nietzsche* (New York: Oxford University Press, 1988), pp. 13–28 at p. 21. If subsistence poverty is a kind of extensional suffering, the negative meaning given to it can be a source of additional,

poverty, but it is impossible to protest against the social assimilation of subsistence poverty to status poverty without in some way taking issue with the very presence of status poverty that makes this possible. Since the added insult to those in the grip of subsistence poverty is unavoidable in a society that also permits status poverty, there is something morally problematic with any society that allows the existence of subsistence and status poverty at the same time. At the very least, until subsistence poverty is overcome through the creation of more wealth or a more equitable distribution of existing wealth, status poverty is a luxury that no reasonably just or decent society can accept with good conscience.[9]

5

It may help move our discussion forward on a surer footing if I bring the distinction developed so far to bear on The People's Republic of China's record of fighting poverty. On the one hand, China is sometimes credited with having made great strides in the fight against poverty since the start of the reform in the late 1970s. On the other hand, it is no less often claimed that poverty has become a worse problem in China today than it was in Mao's time. Both claims contain an element of truth, in my view, and the distinction between subsistence and status poverty is especially useful for capturing what is true in each claim.

Material scarcity was undoubtedly a very serious problem in Mao's time. Generally speaking, however, it was treated as a matter of subsistence poverty alone, with no significant implications for status. The fight against material scarcity thus conceived was in turn framed by the collective pursuit of the goal of communism. Though it was something to be overcome on the road to communism, subsistence poverty was nevertheless a spur to action aimed at bringing about collective prosperity and eventually communism, or so it was believed, and as such it was regarded as the source of the ascetic virtues required for the transition to communism. In this spirit, the entire population embraced the condition of material scarcity, which was a fact of Chinese society to begin with, and in so doing turned necessity into the semblance of choice.

The important thing is not so much that people were by and large equally poor, but rather that in their condition of equal poverty they were

---

intensional suffering. As Danto observes, following Nietzsche, "while extensional suffering is bad enough, often it is many times compounded by our interpretations of it, which are often far worse than the disorder itself" (p. 21).
[9] This is continuous in spirit with Henry Shue's "priority principle" in *Basic Rights* (Princeton: Princeton University Press, 1980), pp. 114–19.

The Insult of Poverty

motivated to wage a common struggle to overcome poverty and realize a better future.[10] Not only did the largely equal distribution of material resources block the rise of status poverty and prevent subsistence poverty from acquiring any negative meaning, the collective cause of communism actually gave positive social meaning to subsistence poverty.[11] In the context of this collective cause, subsistence poverty was not an obstacle to participation in social life and the formation of a valued self. Rather, subsistence poverty made possible participation in a special kind of social life and the formation of a special kind of self – an ascetic self that was based on collectivistic values informed by a communist *telos*. This communist ascetic self was the only kind of self that was socially valued and allowed to serve as a basis of respect. Far from being a barrier to participation in the normal activities constitutive of this self, lack of individual wealth and possession was valorized in political terms and treated as an enabling or even necessary condition for participation in such activities.[12]

Now, some three decades into what is still called the reform, the goal of communism has been given up, except in occasional rhetoric, and the ascetic self that used to make sense in the context of the collective pursuit of communism is no longer a social ideal. As a result, subsistence poverty has become empty of all positive significance – no longer redeemed by association with ascetic virtues, solidarity in a common cause, or the

---

[10] Insofar as some social groups were economically less well off than others, say "workers" and "peasants" in comparison with "intellectuals," the former were compensated, as it were, in the form of higher political standing and greater cultural representation. Against this background, the comparative economic disadvantage of "workers" and "peasants" began to take on a different social meaning under Deng Xiaoping and Jiang Zemin, in that the countervailing factors characteristic of the Mao era had gradually disappeared. In this later period, those who were at the receiving end of political and cultural exclusion on top of economic disadvantage must have felt an especially damaging combination of deprivation and demoralization. This potentially explosive situation may appear to have been ameliorated to some degree in the past several years, but it is increasingly clear that the apparently enhanced representation of the formerly dominant groups by the official media is more propagandist than cultural. For a theoretical account of social relations in terms of multiple dimensions of superiority and inferiority, see Pierre Bourdieu, "The Social Space and the Genesis of Groups," *Theory and Society* 14 (1985): 723–44.
[11] The largely equal distribution was made possible by the state's control of almost all the means of production and its providing almost everyone with a livelihood, however minimal, including such levels of education and medical care as resources permitted.
[12] More extensive discussion can be found in my *Dialectic of the Chinese Revolution: From Utopianism to Hedonism* (Stanford: Stanford University Press, 1994), chap. 4. By way of contrast, it is interesting to note that in Mao's China there was nothing like the kind of competing demands for subsistence and participation discussed in Sen, *Inequality Reexamined*, chap. 7.

prospect of material and spiritual plenitude for everyone with the advent of communism.

This withdrawal of positive meaning from subsistence poverty is compounded by the simultaneous rise of status poverty and a new valorization of individual wealth. Formerly the necessary condition for a kind of valorized (ascetic) self, serious lack of wealth is now an obstacle to participation in the normal activities of education, employment, and consumption that are constitutive of the new kind of (hedonistic) self that is increasingly the social ideal in post-Mao China.[13] With the shift from one paradigm of normal self-constituting activities to another, social exclusion has come to be based on wealth rather than political standing, and so, however substantial the success in reducing subsistence poverty, that success is now part of a larger picture in which the new problem of status poverty looms larger and larger.[14] It is only in the context of the new phenomenon of status poverty that we can grasp the cause and significance of the sharp rise in inequality of income in post-Mao China. The poor are now those who are worst off in both subsistence and status, even though in most cases their absolute level of subsistence is higher than it was or would have been in Mao's time. Thus, the problem of poverty has been reduced in one dimension and enlarged in another.

There is no obvious way of comparing the overall situation of poverty in Mao's time and in ours and saying which is worse. The compounding of subsistence poverty with status poverty in the life of a new underclass definitely makes one hesitant to say that things are better now, as does the pervasiveness of status poverty in a society which, given its general level of material prosperity, still can ill afford it. Even if this is not enough for concluding that things are worse, one can nevertheless say with reasonable confidence that since the start of the reform, poverty has acquired a new dimension and a new meaning and has become a new source of social suffering.

6

The experience of coping with material scarcity in Mao's China provides ample evidence that material scarcity can be treated as a matter of

---

[13] For an account of the shift from asceticism in Mao's China to hedonism in post-Mao China, see my *Dialectic*, introduction.
[14] For a detailed account of the new social exclusion, with special reference to the plight of laid-off female workers, see Shi Tong, *Zhongguo shehui zhuanxing shiqi de shehui paiji* (Social Exclusion in Chinese Society's Time of Transition) (Beijing: Beijing daxue chubanshe, 2004).

subsistence poverty alone and that subsistence poverty on its own need carry no negative social meaning. This experience also suggests that there is a lot to be said for preventing subsistence poverty from taking on negative social meaning, especially under conditions of severe material scarcity. Even more revealing about this experience is that, under certain conditions, subsistence poverty can be interpreted so as to receive *positive* meaning. This is something I want to explore further now, by way of reflecting on the distinction between poverty and asceticism to which I have made a passing reference in my characterization of the fight against poverty in Mao's China.

A poor person and an ascetic are alike in having a minimum of material resources. But this similarity is only external. From the internal point of view, an ascetic, in what may be treated as the typical case, *chooses* to deprive himself of material resources that otherwise would be or might be available, and for this reason we cannot speak of material *deprivation* in the standard sense. Alternatively, an ascetic (as in Mao's China) may embrace a condition of limited material resources that happens to be his lot and thereby turn a life of poverty into an ascetic life. Thus, an ascetic is someone who either chooses to be poor or makes a virtue of the necessity of being poor. In both cases, though more so in the first than in the second, one can be said to *will* a life of material scarcity. To be more precise, what one wills is subsistence poverty, and because one wills it in order to better participate in those activities that answer to one's chosen conception of the good life, no status poverty will result, at least in one's own eyes.

To be sure, the subsistence poverty in question must be of a kind and severity that can be thus embraced, for all the plasticity of voluntary human endurance, just as it may be granted that ascetic practices can at least in some cases be induced and sustained by highly questionable ideologies. But facts such as these do not undermine the conclusion that has emerged from our brief comparison of the unwilling poor and the ascetic: that subsistence poverty can take on positive meaning by being self-imposed or at least willingly accepted.

This is enough to set asceticism apart from simple poverty and to direct our attention to the crucial role of choice in the experience and meaning of poverty. Whereas disrespect is part of the social meaning of status poverty, and all too often even of subsistence poverty through superimposition, it need not be, and tends not to be, part of the social meaning of asceticism – thanks to the exercise of choice. And whereas disrespect is highly reflexive for the unwilling poor, it is not so for an ascetic even in the unlikely event that she is an object of disrespect – again thanks to the exercise of choice.[15] In asceticism, then, status poverty is either absent or non-reflexive, and subsistence poverty is made positive by choice and the resultant intactness of self-respect.

The upshot is that subsistence poverty, normally an undesirable condition, can under certain circumstances be redeemed and made compatible with agency and self-respect; it is indeed required for an ascetic's kind of agency and self-respect. That this is possible – and this is my main reason for examining the ascetic's case[16] – suggests the need for a third, more complex notion of poverty. Some such notion is necessary if we are to make sense of the condition of the ascetic: even if we ourselves do not subscribe to an ascetic conception of the good life, we can at least appreciate what prevents material scarcity from being such a bad thing for someone who does. There is clearly a difference between someone who is materially poor by choice and whom we call an ascetic and someone who is equally materially poor but unwillingly so. The difference, I suggest, is that the latter person, and only the latter person, is in a condition of what I shall call agency poverty, by which I mean a lack of material resources that causes a reduction or loss of agency and with it self-respect. In order to say more about this notion of poverty, I must first say something about my notion of agency, along the way also giving more systematic content to the notion of self-respect.

7

By agency I refer, as I have done in Chapters 3 and 5, to a distinctively human form of meaningful causality in which power, meaning causal efficacy, is appropriated by an emerging or existing subject in the interest of its subjectivity or selfhood. In keeping with my practice in the two earlier chapters, I understand this process of self-formation in terms of "power organized as subjectivity" or "subjectivity achieved through power."

As far as power is concerned, suffice it to say that it is meant here to cover all instances of human causal efficacy. Stripped to its bare essentials, power is generic and neutral and has little meaning or point for the human

---

[15] On the reflexivity of respect and disrespect, see Michael Walzer, *Spheres of Justice: A Defense of Pluralism and Equality* (New York: Basic Books, 1983), pp. 272–73.
[16] What is true of the ascetic can also be true of those who for ecological reasons, say, prefer to live a life that is frugal to the point of poverty from an external point of view. For such people, "physical poverty is not humiliating when it proceeds from choosing to be satisfied with less and not from being relegated to the lower ranks of society" (Gorz, *Ecology*, p. 32).

being as human being until it is organized into subjectivity, until, that is, it becomes the power of a self and, as such, a necessary condition of its subjectivity. What we find at this agency-defining conjunction is neither an indifferent quantum of causal efficacy that is yet to be humanly incorporated, as it were, nor an abstract capacity for subjectivity that is yet to find its concrete realization in meaningful causal efficacy, but an integral experience of agency in which power is organized as subjectivity and thus the self is born or renewed. Only through the continuous recurrence of this conjunction or through the endless supply of subjectively meaningful experiences of power are we able to maintain our distinctively human agency and thereby our humanity.

When one enjoys a subjectivity that is securely grounded on experiences of power, one will have a positive appraisal of oneself and feel good about oneself. Self-respect is none other than this cognitive and affective state – an epiphenomenon that attends upon the unity of power and subjectivity and that, of course, typically relies to some degree on positive feedback from the right quarters. Like the term "subjectivity," "self-respect" connotes the evaluative reflexivity that is an integral part of being a human agent. In thus marking the unity of power and subjectivity, the nature of self-respect shows, on the one hand, that distinctively human power is invariably the power of a self and at the service of a self, or else power no matter how efficacious would be devoid of all distinctively human significance, and, on the other, that a self relies for its existence and growth on experiences of power, or else it would be a metaphysical postulate with no concrete reality or no reality at all. It is this mutually constitutive relation between self and power, with power forming the very stuff of subjectivity and subjectivity giving shape and meaning to power, that I see as the defining characteristic of human agency.

Given this account of agency, agency poverty can be understood in the following way.[17] In agency poverty, the material resources one lacks are those required for self-constituting activities, by some reasonable

---

[17] What I call agency poverty is different from Sen's concept of "capability deprivation" (*Development*, chap. 4). The main difference is that agency, as I use the term, is an internally differentiated concept that gives pride of place to subjectivity and self-constitution over power as such. It is not entirely clear whether capability as used by Sen involves both power and subjectivity or power alone; on the face of it, at least the emphasis seems to be on power. Even if capability is extensionally identical to agency as I use the term, and hence capability deprivation is extensionally identical to agency poverty, the intensional difference remains and is important, not least with regard to the explanatory focus of the two concepts.

standard (a notion I shall later refine in terms of a normal level or range of agency). The significance of this material deprivation is that it leads to power deprivation, which in turn poses a threat to subjectivity, a threat whose adverse effects are registered in the epiphenomenon of lack of self-respect. Thus, what should deeply worry us about agency poverty is not material deprivation as such, though this is important up to a point, nor even power deprivation as such, though this is more directly important, but the fact that material deprivation can lead to power deprivation, which in turn can lead to subjectivity or agency deprivation. Agency poverty is nothing less than a condition in which those involved are prevented by material deprivation from engaging in self-constituting experiences of power and thus from maintaining themselves as subjects. Whenever material deprivation leads to agency deprivation, it undermines the respect for oneself that is part and parcel of a self. More than merely debilitating and humiliating, agency poverty is positively dehumanizing.

Agency poverty, thus understood, is not only bad but unconditionally bad. The same is not true of either subsistence poverty or status poverty. Subsistence poverty is bad, at least in the first instance, but it can be redeemed or made positive by an exercise of choice, as in asceticism. Every instance in which subsistence poverty appears to be unconditionally bad is one in which agency poverty is also present. This can be the case either because subsistence poverty is given a social meaning that undermines agency and self-respect or because the scarcity of resources is so severe that subsistence poverty is no longer compatible with freedom from agency poverty. Otherwise, even when it is not redeemed or made positive as in asceticism, subsistence poverty at least need not be so bad as to be dehumanizing.

Likewise, status poverty, bad though it is, need not be unconditionally bad as long as it does not cause agency poverty. Status poverty and agency poverty have in common the fact that there is a shortfall in resources for participation in activities. But there the similarity ends. To begin with, status poverty is intrinsically relative whereas agency poverty need not be: it does not make sense to say that all members of a society suffer from status poverty or are equal in status poverty, whereas it is possible for all members of a society to suffer from agency poverty, say as a result of extreme material scarcity. Moreover, where both status poverty and agency poverty involve lack of respect, agency poverty occurs only if the lack of respect is reflexive (this is why an ascetic is immune from agency poverty), whereas status poverty does not depend on such reflexivity.

Thus, one can be in a position of status poverty without suffering from agency poverty, thanks to the blocking of reflexivity, just as one can be in a position of agency poverty without suffering from status poverty, as in a situation of evenly distributed extreme material scarcity. It is therefore possible for a society to have agency poverty without status poverty. Whether the converse is also possible is a question I will pick up later.

Thus, it is true of both subsistence poverty and status poverty that what appears unconditionally bad about either is actually the agency poverty that might go with it. In this sense agency poverty may be said to be the real sting of subsistence poverty and status poverty. It is therefore especially important to examine the relation in which subsistence poverty and status poverty stand to agency poverty.

8

One of the lessons that can be drawn from the fight against poverty in Mao's China, as we saw earlier, is that even quite severe material scarcity, short of the magnitude of a disaster, need not prevent a society from developing a range of social activities that constitute the basis of agency and self-respect. It is worth pursuing this line of thinking at a higher level of abstraction, that is, in terms of the general question of what can and should be done to make agency available to all members of society when conditions of subsistence poverty prevail.

On the face of it, a society that lacks material resources for meeting the subsistence needs of its members may be expected also to lack material resources for satisfying their need for agency. Agency requires a level of resources that is sufficient for a degree of power that is in turn sufficient for the formation and continuation of one or another form of subjectivity. Freedom from agency poverty thus conceived seems a taller order than freedom from mere subsistence poverty. The Chinese experience we have considered, however, shows that the opposite can be the case.

Clearly, what a society can do about subsistence poverty depends on the level of material resources available to it. It is entirely possible that even when a society really does as much as it can under the resource constraint, the results may still be insufficient by any reasonable standard of human subsistence. Yet no society can reasonably be required to do more.

If freedom from subsistence poverty is rather rigidly subject to the resource constraint, freedom from agency poverty is not. While subsistence is amenable to relatively clear definition and reasonably objective measurement, participation, power, and subjectivity allow for a considerable degree of social flexibility and cross-societal variability. The important thing is that it is both possible and reasonable to think of the standard that defines agency poverty and informs efforts to prevent or remove it as internal to the society in question. The standard should be internal because of what it measures: not material resources as such, and not powers in themselves, but material resources as constituents of powers and powers in turn as necessary conditions of subjectivity.

Working with this internal notion of agency poverty, we can approach a society's understanding of itself in terms of an organized collection of agents (no society can do without such an understanding, if only implicit), and, by clarifying and extrapolating from this self-understanding, arrive at a standard for the prevention or removal of agency poverty. Thus, the normal range of participation includes those activities that all normally functioning members of society are expected to be able to perform and that serve as the social bases of respect and self-respect. If people are expected to have a job or risk losing respect and self-respect, then having a job is within the normal range of participation. The same is true of being able to find a mate, to enjoy certain consumer goods, and so on, as long as the activities or accomplishments involved make up what it means to be a normally functioning member of society, whether or not these activities or accomplishments are considered worthwhile or necessary from an external point of view. Likewise, being able, and under normal circumstances being motivated, to participate in the political process is an integral part of agency in a society that conceives of itself as a democracy and of its members as equal citizens. The important thing is that we judge a society, in the first instance, by a standard that is implicit in its own understanding of what the society is or realistically aspires to be.[18]

Given this internal standard of agency and agency poverty, a society that suffers from a considerable degree of subsistence poverty despite its best efforts can still meet a sufficient standard of freedom from agency poverty. For the standard is determined in keeping with a society's own (implicit) understanding of agency and of the normal range of activities necessary for such agency, and thus it follows that the society can reasonably be presumed to have the ability to handle its regular level of material

---

[18] How this self-understanding comes about is in turn something to be judged by an internal standard, in the first instance. I say "in the first instance" in both cases in order to leave room for the possibility of legitimate criticism from an external point of view – for example, criticism in terms of adaptive preferences. How such criticism is exactly to be conceived is beyond my present concerns, however.

scarcity in such a way as to place every member within *its own* normal agency range.[19] Here, "ought" is supported by "can" according to a society's self-understanding and self-assessment. If a society fails to bring its standard of normal agency within the reach of every member, therefore, it will not be for lack of resources, the resource constraint notwithstanding.

Instead, every kind of material deprivation that systematically pulls a disadvantaged group of people below the normal agency range implicit in the society's self-image must be blamed on the society's failure to attach sufficient priority to this most fundamental of its moral responsibilities – the responsibility to establish and implement an alignment of its standard of human agency and its material conditions so as to bring within the society's normal agency range every member of society who makes a reasonable effort. Since this responsibility is internally generated, a society that fails to meet it exposes itself to the charge that it is not taking its own moral standards seriously. Behind this charge is an internal argument for – or internal critique in support of – the right to freedom from agency poverty even under conditions of subsistence poverty.

There is no guarantee, to be sure, that a society will not have a self-understanding that is very undemanding in its conception of agency and hence of what it can reasonably be expected to do about agency poverty. Given such a conception, the society in question will not have to do much even by its own lights or under the pressure of its own collective self-understanding. To this possible scenario the best answer is a democratic organization of society; indeed, the possibility of such a scenario and the need to avoid it constitute in themselves a distinctive argument for democracy. To the extent that a society is democratically organized, the state is under pressure to secure legitimacy by pitching its notion of normal human agency and of its corresponding responsibility toward its citizens at a reasonably high level. Think of this pressure in terms of a choice: the choice between, on the one hand, an *agency deficit* that is likely to occur if agency is pitched at a sufficiently high level for purposes of winning popular support, with the inevitable result of raising the probability of a failed promise, and, on the other, a *legitimacy deficit* the probability of which is increased in proportion as the standard of agency is lowered and the likelihood of agency deficit thereby reduced. Not surprisingly, in a democratic society the choice tends to be made in favor of aiming for a relatively high standard of agency and tolerating the resulting risk

---

[19] With due allowance for some types of exceptions, such as the severely handicapped, the satisfaction of whose needs for agency presents a different kind of challenge.

of an agency deficit, if only because a government or political party that promises very little and is prepared to do very little, even in political rhetoric, lays itself open to competition and attack from those who will have an easy time showing that more can and should be done. It is true that the existence of any serious agency deficit by a society's own standard has the potential to internally undermine claims to legitimacy based on that standard. After all, legitimacy requires not only promising a reasonably high level of agency but also making good on that promise. Thus, pitching agency at a reasonably high level to satisfy the need for legitimacy is itself the source of a different kind of threat to legitimacy. But even this does not weaken the need to pitch agency at a reasonably high level in order to win popular support and secure the right to govern in the first place.

It is this need to aim for a reasonably high standard of agency, with the ever-present threat of agency deficit as a result, that prevents a society's self-understanding of agency from being so undemanding as to leave little room for internal critique. The unconstrained use of the space for internal critique presupposes a truly democratic organization of society with its attendant effectual freedoms. Indeed, this presupposition can be regarded as an *internal* argument for democracy.[20] One of the grave defects of a nondemocratic society is precisely that its members cannot freely and effectively hold their government, and their society at large, to account for failing to operate with a reasonably high standard of normal agency and failing to eliminate agency poverty by such a standard.

In the world as we find it, it can reasonably be claimed that few states are truly democratic, although it would also be hard to deny that some states are significantly more democratic than others. Thus, the fight to remove agency poverty is at the same time a fight for democracy. This does not mean that the room for internal critique that democracy opens up is unlimited, but such room should be quite large. Nor does it mean that the size and locus of this space are fixed and the same for all societies, for such things are properly subject to democratic contestation and revision and therefore may be expected to vary from society to society and to change

---

[20] A similar argument for democracy can be derived from Pogge's institutional (as opposed to interactional) understanding of human rights, in that members of a nondemocratic society cannot be held responsible, with any reasonable degree of stringency, for harm arising from an unjust institutional order and for not taking strong action to reform that order. For the distinction between an institutional and an interactional understanding of human rights, see Pogge, *World Poverty*, pp. 64–67.

over time. What informs the combined fights for democracy and for freedom from agency poverty is the substantively flexible claim that any society can and should remove agency poverty according to a reasonably high standard that is part of its self-understanding as a democratically organized collection of agents, or else it must either be in a situation of extreme material scarcity or deserve to suffer a serious legitimacy deficit.

I make this claim on the assumption, of course, that the standard of agency that serves as the point of reference here is a society's own. This claim is meant to hold even under the insistence that the standard be reasonably high. What makes the standard *reasonably* high is that it allows *as much as possible* to be done to promote agency and respect under conditions of subsistence poverty. It is necessary to elaborate on the idea of a reasonably high standard, and this brings me to the core of the internal argument for freedom from agency poverty despite subsistence poverty.

The most important feature of an internally generated standard is its flexibility, and what is most flexible about it is the relation between agency and material conditions. Agency poverty, as we have seen, consists in a particular relation between the level of material resources and the level of agency rather than in any absolute level of material resources itself. Given that agency poverty is relational, the task of doing something about it must be relational, too: a matter of finding the right relation between the two elements involved. Thus, a society's task to remove agency poverty is a matter not of lessening the resource constraint (this would be covered by the task of removing subsistence poverty) but of aligning its understanding of agency with its resource constraint, such as it is, in such a way that it is possible for every member to have enough resources for purposes of agency and respect by the society's own standard.

The flexibility of this task gives a society a special power and responsibility with respect to the prevention or removal of agency poverty within it. It follows that, barring conditions of extreme scarcity, if a society's resource constraint is such as not to allow each and every member access to sufficient resources for agency and respect, then, given its power and responsibility, the society is itself to blame for sticking to a norm of agency that is out of keeping with its material conditions. Accordingly, the moral burden is on the society either to modify its norm of agency, with its range of self-constituting activities, or to improve its material conditions so that these two elements can be properly aligned. A society must stand accused of fundamental injustice if it does not reform itself to bring about an alignment of agency and material conditions that gives each and every one of its members the wherewithal to participate in self-constituting activities and live the life of an agent worthy of respect and self-respect by the society's own standard.

It is worth emphasizing that a society's modification of its norm of agency to be in line with its unfavorable material conditions does not imply a lowering of the norm of agency. What is higher or lower is the level of material resources required for normal agency, not the level of agency itself. For example, in a very poor society it would be a bad idea to expect a normal agent, say in the process of acquiring and maintaining a job, to display a degree of cleanliness that only easy access to a washing machine and a shower facility makes possible. Depending on the exact material conditions, it could also be misguided to include among the necessary means of normal agency the possession of a computer and a mobile phone, access to the Internet, the ability to afford to dress according to ever changing codes of fashion and to go to the right places of entertainment or consumption, and so on, not to mention ownership of a sizable and comfortable apartment, a suitable kind of car, and the financial means to travel regularly for pleasure. As a matter of fact, almost all of these things have become more or less necessary conditions for normal agency and respectability in China today, while none of them or of their equivalents (the possession of a television set or a telephone, and so on) was in Mao's China. As these examples show, when a poor society aligns its standard of normal agency with its unfavorable material circumstances, it is not thereby adopting a lower standard of agency. Instead it is simply making sure that the standard of normal agency is not pegged to things that only some members of society would be able to afford. Of course, the level of material resources required for normal agency is lower, but this need not mean that the standard of agency itself is lower, except on the (unsupported) assumption that there is a straightforwardly positive correlation between level of material resources and level of agency. My idea of alignment of agency and resources thus boils down to this: a society's standard of normal agency should be so conceived that it does not require the production and consumption of things of which there could not be enough for everyone, given the resource constraint.

This is not to suggest, of course, that satisfying the imperative of alignment will be easy, but it makes a world of difference that the difficulty does not issue in any inflexible way from the resource constraint. Bear in mind that we understand material scarcity here in terms of its effects on agency and understand agency in turn in an internal fashion, such that material scarcity is strictly relative to the self-constituting activities that happen to matter in the society in question. Given this understanding, relative material abundance is neither a necessary nor a sufficient condition for bringing about the alignment.

That relative material abundance is not a necessary condition for fulfilling the imperative of alignment makes it possible for a relatively materially poor society to be free from agency poverty. Thus, a society that is regarded as materially poor by some external standard can do very well, by its own standard and to its credit, if it secures for each of its members sufficient material resources for purposes of agency and respect. In such a society (think of the examples I have given of Mao's China), material possessions are unlikely to figure as one of the defining bases of participation and recognition; or, to the extent that they do, they are likely to be more or less equally distributed. In either case, resources that may look meager from an external point of view do not lead to agency poverty from an internal point of view because they suffice for internal purposes of participation in normal self-constituting activities.

By the same token – and this shows that relative material abundance is not a sufficient condition for satisfying the imperative of alignment – a society that is materially rich by some external standard can do a bad job of preventing or removing agency poverty, by its own standards, if it attaches great importance to individual income as a means of social participation, systematically linking wealth to recognition, and at the same time permits a sharp inequality in wealth, with many people falling below the level that is socially deemed necessary to support a normal level of agency and respect. What is important is not material abundance as such, nor even a relatively equal share in material abundance, but rather the alignment of a society's standard of agency with the material resources at its disposal, an alignment that should allow everyone to live a life compatible with respect and self-respect.

The imperative of alignment is, as I have emphasized, a requirement of an internal kind that calls for the provision of sufficient resources to every member of society for purposes of agency and respect as conceived by the society itself, subject to its own resource constraint. As such, the imperative is flexible, and the only fixed point of reference is the avoidance of agency poverty, whatever the level of subsistence. There is one particular form, however, that the alignment may have to take in the case of extreme or nearly extreme subsistence poverty. When subsistence poverty reaches a critical level, the struggle against it can turn into a desperate fight for survival. In such a fight, the human need for agency and respect, though still at stake, is pushed into the background, so desperately absorbing is the struggle to maintain life itself. It is understandable if, for those who happen to be in such dire straits and for those others who identify with them in their fight against poverty, the *only* stake in poverty appears to be subsistence and survival.

In the event that a society finds itself in this kind of crisis, it may well be that the only proper alignment of agency and material resources is complete de-alignment: the severing of any links that happen to exist between socially valued forms of agency on the one hand and levels of income on the other, so that agency can no longer be undermined by low levels of income. Once such links are severed through a revolution in the society's conception of agency, the twofold threat that extreme subsistence poverty poses in the case of the worst-off – to their agency and their sheer life – becomes simplified into a single threat to sheer life. This is no mean outcome, halving the pain of poverty, as it were, by effectively removing the insult and leaving only the injury. In this way agency and respect are preserved because they are no longer tied to income and material possession – and this for the simple yet all-important reason that under the circumstances such links would be incompatible with making available to every member of society enough resources to live a life of normal agency and perhaps even with the preservation of every member of society.

Two important implications flow from the uncoupling of agency and income. First, given that agency and respect are no longer tied to material possessions, all values and institutions that rest upon this connection (not least private property rights), along with the inequalities they justify, cease to have any basis. Second, given that the only thing that remains at stake in the access to material resources is subsistence, all values and institutions that serve to regulate the distribution of resources for purposes beyond subsistence (private property rights again being a preeminent example) must be adjusted or abandoned in favor of the most effective preservation of human life. These implications will hold until the crisis of extreme subsistence poverty is sufficiently lifted that an alignment of agency and resources can be brought to bear on it without having to cut the connection between agency and resources altogether.

9

To my earlier discussion of subsistence poverty and status poverty in China, it is worth adding a brief account of agency poverty. When Mao's

China is said to have an impressive record of fighting poverty, it is usually subsistence poverty that is implicitly under consideration. What I believe is more distinctive of that record, however, has to do with the prevention or removal of agency poverty. This was accomplished by cutting the link between income and all socially valued forms of agency, including self-respect as their epiphenomenon. Not only was individual wealth no longer treated as a necessary condition for any socially valued form of agency, it was perceived as a source of bourgeois vices and, as such, an obstacle to the realization of the forms of agency envisioned by socialism. As part of this realignment of values, individual subsistence poverty came to be socially regarded both as a marker of membership in politically progressive classes and as a source of proletarian virtues. What remained undesirable about poverty – the miseries of hunger and cold and so on – had to do with the material dimension of human life alone. Poverty was a matter of subsistence rather than participation, agency, and respect.

In this way, the daunting problems of material scarcity the Communist Party inherited were reconceived through the simplification of poverty into a problem of sheer subsistence on the one hand and through the revaluation of subsistence poverty on the other. This radical reconceptualization of poverty laid the foundation for instituting a scheme of largely equal distribution of material resources.[21] To be sure, this scheme was somewhat compromised by the haphazard application of the so-called socialist principle of reward based on contribution and was severely compromised by the city/countryside divide and the relegation of the entire rural population to effectively second-class status with respect to a range of what we would now call rights and entitlements.[22] These compromises notwithstanding, the reconceptualization of poverty and the largely equal

---

[21] This equality did not amount, however, to the disappearance or even reduction of the hierarchical nature of Chinese society. What happened was not the removal of hierarchy as such but the removal of wealth as a basis of hierarchy and hence the removal of status poverty. It is arguable that the replacement of one basis of hierarchy (wealth) with another (political performance) was a rather limited achievement, if at all, in its own right. Nevertheless, there seems little doubt that this replacement helped prevent the already serious subsistence poverty prevalent in China at the time from being compounded by agency and status poverty, a scenario which would have been morally less acceptable.

[22] For an analysis of the city/countryside divide in terms of political economy, see John Knight, Li Shi, and Song Lina, "Zhongguo chengxiang chaju de zhengzhi jingjixue fenxi" (A Political-Economic Analysis of the Gap between the City and the Countryside), in Yao Yang, ed., *Zhuangui Zhongguo: Shenshi shehui gongzheng he pingdeng* (Equity and Social Equality in Transitional China) (Beijing: Zhongguo renmin daxue chubanshe, 2004), pp. 176–97.

distribution of resources informed by it added up to a momentous, indeed foundational, success in the fight against material scarcity. A rather different, and narrower, kind of success came only later, this time in the already simplified struggle against subsistence poverty – a success that took the form of increased agricultural outputs and so on.[23]

There is little doubt that the fight against subsistence poverty has been taken much further since Mao's time.[24] But then precisely because material conditions have improved it has become harder to conceive poverty as essentially a problem of subsistence. One of the most profound changes that have taken place in post-Mao China is the gradual but unmistakable recoupling of agency and wealth. Divested of all positive value in Mao's time, individual wealth has made a resounding comeback as a basis of agency and status since then – so much so that, as one (by no means unrepresentative) rural slogan has it, it is glorious to become rich and cowardly to remain poor.[25] In this new ethos, an extremely large number of people whose condition of subsistence has improved compared with their own condition or their counterparts' in Mao's time find themselves having to cope with a problem that did not exist then: the problem of agency poverty. It should come as no surprise that agency poverty in the absence of acute subsistence poverty can feel a lot worse than a

[23] The record of combating poverty in Mao's China is far from one of unmitigated success. After all, a disaster in a class of its own happened in the domain of sheer subsistence as a result of the huge political mistake known as the Great Leap Forward. That this mistake was clearly avoidable both makes those responsible for it (especially Mao) less forgivable and preserves the otherwise positive lessons of the Chinese experience as a whole.

[24] The extent of subsistence poverty that remains or has emerged since must not be underestimated, however. Perhaps the most threatening element of subsistence poverty in China today is the unaffordability of medical treatment (especially for relatively serious conditions) for extremely large numbers of people, who regularly have to choose between food and medical care. This situation is made worse by the increasing costs of education, which can lead to agency poverty and status poverty directly and to subsistence poverty both directly and indirectly. All too often, the poor in China today have to strike an impossible, and degrading, balance among the needs for food, for health, and for (their children's) education. Something is being done about this, but it is obviously too little, if not too late. For an empirical account of increasing inequalities in health care and education, see Zhang Xiaobo, "Zhongguo jiaoyu he yiliao weisheng zhong de bupingdeng wenti" (Issues of Inequality in Education and Health Care in China), in Yao, ed., *Zhuangui Zhongguo*, pp. 209–28.

[25] See Cao Jinqing, *Huanghebian de Zhongguo* (China along the Yellow River) (Shanghai: Shanghai wenyi chubanshe, 2000), p. 263. The idea contained in this slogan is endorsed by Zhang Shuguang, "Jingjixue (jia) ruhe jiang gongping" (Fairness as Viewed by Economists and in Economics), in Yao, ed., *Zhuangui Zhongguo*, pp. 635–59 at esp. p. 650. Zhang's position is quite in keeping with the general spirit of the reform era.

considerably higher degree of subsistence poverty that is not compounded by agency poverty. In this sense it may even be said that poverty is a worse problem in China today than in Mao's time – an assessment that is pointedly expressed in a popular saying that has the worse-off (not the absolutely worst-off) of today cursing even as they have at long last become able to afford a diet rich in meat (a luxury in Mao's time).

What is responsible for this state of affairs is, of course, not that material conditions have improved, nor even that wealth is more unevenly distributed, but rather that more is now at stake in wealth. The growing inequality, with its devastating effects on the poor, is but a by-product of the increased stakes in the competition for wealth as a means of social participation. The Confucian idea that what is to be feared is not scarcity but unequal distribution acquires a poignant resonance in China today if interpreted in this light. Not that scarcity is not a bad thing, but, after sheer survival, the worst threat poverty can pose to a human being is meager recognition as long as society sees fit to maintain a significant link between wealth and recognition. Such a threat has returned to the formerly socialist land of China with a vengeance.

10

The last issue we must consider within my typology of poverty is the relation in which status poverty stands to agency poverty. Status poverty is obviously problematic, as we have seen, when conjoined with subsistence poverty, assimilating the latter to itself and adding insult to injury. Status poverty is also obviously problematic, as I have observed, if it causes agency poverty. The question that remains to be addressed is whether in a society free of subsistence poverty it is possible for status poverty to be compatible with freedom from agency poverty. Since status poverty clearly can translate into agency poverty – a situation in which it is difficult or impossible for those who have the lowest economic and social status to achieve a normal level of agency – the question can be formulated more precisely as asking whether, and in what ways, such translation can be prevented.

It may be thought that in a book about China such a question is premature. But if there is one thing that is perhaps truer of China today than it is of most societies in the world, it is that nothing in China is standing still, and this includes the most urgent problems and the most needed solutions. Thus the question of the possible threat of status poverty to agency may soon cease to be a luxury even if it is so regarded with a measure of plausibility in China today. If we add to this the all too common tendency for modern-minded Chinese to look to Western liberal democracies for broad hints of solutions to China's problems, a tendency increasingly supported by the nature of China's current socioeconomic transformation, then spelling out the logic, merit, and deficiency of the liberal democratic approach to this question has an obvious relevance for China.

Now, whether status poverty causes agency poverty (even in the absence of subsistence poverty) is a matter of the relation in which those who suffer from status poverty stand to the normal level of agency of the society in question. To be sure, there is nothing positive about status poverty in itself. It is not simply a function of comparative lack of material resources but is a relational condition of a worse kind, one in which those who occupy the lowest economic position stand in a relation of *social* inferiority to *all* other members of society. To the extent that status poverty implies comparison, the poor are worse off than not just some but all other members of their society. It is this *absolute* status of being at the bottom that can make the poor stand apart from the rest of society, where most people are worse off than only some people. Despite the unattractiveness of status poverty as such, its normative (and psychological) acceptability depends on whether status poverty leads to agency poverty. It is one thing if some members of society suffer from some degree of status poverty and yet have enough resources to attain the normal level of agency. It is something altogether different if their status poverty places them below the normal level of agency.

How can the first situation (as a minimum) be achieved and the second avoided? In a manner of speaking, the trick is to bring it about that the so-called middle class absorbs all members of society below it into its ranks, since it is safe to assume that members of the middle class already attain the normal level of agency. One consequence of this leveling-up is, of course, that the middle class will cease to occupy the middle position (and so cease to be the middle class, literally speaking), for there are no longer members of society below it, nor indeed any category of such members of society. In thus becoming part of the bottom of society, as it were, members of the hitherto middle class will find themselves in a new situation of status poverty. Since this happens as a result of the formerly worst-off rising to the level of the middle class instead of the latter sinking to theirs, however, neither the old nor the new members of the now defunct middle class need suffer from agency poverty, although both will be in a condition of status poverty.

Thus, the reason for which it is conventionally considered desirable to have a sizable middle class should be just as compelling a reason for having no members of society living below the level of what would otherwise be the middle class. The underlying rationale is that what is essential about members of the middle class is not so much their being situated in the middle in terms of economic and social position as their being able to meet their society's standard of normal agency – at least the lower end of that standard, as it were. If this rationale is at all plausible, we may hypothesize that what keeps the middle class reasonably happy despite their economic and social inferiority to those in the upper reaches of their society will remain true even in the event that all those who have hitherto made up the bottom of society rise to their level so that the middle class retain their level of agency but cease to occupy a middle position. What is crucial, on this hypothesis, is not how many people occupy the so-called bottom of society but whether those who do will have to suffer from agency poverty on top of status poverty.

This hypothesis, no doubt rather optimistic, supports the hope that agency poverty can be avoided without removing status poverty altogether – on the assumption that the removal of status poverty is a much more difficult and normatively contentious task. The biggest obstacle to the realization of this hope is what appears to be an ineradicable feature of human society: the need for social hierarchy as caused by human beings' desire to feel superior to (at least some) others in order to feel good about themselves. It is not impossible that such a desire informs the self-understanding of the middle class to some degree, and if so, one defining feature of members of this class is their *middle* position – their superiority to the underclass called the poor.[26] In other words, the middle class, on this understanding, defines itself in relation to the class that is socially and economically situated below it (as well as, of course, in relation to the class above it), and not on the basis of some standard that could in principle be simultaneously reached by all members of society. Implicit here is an acknowledgment that at least to some extent social hierarchy and the desire for superiority are unavoidable.[27] If this is true, and it seems naive to rule out this possibility, then the challenge is to

---

[26] Raymond Williams says of the modern British class system that "this fundamental class system, with the force of the rising middle class right behind it, requires a 'lower' class if it is to retain any social meaning." See his *The Long Revolution* (London: Chatto & Windus, 1961), p. 320.

[27] See Walzer, *Spheres*, p. 274. As Walzer puts it, "men and women value themselves – just as they are valued – in comparison with others."

eradicate agency poverty not only despite status poverty but also despite the troubling desire for superiority that may underpin it.

Perhaps the most promising response to this challenge consists in the bifurcation – especially characteristic of modern, liberal democratic societies – of recognition into respect and esteem.[28] Corresponding to this bifurcation is the division of human activity into two broad domains (call them domains of agency), the public domain of citizenship and the private domain of work, family life, and consumption. This division makes possible a certain equality of respect in the first domain while a certain inequality of esteem is permitted in the second domain subject to considerations of fairness and efficiency. In other words, instead of being a single property subject to either equal or unequal distribution, recognition is split into two, whereby respect becomes a function of citizenship and is distributed equally, or so it is supposed, and esteem becomes a function of personal qualities and accomplishments and is distributed according to merit and, in practice, unequally.[29] Thus, even those who fare worst in the second domain and as a result have the lowest esteem can still enjoy equal citizenship with others, inasmuch as "democratic citizenship is a status radically disconnected from every kind of hierarchy," as reflected in "a kind of self-respect that isn't dependent on any particular social position."[30] With this bifurcation, what we have been calling status poverty is confined entirely to the second domain, at least in theory.

Is this bifurcation sufficient to raise every member of society to a normal level of agency and thereby eliminate agency poverty despite the continuing presence of status poverty (in the second domain)? It all depends on whether the first domain is sufficiently important and the second sufficiently unimportant that equality in the first can outweigh inequality in the second.

It is generally assumed in liberal political philosophy that the first domain of agency is more fundamental than the second. It can be granted, even before examining this assumption, that the bifurcation of recognition into equal respect and unequal esteem is already a great improvement over an unequal distribution of an undivided good of recognition. It can also be granted that the bifurcation is real to a significant degree, rather than merely ideological. Still, a great deal of its force rests on the assumption

---

[28] For the distinction between respect and esteem, see Walzer, *Spheres*, chap. 11.
[29] See Axel Honneth, "Redistribution as Recognition: A Response to Nancy Fraser," Nancy Fraser and Axel Honneth, *Redistribution or Recognition* (London: Verso, 2003), pp. 110–97 at esp. pp. 140–41.
[30] Walzer, *Spheres*, p. 277.

The Insult of Poverty

that the first domain of agency matters more fundamentally than the second. For the achievement of equal respect is consequential only to the degree that the domain in which it happens is important.

It is here that the significance of this achievement can be exaggerated. It is not a coincidence that the bifurcation of recognition into equal respect and unequal esteem has been accompanied by a shift in importance, famously noted by Benjamin Constant, from the so-called freedoms of the ancients to those of the moderns.[31] Put in the terms we are using, Constant is in effect saying that the second domain of agency is more fundamental than the first for members of modern societies. This is because it is in the second domain that members of modern societies can find the most extensive scope for self-constituting activities – activities that are required for the normal level of agency. If Constant is largely right about this, and I think he clearly is, then it must be admitted that the achievement of equality, however indispensable, has occurred in a domain that cannot be said to be more fundamental than the domain in which inequality remains.[32]

Thus, the bifurcation of recognition into respect and esteem and the establishment of equal respect are not enough to ensure that every member of society attains the normal level of agency. A large part of being a normal agent in any modern society involves enjoying a minimal degree of esteem based on self-constituting activities in the private domain, together with the equality of respect guaranteed in the public domain. What this minimal degree of esteem actually consists in is not something about which much can be said, since it is relative to what happens to be the normal level of agency operative in any given society, and this level is in turn a matter internal to that society. Nevertheless, it is possible to indicate in a general way what it takes to make this minimal degree of esteem available, whatever a society's normal level of agency.

It is important for ensuring a minimal degree of esteem that the distribution of esteem proceeds in a way that is regarded as fair. One particularly influential construal of this condition is couched in terms of some notion of equality of opportunity such that those who receive less esteem are not unfairly disadvantaged in the competition for more. What counts as fairness in the distribution of esteem is open to contestation, but one thing is clear: no matter what conception of fairness is adopted, the

---

[31] See Benjamin Constant, *Political Writings*, trans. and ed. Biancamaria Fontana (Cambridge: Cambridge University Press, 1988), in particular "The Liberty of the Ancients Compared with That of the Moderns," pp. 309–28.

[32] See my "Political Agency in Liberal Democracy," *Journal of Political Philosophy* 14 (2006): 144–62.

distribution of esteem, unlike of respect, is an inherently competitive and differentiating practice, one that ranks people higher and lower according to some standard of merit or achievement. Even if this practice is based on the least objectionable conception of merit or achievement that can be agreed upon, some will still rank lower than others, and some will rank the lowest of all.

The best thing about a "fair" distribution is that it gives those who fare less well or even least well very little to complain about. But this is also the worst feature of the distribution, in that the only thing the less successful members of a society can fairly complain about is some aspect of themselves, depending on what they take to be the cause of their lower or lowest level of achievement and hence esteem. In this way, resentment of society may be blocked, but only at the expense of self-esteem: the already low self-esteem that results from low achievement and low esteem is compounded by the attribution of low achievement and low esteem to some fault of one's own. Indeed, the fairer one takes the system to be, the more one is forced to blame oneself and hence the greater one's loss of self-esteem. When status poverty happens under fair circumstances, what hurts is not only the relative lack of material resources but, far more importantly, the meaning of such lack as a *deserved* lack of esteem and self-esteem. Even at its fairest in its own terms, the inherently unequal distribution of esteem is capable of producing what have been aptly called the "hidden injuries of class."[33]

Given that the distribution of esteem has no internal mechanism for preventing too low a level of esteem by the normal standard of agency, any solution to this problem will have to be introduced from the outside. One such solution, in theory, is to make esteem and self-esteem carry significantly less weight in the constitution of normal agents than they do now. This would mean giving equal citizenship a far greater scope and importance in the lives of members of modern societies than it now has, at the expense of the so-called freedoms of the moderns through the exercise

---

[33] See Richard Sennett and Jonathan Cobb, *The Hidden Injuries of Class* (New York: Knopf, 1973). As they point out, "a system of unequal classes is actually reinforced by the ideas of equality and charity formulated in the past. The idea of potential equality of power has been given a form peculiarly fitted to a competitive society where *in*equality of power is the rule and expectation. If all men start on some basis of equal potential ability, then the inequalities they experience in their lives are *not* arbitrary, they are the logical consequence of different personal drives to use those powers – in other words, social differences can now appear as questions of character, of moral resolve, will, and competence" (p. 256). See also Honneth's discussion of the achievement principle in "Redistribution," esp. p. 148.

of which, more than anything else, members of modern societies constitute themselves as subjects leading meaningful lives. If such a prospect faces overwhelming odds against it that lie in the very nature of modern societies, another possibility is to enlarge the range of esteem-supporting rights and entitlements that are independent of actual achievement even though they may not generally be treated as part and parcel of equal citizenship.[34]

As long as the freedoms of the moderns retain their central importance and thus differential esteem, as distinct from equal respect, continues to play a central role in the constitution of normal agents, however, there is a limit to how much can be achieved by modification from the outside. Quite clearly, beyond a certain level wealth has meaning for human beings only in their capacity as agents. This level is easily reachable for every member of any relatively affluent society, provided that wealth is not distributed too unevenly. The question is why, beyond this level, anyone would still have a strong preference for a higher over a lower income and join the race for wealth. The only plausible answer I can think of is that in any society in which such a race draws in large numbers of people, wealth has *not* been relegated to a domain of secondary importance. It is only to the extent that the bifurcation of recognition fails to make equal citizenship (as an expression of equal respect) the primary basis of a normal level of agency that wealth (as a marker of unequal esteem) can matter enough to motivate a keen competition for it throughout a society. In such a society, the principal if not sole stake in the competition for money, beyond the modest level of resources needed for subsistence, is the esteem that is accorded to certain forms of agency for which income serves as a proxy.[35] This fact in turn gives distributive justice its precise meaning in those modern societies that are more or less free from subsistence poverty: what distributive justice regulates in such societies is, at bottom, the distribution of things that form the social basis of (unequal) esteem, which in turn contributes significantly to the constitution of (unequal) agency.

Thus, neither of the two options considered so far can do the trick: it does not seem possible to devise a system for the fair distribution of esteem that can by itself prevent an excessively low level of esteem for

---

[34] See Honneth, "Redistribution," pp. 149, 188.

[35] Gorz is right on the mark when he says that "differences in consumption are often no more than the *means* through which the hierarchical nature of society is expressed" (*Ecology*, p. 31). This is true of differences in income in general, and the hierarchy in question is ultimately that of esteem as a social basis of self-constitution.

some members of society; nor is it possible to reduce the importance of esteem for the constitution of normal agents to a sufficient degree to counteract the inequality of esteem. So a third option, simple and traditional-looking as it is, has an indispensable role to play. That is to find a way of ensuring, in addition to equality of respect, that the distribution of esteem – that is, the distribution of things that form the social basis of esteem – is sufficiently equal that no one has less than is required for functioning as a normal agent and hence that no one will suffer from agency poverty as a result of status poverty. The equality that ultimately matters is neither of respect alone nor of esteem alone but something comprehensive.[36] If it is inadvisable to cut the link between wealth and agency altogether in an affluent society, it is clearly necessary to weaken this link through a relatively equal distribution of wealth – on the assumption that wealth matters for agency and recognition and therefore is worth equalizing. Otherwise, in a society in which wealth is neither largely uncoupled from agency nor relatively equally distributed, there is scant guarantee that status poverty will not turn into agency poverty despite affluence and the bifurcation of recognition.

II

Ultimately, the worst evil of poverty is its detrimental effect on agency. In the absence of agency poverty, status poverty need not be a cause for moral alarm even though some of us prefer a society that recognizes "a diversity, rather than a hierarchy of talents."[37] And in the absence of agency poverty (and of status poverty as a potential cause of agency poverty), subsistence poverty is a lesser and, just as importantly, a more easily resolvable evil. Much of the poverty in China and the world today that may pass for simple material scarcity is in fact the worst possible combination of subsistence poverty, status poverty, and agency poverty.

---

[36] David Miller's idea of a fundamental equality of status, developed as an interpretation of Michael Walzer's notion of complex equality, is suggestive as an attempt to bring about this comprehensive equality. Miller's main argument, a reformulation of Walzer's, is that equal citizenship complemented by distributive pluralism can yield equality of status. Whether this argument will work depends, in my view, on the effectiveness of distributive pluralism in bringing every member of a society to its normal level of agency and recognition, not in preventing systematic outranking as such. See Miller, "Complex Equality," in David Miller and Michael Walzer, eds. *Pluralism, Justice, and Equality* (Oxford: Oxford University Press, 1995), pp. 197–225.

[37] Sennett and Cobb, *Hidden Injuries*, p. 261. See also Gorz, *Ecology*, pp. 34, 41.

True, the subsistence poverty that figures in this combination is sometimes of such severity and magnitude that in comparison status poverty and even agency poverty pale temporarily into insignificance. Many of the world's poor are so devastated and numbed by the sheer injury of subsistence poverty that they can hardly recognize the insult of status and agency poverty. That this is all too often the case, and that relieving the plight of these people commands the highest moral priority, do not reduce the gravity of the insult but only show how desperately poor many of our fellow human beings are, and how far there is to go before the injury of subsistence poverty is sufficiently ameliorated to reveal the hidden insult of agency poverty.

8

Democracy as Unmistakable Reality and Uncertain Prospect

1

After three decades of massive economic and social transformation, China has become a society in which democracy, like freedom, is both a limited reality and an unavoidable question for the future. It is precisely because democracy is already a limited reality, in a sense that I shall spell out in the course of my discussion, that we both can and should approach the question of democracy in China as a question immanent to Chinese society, as I have done with freedom (in Chapter 3). This means, in turn, that my first order of business must be to give a reasonably accurate characterization of the relevant aspects of Chinese society. Together such aspects make up a social reality – the kind of society China has become in the past three decades or so and is likely to remain in the foreseeable future – that will serve as my point of departure and return for thinking about the question of democracy. Indeed, I believe that once we have formed a reasonably accurate picture of this social reality, a good deal will follow from it, and the rest of the argument will be relatively easy; at the very least we will have a clearer sense of what we are talking and debating about at the level of fundamental political choices.

2

My reasons for this belief have to do with the question of the nature of normative reasoning. And my heightened awareness of the importance of this question is in turn prompted by the observation that democracy is a highly vexed question in China today and discussion of it all too often has, quite frankly, a hastily partisan character. I cannot pretend to be objective or impartial on so unavoidably evaluative and potentially polarizing a question. But there is much to be gained, both cognitively and politically, from taking a step back from the conflicting positions on democracy and making perspicuous what such positions are in conflict about, or should be understood to be in conflict about if they are to make good and significant sense. To this end, I want to propose a simple and, yet I hope, fruitful approach to thinking and debating about normative and political questions such as democracy.

At the first step of such an approach, we try to come up with a reasonably accurate picture of the relevant aspects of the reality of Chinese society today. The next step then involves asking, in terms of our normative discourse, what stance we take toward this reality, whether on the whole we are positive or negative about it. If we are basically negative about this reality, our normative discourse about it will, quite obviously, have a strongly counterfactual character. It will be an *ideal* discourse – a revolutionary or utopian or otherwise radically transformative discourse of some kind. Such discourse, as a category, is not only legitimate but also often necessary, and it is in my view definitely not to be dismissed in China at the present moment. But I will not take up such discourse in this chapter. Instead, I will experiment with the other alternative, in the shape of what may be called normal normative discourse. Such discourse is *normative* in a straightforward sense, and it is *normal* in the sense that it more or less accepts a society's reality as given and explores the possibility of improving or ameliorating this reality largely within the latter's parameters. This kind of normative discourse need not be conservative or uncritical (it is normative discourse, after all), but it is both defined and limited by its broad acceptance of a given social reality. Thus, with regard to democracy, the questions it poses and the answers it provides have to do not with whether democracy is a normatively desirable (or the most normatively desirable) form of government but with whether democracy is such a form of government *given social reality as it is and is likely to remain*. We are here in the business of drawing the most reasonable and appropriate normative conclusions *in the light of the nature of existing society*. The normative conclusions that are reached in this way are thus strictly circumscribed conclusions and have a kind of validity – if and when they do – that is likewise circumscribed.

This reasoning from a certain social reality to certain circumscribed normative conclusions commits us to thinking in a certain way as long as we, for one reason or another, or even hypothetically, take for granted the social reality as we find it instead of promoting its radical transformation. It forces upon us, on pain of inconsistency, the choice of embracing certain normative conclusions, however unpalatable they may appear at first sight, or else desiring the radical transformation of existing society.

This is exactly the radical choice I want to present to those who take part in the debate about democracy in China today. To bring this choice under sharper focus, I want to take up, entirely in the spirit of a thought experiment, what I have earlier called the normal normative point of view and see where that will lead us. The upshot of this thought experiment is, on the empirical or factual question of what Chinese society is like, that China is already what I would call a proto-liberal-democratic society, and, on the normative question of where China should be heading, that China should move in a broadly liberal democratic direction. I am suggesting that (a) *if* it is true that China is already a proto-liberal-democratic society, in a sense I will soon explain, and (b) *if* (a big "if") one thinks that such a society is basically on the right track, that is, sufficiently so that its radical transformation is not desirable, then (c) it clearly makes sense for China to improve itself and overcome its problems by moving further in this direction – prudently of course and therefore perhaps slowly and gradually, but without fundamental hesitation. There is no reason, however, why one has to believe (b), and hence no reason why one has to accept (c). But, and this is the crux of my argument, I think it is difficult to deny (a), and thus to the degree that one rejects (c), one must be motivated, with regard to (b), to radically transform existing Chinese society until (a) is no longer true.

If one were to accept (a) and yet reject (c) without desiring and promoting radical change, one would fall into serious inconsistency. What is important about this inconsistency is not logical but moral and practical, in two senses. First, it is a straightforward matter of moral entitlement that, if a society is so organized that people need certain freedoms in order to make a living and lead meaningful lives, then they should enjoy these freedoms. Likewise, if the goods and goals of human life are so understood in a society that with respect to them people are, as a matter of fact, more or less equal, then they deserve to be treated as equals, and such treatment should include a generally democratic form of government. Secondly, it is both a moral requirement and a matter of prudence that, given a society's form of life, a political system should be developed that is more or less, if not ideally, suited to bringing out its best and preventing its worst. If a form of life does not have a political system that is appropriate for it, its endemic injustices and ills will go unchecked and be worse than they need be. This worse-than-necessary scenario will happen even if one does not accept (a) and rejects (c) without desiring and promoting radical change and yet (a) nevertheless happens to be true. Thus a great deal hangs on whether (a) is true, and for this reason I will devote much of my discussion to showing that (a) is at least plausible.

It is worth stressing again, however, in order to forestall misunderstanding, that taking (a) to be true or plausible does not in any way commit one to embracing (c). So the thought experiment does not favor any substantive normative conclusion. All it does is to compel us to be consistent if we have reason to find (a) true or plausible. With respect to (b), there may well be good reason to think that what I have called normal normative discourse is too timid and impoverished and that some form of utopian or revolutionary discourse is much to be preferred, although I will not pursue this alternative in the present context. Thus our thought experiment is neutral and open-ended. And since so much rides on whether (a) is true, the thought experiment has the further salutary effect of forcing us to take a hard look at the reality of Chinese society. This is what I will do next.

3

In some important respects, not least its political and bureaucratic structure, China has remained pretty much the same despite three decades of reform, and yet in other, no less important respects, it would be no exaggeration to say that China has changed beyond recognition. Changes in these latter respects add up to a wholesale, if incomplete and contradiction-ridden, transformation of Chinese society, if not so much of Chinese politics, in a broadly liberal democratic direction. We may or may not like this transformation, in its individual elements or as a whole, and, accordingly, we may want to aid its progress or stop it in its tracks before things get even worse and even more irreversible. In either case we need a clear-eyed and illusion-free understanding of the kind of society China has become. My own very tentative attempt at such understanding, for the purpose at hand, has led me to identify profound change in five closely related respects.

(1) Nothing has been more important for the fate of China in the three decades of reform than the abandonment of communism as a goal for Chinese society and its individual members. The abandonment of this goal involves not only the disappearance of belief in a certain kind of future but

also the loss of the rationale and motivational basis for a certain ascetic organization of libido and for a certain altruistic morality. We may think of the three dimensions of this process in terms of disenchantment (the breakdown of belief in a communist future), desublimation (the unraveling of the ascetic, highly sublimated organization of individual desires), and demoralization (the collapse of a morality enjoining self-sacrifice and altruism).[1] The upshot is that the legitimate goals of individual life no longer have to be highly idealized or moralized; they need only to stay within the bounds of the legally permissible.

(2) The state is no longer in the business of providing every citizen with a livelihood and indeed the meaning of life through the exclusive control of the means of production and the organization of all citizens into units of production and other essential activities. Regardless of whether anything like "individualism" has emerged as a result of this profound change, there is no doubt that members of Chinese society today have to fend for themselves as individuals, whether they like it or not. This new necessity, which is also a new freedom, covers not only the mundane business of making a living but also the quest for meaning in life. The protagonist in the drama of a radically altered China is the atomistic and lonely individual in pursuit of goals of employment, property, consumption, pleasure, lifestyle, and, in a nutshell, personal status and happiness. Such an individual is none other than a (potential) modern bourgeois subject.

What we have here, then, is a momentous change not only in the substance of the goals pursued – from communism to individual prosperity, with the residue of collectivism now channeled into a substantively highly flexible nationalism – but also in the very conception of the agents who are fit to pursue such goals – from members of a society together pursuing the intrinsically collective goal of communism to isolated individuals each out to realize his or her own interests even when such interests may, if the individuals so choose, include the interests of others and society.

(3) Against the background of the last two developments, it is not surprising that there has emerged in Chinese society a brand-new idea of equality. *Given that* the legitimate goals of life have descended to the

---

[1] See Chapter 2. The concepts of disenchantment, desublimation, and demoralization, as I use these terms, are also explained in my "Disenchantment, Desublimation, and Demoralization: Some Cultural Conjunctions of Capitalism," *New Literary History* 30 (1999): 295–324.

mundane level of individual prosperity and happiness, it is inarguable that all individuals are, *as a matter of fact*, more or less equal as agents, as people who are able to choose goals for themselves, to exercise instrumental rationality in pursuit of these goals, and to form an identity and find meaning in doing so. If we bear in mind the nature of the goals that people actually pursue in such a society, this equality of agency is, specifically or substantively, the equality among agents as (potential) bourgeois subjects. This equality is simply a fact – not a fact of human nature but a fact in which is congealed the historical reconstitution of Chinese society in the past three decades. Once we acknowledge this fact, it has an inescapable normative implication, namely, that people ought to be treated equally – in keeping with the fact that they are actually equal (in the socially relevant respects).

The equality here is a qualitative one, in the sense that people are equal with regard to a socially valorized human quality, that is, a generic agency with its content left open, or that they are more or less equally in possession of this quality. This qualitative equality is different from, and quite compatible with, what we may call quantitative inequality. It is quite possible for people to think of themselves as qualitatively equal, that is, equal in their status as agents, and treat one another accordingly and yet be quantitatively unequal, that is, unequal in the amounts of goods they have, such as income or achievement. Neither fact need make impossible the other. Warren Buffet and ordinary investors, for example, are obviously quantitatively unequal but this does not undermine their equal status as agents, as bourgeois subjects.

We need to be careful in determining in what way and to what extent the new idea of equality has become a fact of Chinese society. There is a sense in which the new idea of equality has emerged negatively or by default. Once the ideal of a communist future has made way for thoroughly mundane goals of life here and now and, in keeping with this, the state has shed both its control over and its responsibility for the livelihood and spiritual life of its citizens, members of this new society are, simply as a matter of fact, left to their own devices. They become individual agents by default and, by the same token, individual agents of a certain kind – atomistic individuals who are at once (potential) bourgeois subjects and subject to the alienating, competitive capitalist order. That they are thus rendered free and equal as atomistic individuals is not the outcome of a positive struggle for equality, and thus the resultant idea of equality is more tacit than expressed, more latent than manifest, more an inference from a new form of life than a consciously affirmed value. Even to the limited extent that the new fact of equality of atomistic individuals as agents – the fact of people being equally left to their own devices – has given rise to a consciously affirmed value of equality, this value is severely compromised in practice by widespread social injustice, such as lack of equality of opportunity. But despite its negative origins and lack of conscious affirmation, and despite the fact that the equality of atomistic individuals is a dubious value and its realization at best a mixed blessing, there is no denying that the new idea of equality has taken on a life of its own and therefore it must be taken seriously, whether one likes it or not.

It is a fact of enormous significance, in this connection, that the state no longer sees it as its business and prerogative to tell ordinary citizens what they ought to want but instead tries to secure legitimacy by acting effectively to deliver what ordinary citizens actually do want. Under such rubrics as "*minsheng*" (the livelihood of the people) and "*xiaokang*" (moderate prosperity), the state does what it can to help people become the property-owning and consuming subjects that more and more of them actively desire to be, having constituted or reconstituted themselves in the image of the new Chinese society. In this sense, present-day Chinese society, however elitist in its political arrangement and however unequal in its distribution of income and opportunity, is marked by populism with respect to values.[2]

It is in large part thanks to this populism that people react with such resentment to official corruption and social injustice – to the fact that those in positions of power help themselves with lawless abandon to all the objects of bourgeois desire. It is indeed only in the context of this populism, this complete lack of "leadership" in the sphere of values, that we can understand why there exist so much corruption and social injustice in the first place. In a seemingly strange yet easily comprehensible way, the systemic character of corruption and the prevalence of resentment against it provide evidence, if of the most undesirable kind, of the leveling down of values across the entire Chinese society to the lowest common denominator as represented by the atomistic bourgeois individual. Just as important, these phenomena also constitute evidence of how seriously Chinese society fails even to live up to the new idea of qualitative equality or equality of agency. We now inhabit a form of life that clearly expresses

---

[2] On populism in this sense, see John Skorupski, *Ethical Explorations* (New York: Oxford University Press, 1999), pp. 193–94.

and rests upon this new idea, if only or largely by default, and normatively questionable as this idea is, we now confront a social reality that falls considerably below it while expressing and presupposing it and hence a social reality that is worse than it need be.

But even to speak in this way of the gap between idea and reality and to imply the need either to bridge the gap or to radically transform existing society, is already to acknowledge that the idea of qualitative equality, of people as equal agents and choosers, is now firmly part of the new Chinese social imaginary that has taken shape in the era of economic and social reform. This is an idea that increasingly informs and motivates ordinary people in their struggle for recognition, no matter how questionable it may be as a value, just as it is an idea that no one, official or unofficial, sees fit to publicly argue against, no matter how seriously the reality of Chinese society falls short of this idea.

This new idea of qualitative equality is a far cry from the notion of equality that figured in Mao's China. It may appear that equality was in some ways a more prominent value in Mao's China than it is now, but we are not talking about the same value of equality. Under Mao, equality was defined and limited by two things, among others. First, the pursuit of communism was a heavily theoretically informed project and as such required an exceptionally high level of proletarian class consciousness which only a small minority, the vanguard, was supposed to possess in sufficient purity. This vanguard was not qualitatively equal with the proletarian masses. Second, the discourse of class and class struggle left class enemies out of the scope of equality enjoyed by the proletarian class and its allies. Both of these features have disappeared in the past few decades. Now that the elevated collective goal of communism has been replaced by the mundane, largely individual-oriented goal of some getting rich first and others desperately trying to catch up later, the value of equality has for the first time come to apply to people as agents, as decision makers for themselves as opposed to followers of the Party and recipients of benefits from the state. Moreover, this equality now extends to everyone because the abandonment of the discourse of class and class struggle means that no one is excluded from the right to pursue property, prosperity, and all the other mundane goals of life. In terms of *conception*, then, the new equality is that of agency rather than of followership or of goods obtained or received, and in terms of *scope*, this new idea of qualitative equality is in principle universal, covering everyone in the rights and responsibilities it generates. All this is true despite the fact that post-Mao China has seen a dramatic increase in quantitative inequality.

(4) The new idea of equality has arisen, as I have said, in a manner and a context from which it derives its precise meaning and significance, much of it undeniably ideological. As long as we are mindful of this, we need have no hesitation in acknowledging, as a fact of the new Chinese social imaginary, that in view of the new values and goods constitutive of individual identity and desire in post-Mao Chinese society, people have for the first time come to be conceived as equal in their status as agents, choosers, or decision makers for themselves. This is truly a metamorphosis in the notion of equality, with far-reaching implications for politics and society. Where we used to have *leaders* whose wisdom was supposedly all encompassing and who had the prerogative to set goals for the entire society and all its members, we now have *public officials* or *administrators* who, however powerful, are essentially charged with the task of realizing given, socially popular goals through means-ends rationality. For the latter, mundane task, the appropriate requirements are no longer exceptional class consciousness and political vision but only superior planning and management skills. The supposed possession of such superior skills may put public officials in positions of immense power, but the rationale for this power means, in principle, that such officials must be held accountable for their *performance* – their efficiency (means-ends rationality) and integrity (adherence to the ethical and professional requirements of their office). And it is ordinary members of society who, as equal agents fully on a par with public officials despite their lack of administrative power, are supposed, in principle, to be the ultimate judges of such performance.

(5) In the context of the profound change in the conception of the ruler-ruled relationship, itself made possible by other, equally profound changes, it has become increasingly true in post-Mao China that any justification of state power must refer to, or at least be consistent with, the *consent* of the governed. Hence, to use Gramsci's terms, the integral state is relying increasingly on hegemony as opposed to sheer domination.[3]

To be sure, hegemony was part of Mao's rule, too, and thus along with coercion there was also the active manufacturing of consent, through propaganda and various other methods of mobilization. So even back

---

[3] See Antonio Gramsci, *Selections from the Prison Notebooks*, ed. and trans. Quintin Hoare and Geoffrey Nowell Smith (New York: International Publishers, 1971), pp. 12, 57–58, 80n49, 239, 263.

then, consent played a part in securing legitimacy for an otherwise quite obtrusively coercive state. But this highly distinctive form of consent was marked by the fact that there was no choice but to give consent, for the only realistic alternative to consenting was to be consigned to the category of class enemies. Indeed, the fear of being placed in this deadly category was as much a factor in the manufacturing of consent as the opportunity to acquire a positive identity by responding to political mobilization. In China today, by contrast, consent is no longer coerced to nearly the same degree, and correspondingly the state has to perform in order to win such consent.

Consent involves both *form* – how consent is expressed, whether it is explicit or only tacit, and so on – and *substance* – what consent is about, the substantive goods with regard to which people appraise the performance of the government and give or withhold consent. With this distinction, I want to capture the fact that the substantive dimension of consent has a certain measure of independence from the expression of consent such that it is possible to make relatively reliable inferences about consent with regard to the performance of a government even in the absence of well-established channels for the expression of consent. It is for this reason that talk of tacit or implied consent, given the relatively plentiful and equitable provision of goods generally important in a society, can make some sense, even if lack of opportunities for explicitly giving or withholding consent can be a legitimate source of complaint.

Drawing on the distinction between the form and substance of consent, we can roughly say that in China today the form of consent largely consists of consultation of various kinds and a modicum of local elections while the substantive dimension of consent revolves around individual prosperity, national power, and a certain threshold of social justice. As far as the substance of consent is concerned, China is now characterized, as I have said, by populism. The state is at one with the vast majority of the citizenry when it comes to the most important goals and values. This is a function of reciprocal influence, with the state still serving as by far the most important socializing agent and the people in turn pressuring the state to deliver the goods the state has largely taught them to want. The fact that the state may seriously fall short of the socially popular goals, especially the last one, social justice, does not change the fact that the state is pursuing popular values and goals, and only those. We may describe this fact in terms of *substantive populism* – substantive in the sense just explained and in the further sense that this populism does not extend to active public participation in the *process* whereby the state goes about pursuing the socially popular goals.

Given this substantive populism, it is not surprising that there is much greater voluntariness, as I have said, in the consent of the governed today than in Mao's time. Mao may have been a populist in the means he used for mass mobilization, especially during the Cultural Revolution, but he was anything but a populist with respect to the agenda he set for China. It is a measure of the sheer terror of the class struggles Mao waged, aided no doubt by his charisma, that he was able to manufacture consent for as long as he did. With the passing of the Mao era, the terror is gone, along with the charisma, and thus consent takes on a more voluntary and calculated character. Gone too is the very category of class enemies, and thus consent must be secured across the board. Whether consent thus understood is effectively procured by the current government is a question we need not take up here, beyond pointing out that the legitimacy of the state at the present moment rests as much on aggregate economic development as it is compromised by the corruption and social injustice that mar its distribution. The important thing for our purposes is that the state must actively seek, as a necessary condition of its legitimacy, the *voluntary* consent of *all* under its rule. What I have called substantive populism is both a cause of this condition and a significant part, though by no means the whole, of its fulfillment.[4]

4

Taken together, the five developments I have just sketched – (1) the abandonment of the highly sublimated goal of communism in favor of much more mundane goals, (2) the emergence of the individual as the main agent in everyday life, (3) the rise of a brand-new idea of equality that sees people as equal individual agents largely in the mode of bourgeois subjects, (4) a profound change in the ruler-ruled relationship from comprehensive leadership to instrumentally rational administration, and (5) the greatly increased need to secure popular consent as a basis of the legitimacy of state power – add up to a certain form of life that it is not farfetched to describe as liberal democratic or at least proto-liberal-democratic. To the

---

[4] Changes of the kind just described are hardly deniable, and it is largely a matter of how one formulates them. For a different formulation, see Zhou Guanghui, "Dangdai Zhongguo zhengzhi fazhan de shida qushi" (Ten Major Trends in the Evolution of Contemporary Chinese Politics), *Zhengzhixue yanjiu* 1 (1998): 29–42.

degree that (1) and especially (2) are true of a form of life, the very viability of that form of life requires that people actually enjoy some, though not necessarily all, of the freedoms characteristically present in a *liberal* society, whether or not such actual freedoms are apprehended in terms of the value of freedom.[5] Likewise, insofar as (3), (4), and (5) are true of a society, that society cannot be very far removed from a *democratic* society in sentiment or spirit, whether or not this sentiment or spirit is matched by appropriate institutions. Thus, if we think of liberal democracy broadly as a social setting marked by a combination of certain basic facts of everyday life and a certain widely shared general value orientation (i.e., an endorsement of these basic facts), rather than narrowly as a form of government, then China already finds itself in such a setting, not yet entirely to be sure, but already perhaps irreversibly, at least for the foreseeable future.

Given the approach to normative reasoning as set out earlier, this is a claim that is not only descriptive but also normative – or descriptive with normative implications. It is descriptive in the sense already explained: namely, that it is a matter of fact that Chinese society is constituted today by the pursuit of mundane values and goals centered round the individual's good life, by a conception of people as equal agents or choosers given such values and goals, and by the abandonment of the old style of comprehensive leadership and the consequent need to appeal to popular consent and satisfaction as a basis of governmental legitimacy. It is normative in the sense that such a social setting, as long as we take it for granted, gives rise to an entitlement to a certain range of freedoms and democratic institutions that is morally difficult to deny, and in the further sense that only when the nature of a society, in this case Chinese society, is allowed to determine the shape of its political institutions can the goods characteristic of such a society be best promoted and its typical ills and injustices best prevented. Thus, for example, if the goods that members of present-day Chinese society generally pursue and whose production and distribution political institutions exist to facilitate and regulate are mundane ones with regard to which people are as a matter of fact more or less equal, then as long as this is a fact of life that we cannot change or do not wish to change, it is only fitting that we evolve toward a form of government that is consistent with this equality, and it is only right and

---

[5] For the distinction between actual or de facto freedom and the value of freedom, see Chapter 3.

prudent that we seek not to create excesses of social injustice by resting government on contrary and false assumptions.

On this view, liberal democratic institutions, that is, good and effective liberal democratic institutions, have their raison d'être in serving as favorable conditions for the best that is possible, and as antidotes to the worst that is possible, in a corresponding type of society. Even at its best, such a society may leave a great deal to be desired, in terms of ethics or social justice, but the deficiencies that remain will be different in kind and magnitude from those that can come about when a proto-liberal-democratic society has superimposed upon it a political structure ill suited to the distinctive advantages and liabilities of such a society. It is the deformities in ethics or social justice caused by such a mismatch that make up what I have earlier called a *worse-than-necessary* scenario. One symptom of such a scenario, in the domain of social justice, is the rampant collusion of power (still exercised in the name of socialist values and principles) and money (no less valorized than in any openly capitalist society) in the absence of appropriate checks and balances and an effective rule of law.[6] Another, in the domain of ethics, is the continuation of a style of moral education and propaganda that largely presupposes a socialist society that no longer exists except in the most attenuated and fragmented form, with the result that such moral education and propaganda succeed only in feeding a deadly cynicism about all things moral and creating a moral wasteland significantly worse than the uninspiring scene in full-fledged liberal democratic societies.

The unavoidable normative implications of the proto-liberal-democratic social setting of China today do not mean, however, that we must accept the ideal of liberal democracy in China and work toward the realization of its full-fledged form. They only force upon us the requirement to be consistent as a matter of intelligibility and integrity. The record of liberal democracy – not least since its triumph in the Cold War, with the alleged "end of history" in the realm of values and the accelerated pace of globalization – leaves ample room for radical critique, especially from those who find liberal democracy too weak in the face of the

---

[6] A simpler case is that of capital enjoying freer rein than it would in a society with better regulation and more effective trade unions. For discussion of Foxconn's operations in mainland China as an example of this, see Ding Xueliang, *Bianlun "Zhongguo moshi"* (Debating the "China Model") (Beijing: Shehui kexue wenxian chubanshe, 2011), pp. 117–19. It is also arguable that the gross inequalities in China today have their cause, or at least one of their main causes, in the lack of a political arrangement capable of producing greater distributive justice in a capitalist society. See ibid., pp. 178–80.

capitalist onslaught on human flourishing and the natural environment, if not complicit in this very destruction. If we belong in such company, we must take up a discourse that cannot but be *ideal* in relation to present reality. This is a perfectly legitimate exercise, indeed a much needed one in our world, although of course it carries its own uniquely challenging burden of argument. But our present discussion is confined to what I have called *normal normative discourse* in response to the proto-liberal-democratic way of life in China, and it is with respect to this discourse that the requirement of moral and practical consistency kicks in with particular force.

Thus, if for whatever (actual or hypothetical) reason we accept the proto-liberal-democratic social reality of China today, then the question is no longer whether we should want the liberal democratic type of government but what precise form of such government we should want. We can argue against this or that way of understanding liberal democracy – for example, against libertarianism in favor of liberal egalitarianism, or against any crude version of electoral politics in favor of seriously deliberative democracy.[7] If this does not go far enough, we can subject liberal democracy to ideology critique from within in order to hold it to the highest internal standards and insist that it live up to its professed moral and political potential instead of serving as an ideological justification of a severely compromised status quo.[8] We can also argue against one agenda or another for political transformation or evolution – for, after all, real political change with such high stakes in a society as complex as China is anything but the simple translation of theory into practice. And we can argue about as many other related matters as we care to think of, but we are no longer really in a position to argue against liberal democracy in principle. Liberal democracy thus becomes something we fight over, not against, and as such, it is what is called an essentially contested concept. The only intelligible and honest alternative to such acceptance of liberal democracy is not the rejection of liberal democracy itself but the *prior*

---

[7] An example of an argument for liberal egalitarianism in the Chinese context is Zhou Baosong, *Ziyouren de pingdeng zhengzhi* (The Politics of Liberal Equality) (Beijing: Sanlian shudian, 2010).

[8] I myself have pursued this tack in a series of articles including "Redeeming Freedom," in Stan van Hooft and Wim Vandekerckhove, eds., *Questioning Cosmopolitanism* (Dordrecht: Springer, 2010), pp. 49–61; "Political Agency in Liberal Democracy," *Journal of Political Philosophy* 14 (2006): 144–62; "Taking the Reasons for Human Rights Seriously," *Political Theory* 33 (2005): 243–65; and "Liberty Rights and the Limits of Liberal Democracy," in Rowan Cruft, Matthew Liao, and Massimo Renzo, eds., *Philosophical Foundations of Human Rights* (Oxford: Oxford University Press, forthcoming).

refusal to embrace the proto-liberal-democratic social reality that makes it morally unavoidable and prudentially necessary. By the same token, for those who are repelled by the thought of following in the footsteps of Western societies in the design of China's political system and institutions, the only intelligible and honest alternative to the Westernization of Chinese politics is not opposition to the introduction of elements of Western political systems themselves but the prior refusal to embrace the Westernization of Chinese *society* that makes the adoption of such politics morally unavoidable and prudentially necessary. Whether such refusal in either case is realistic and informed by a vision of human life and society superior to the Western liberal democratic one is a separate and open question that is outside the scope of the present discussion.

5

It is one thing to claim that China is already a proto-liberal-democratic society, something else to claim that acceptance of this fact entails a certain normative pressure toward promoting a full-fledged liberal democratic society, and yet something else if one were to further claim that China will actually develop into a full-fledged liberal democratic society. I make the first two claims but not the third. But I do want to say something about the internal pressures and contradictions within Chinese society in terms of which one might discern the likely shape of things to come. To this end, we need to take apart the notion of a liberal democratic society, examine separately its liberal and democratic components, and come to a reasonably accurate understanding of the relation in which these two distinct yet closely related components of liberal democracy stand to each other.

Now, if we take a close look at each and all of the five features of Chinese society I have briefly identified, we will see that this society is both proto-liberal and proto-democratic, and hence what I have called proto-liberal-democratic. And it is proto-liberal-democratic in roughly the same way that a modern Western society is liberal democratic. This is so not only in the sense that certain features of a society, say, (1) and (2), are liberal or proto-liberal and other features, say, (3), (4), and (5), are democratic or proto-democratic but also in the further sense that the liberal and the democratic dimensions of such a society are so related that the liberal may be said to take precedence over the democratic. I will discuss this precedence in more detail later. For now it suffices to note, following Benjamin Constant's well-known observation, that members of a modern society, in a way that is as true of Chinese society today as it is of Western societies, pursue their most important activities and constitute their most important identities in the domain of private life and that their participation in public life has only a secondary importance, much of which, moreover, is only or largely instrumental to what goes on in private life. Even where public life draws the widest interest and keenest participation, it still mostly revolves around issues that have to do with conditions necessary for the individual pursuit of the good life rather than around activities essentially constitutive of a shared political life. Inasmuch as this is the condition of modern life, that is, inasmuch as the human need for agency finds expression, in modern societies, predominantly in private rather than public life, it is only natural that members of such societies value freedom more than they value democracy. Thus, the formulation "liberal democratic" does not mean some unordered conjunction of the liberal and the democratic but a certain priority of the liberal in that conjunction.

To understand precisely what this priority means, we need to distinguish three dimensions of the freedoms that make up the liberal component of liberal democracy. These freedoms have in common the fact that the agents who enjoy them determine for themselves, within certain human and social limits, what they do and who they are, understand themselves as thus self-determining, and thereby constitute a certain (generic) identity as free individuals. This self-determination is a good that all exercises in freedom manifest, whatever else they accomplish, and since the good is that of self-determination as such, we may call it *the agency good of freedom*. While the agency good of freedom is important in its own right for those whose self-understood identity is that of free individuals, this generic or formal (form-giving) good is at the same time directed at specific goals or objects. People realize their (generic) identity as free individuals in pursuing the specific goals they have as citizens of a democratic polity and, especially, as private persons in a liberal, capitalist society, as well as in pursuing, in the spirit of instrumental rationality, the resources deemed necessary to achieve such goals. Such specific goals of freedom and the specific resources they require are various, and let us call these *the substantive goods of freedom*. It is true that members of a liberal democratic society pursue the substantive goods of freedom in their self-understood capacity as free individuals. But they do so, more precisely, as members of a society of free individuals, and, as such, they pursue the substantive goods of freedom in the context of a struggle for recognition. It is for this reason that social justice, designed to ensure fairness of the struggle for recognition, is of prime importance in a liberal democratic society. Freedom in a liberal democratic society is thus nothing but the equal opportunity to participate in the acquisition of the substantive goods of freedom as part of a fair struggle for recognition and at the same time to constitute oneself as a free individual in a society of such individuals. Freedom thus understood is intrinsically subject to social justice: call this *the social justice constraint* constitutive of freedom in a liberal democratic society.

In what relation does the democratic component of liberal democracy stand to the three goods of freedom just identified – the agency good, the substantive goods, and social justice? It stands, first and at least in theory, in a relation of independence, insofar as members of a liberal democratic society see their participation in the democratic process as constituting an important part of their collective and individual identities and thus as a valuable activity and experience in its own right. To what precise extent actual members of actual liberal democratic societies do so is an empirical question, but it seems reasonably accurate to say that they do so to a significant degree that nevertheless does not nearly match the importance they attach to individual freedom. The degree in question warrants the attribution of intrinsic value to democracy, and we can think of this intrinsic value as *the agency good of democracy*. It is a serious mistake to understand this agency good as having to amount to the people literally governing themselves or exercising power over themselves. Modern representative democracies simply do not work in this way, and thus, strictly speaking, democracy may be a misnomer when applied to such societies. But it remains a fact that the people do exercise a significant measure of power in determining who will govern, even though they do not themselves thereby become the ones who govern. This measure of power is the real basis for a certain understanding of members of a liberal democratic society as collective political agents, as citizens who actively help shape the course of politics rather than mere recipients of the benefits and harms of politics. As long as we have a sober and reasonably accurate assessment of this measure of power and as long as we bear in mind how the very fact of representative institutions makes "democracy" to some degree a misdescription of the reality of power in a liberal democratic society, we are not far wrong in identifying an intrinsic agency good of democracy.[9]

---

[9] See my "Political Agency."

Democracy as Unmistakable Reality and Uncertain Prospect 173

This intrinsic agency good of democracy, considerable as it is, does not change the fact that democracy plays a far less crucial role than freedom does in the everyday life and identity-formation of members of a modern, liberal democratic society. This is one sense in which the liberal component takes precedence over the democratic component in liberal democracy – a matter of the relative importance of the agency good of freedom vis-à-vis the agency good of democracy in the constitution of modern subjects. There is a further sense in which this precedence is true of the relation between the two components of liberal democracy, namely, that the democratic component stands in an instrumental relation to the liberal component. This means, first and foremost, that democracy helps safeguard the very precedence of freedom over democracy, in that members of a modern, liberal democratic society have a vested interest in maintaining this precedence and they may be expected to act on this interest through their participation in the democratic process. There is simply no better guarantee of freedom than democracy.[10]

It is a separate and, in some cases, somewhat less determinate question what instrumental function, if any, democracy performs in relation to the three goods of freedom. With regard to the agency good of freedom, it is clear that whatever democracy does in safeguarding the priority of freedom also covers the agency good of freedom; after all, the agency good of freedom is what constitutes members of a liberal democratic society generically as free individuals. When it comes to the substantive goods of freedom, it is difficult to say, especially in advance, what role, if any, democracy plays in promoting them. It depends on what the goods happen to be and on the circumstances of the society in question. Even when it is obvious what the relevant goods are, say, social stability and economic growth, it is much less obvious that democracy is more suited to delivering such goods than some other political arrangement given the kind of political culture and social psychology that may prevail in the society in question. What one can say with reasonable confidence is only that, thanks to the nearly mythical status of democracy as a moral and political value in the world today, whenever the substantive goods of freedom are not provided in sufficient abundance, this is likely to lead to calls for democracy or for greater democracy if the society in question is

---

[10] As Benjamin Constant famously puts it, "Individual liberty...is the true modern liberty. Political liberty is its guarantee, consequently political liberty is indispensable." See his *Political Writings*, trans. and ed. Biancamaria Fontana (Cambridge: Cambridge University Press, 1988), p. 323.

regarded as undemocratic or insufficiently democratic. The same seems to be true of the relation between democracy and social justice: other things being equal, the more perceived social injustice, the stronger the public demand for democracy or for greater democracy. But there is clearly more to the relationship between democracy and social justice than this. For one thing, in a society whose members are qualitatively equal as agents, democracy itself is a matter of social justice and, for another, democracy is an antidote to political corruption as a source of social injustice, especially when it is combined with measures against social injustices at the expense of the minority. Thus, to conclude, with some simplification, we might say, first, that democracy is instrumentally useful for ensuring the agency good of freedom, second, that whether democracy is instrumentally important for the substantive goods of freedom is a question that is best left open and thus, for our purposes, best left aside, except that there is an inverse relation between abundance of such substantive goods and strength of interest in democracy, and, third and finally, that democracy is both expressive of and instrumentally conducive to social justice.

6

As we turn to consider the prospect of liberal democracy in China, it is important to bear in mind the precedence of the liberal over the democratic in the modern, liberal democratic way of life. Insofar as China is a proto-liberal-democratic society, then, its internal pressures toward a full-fledged liberal democratic society come mainly from the liberal side of the liberal democratic complex. What this means, first of all, is that interest in the intrinsic agency good of democracy is relatively weak. There is no cause for surprise here, given the balance of importance between individual freedom and collective democratic process in the very conception of liberal democracy, and Western societies show scarcely more genuine and sustained passion for democratic participation for its own sake, for reasons Constant illuminated long ago.[11] Thus, if the development of a proto-democratic society into a full-fledged democratic one consists in the establishment of the democratic form of government, the momentum for such a development will not come from any strong appreciation of the value of democracy as an agency good in its own right.

It is less immediately clear what the priority of individual freedom should lead us to expect with regard to China's possible change from a

---

[11] See my "Political Agency."

proto-liberal society into a full-fledged liberal one. In thinking about this prospect, it is useful to start from a fairly obvious and yet fundamental fact, namely, that in the course of its gigantic economic and social transformation over the past three decades China has become a society in which people have both to make a living and to find meaning in life for themselves in increasingly conscious awareness of their independence or isolation and their responsibilities as individuals. It is a sheer necessity in such a society that people have the freedoms that are required for their self-preservation and self-constitution as individuals and are commensurate with their self-understanding as such. Small wonder, then, that a vast space of freedoms has gradually opened up since the start of the reform in the late 1970s, and it is in this space, with its distinctive possibilities and pressures, that members of Chinese society have come to be the kind of individuals that they now are. This very fact – the undeniable metamorphosis of Chinese men and women from members of a communism-seeking collective into a crowd of lonely individuals each locked in their own quest for a living and a good life – bears witness, both direct and inferential, to the staggering expansion of freedoms in the past three decades. Yet what is most distinctive of the freedoms that have become available in this process is that they are essentially *de facto freedoms*, freedoms that are simply there in the form of possibilities of action. Some of these freedoms are, to be sure, codified in laws and regulations, but on the whole, and in a fundamental sense, they are not raised to the level of a society-defining value. This situation may be captured by saying that certain de facto freedoms exist in plenty, but freedom has not established itself as a value in terms of which people see themselves, give meaning to what they do and who they are, and safeguard certain possibilities of action and identity against interference from others and especially from political authority.[12] There are various reasons, among them political ones, why this is so, but I will not look into them here. The important thing in the context of our present discussion is that in China today freedoms exist in an in-between or interim sense, and this peculiar situation contains an ambiguous social dynamic as we look to the future.

Insofar as certain freedoms exist in a de facto sense and provide relatively ample possibilities for self-preservation and identity-formation, there is little pressure for a second metamorphosis – from a proto-liberal-democratic society into a full-fledged one. But de facto freedoms, no matter how expansive they happen to be, are inherently precarious and

---

[12] See more detailed discussion in Chapter 3.

cannot serve as a stable basis for life and meaning. And, just as important, we may expect that those whose actual situation, with its many de facto freedoms and corresponding pressures and responsibilities, already means that they are *independent* or *isolated* individuals cannot but experience a gap in their status as agents and in their individual-centered quest for meaning until they are able to form a conception of themselves as *free* individuals and to act on that conception in real life. Thus, we have in the precariousness of de facto freedoms and in the gap of agency and meaning inherent in such merely actual freedoms a certain built-in dynamic toward the sublimation of de facto freedoms into the value of freedom. It is difficult to say how strong this dynamic is, but it seems a fairly safe conjecture that given the existing scope of de facto freedoms and given their sufficiency for a certain kind of life and a certain level of meaning, though these may fall short of some higher standard, and given moreover the political obstacles facing the elevation of freedom into a value, there is unlikely to be widespread and overwhelmingly strong interest in any major change in the current situation of freedom. By the same token, there is unlikely to be any strong pressure for democracy on account of democracy's important instrumental function with regard to freedoms. It is as if there is a contract between the government and the people whereby ample de facto freedoms are allowed in exchange for absence of demand for freedom as a value or for democracy as a guarantee of freedoms. Other things being equal, the fact that China is already a proto-liberal society contains in itself a certain inertia or equilibrium that is unlikely to be outweighed by the simultaneous presence of a certain instability and dissatisfaction.

Neither this nor the lack of strong interest in the intrinsic agency good of democracy means that the pressure for democracy is off. For there is another source of pressure for democracy, and that is the concern with social justice coupled with the understanding that much of the social injustice in China today has its main cause in the lack of democratic supervision of political power. The concern with social justice here is a concern with freedom – with making sure that the exercise of freedom in the struggle for recognition proceed in social conditions that are fair and do not undermine the very raison d'être of freedom. Thus the pressure for democracy as motivated by this concern with social justice reflects an appreciation of democracy's instrumental function in relation to social justice as a constitutive dimension of freedom. It would not be off the mark to say that the concern with democracy in China today is chiefly a concern with social justice. There is nothing odd about this; Western liberal democratic

Democracy as Unmistakable Reality and Uncertain Prospect 177

societies are not much different, and the deeper reasons for the preeminence of social justice are well captured by Hannah Arendt in terms of the eclipse of the distinction between the public and the private by the rise of the social.[13] In present-day China, where gross social injustice is endemic and rising, we may expect the pressure for democracy to remain strong, but we must not make the mistake of thinking that such pressure is in any significant way informed by a quest for the intrinsic agency good of democracy. Otherwise we would fail to appreciate the logic of the struggle for democracy in China and fail to understand the possibilities and challenges of social and political amelioration and the loci of potential or perhaps already actual crises.

7

The claim as I have laid it out – that China is already a proto-liberal-democratic society – is a claim that, in its purely descriptive aspect, is meant chiefly to apply to Chinese *society*. I mean Chinese society as distinct from China's political system and from Chinese culture. The five changes I have identified earlier are, first and foremost, changes that have happened to Chinese society and to the Chinese social imaginary. These changes have political implications, of course, and the last two are of a directly political character. But they have not led to corresponding changes in the political system, and there is no reason to think they must: in politics things have no natural course to run. After three decades of profound economic and social transformation, China remains a one-party state, and even though the party itself has become more of a functional one, the one-party state has as strong a vested interest in keeping China from evolving into a full-fledged liberal democratic society as it did in setting in motion the economic and social reforms that have led to the emergence of the proto-liberal-democratic society in the first place. Nor is this a state of affairs imposed on Chinese society by an oligarchy that pursues an agenda at odds with the interests of the governed and is able to have its way only because of its effective monopoly of force. The one-party state finds a potent source of legitimacy in its embracement of a substantive populism, as we have seen, and it finds yet another, related source of legitimacy in its successful makeover of itself into an increasingly functional organization that knows it must perform up to a

---

[13] See Hannah Arendt, *The Human Condition* (Chicago: The University of Chicago Press, 1958), chap. 2.

certain level, especially with regard to the economy, if it is not to fall victim to seriously delegitimating and destabilizing public discontent. If the one-party state has performed badly with regard to social justice, it has surpassed all expectations in presiding over three decades (especially since the early 1990s) of rapid and sustained economic growth and in reducing absolute poverty. The consequent "rise of China," though greatly exaggerated and vulnerable to an increasingly uncertain future, has done more than anything else to lend respectability to China's political system in our age of nearly universal worship of electoral democracy and to blunt the edge of calls for political reform – a euphemism for democratization. With this widely acknowledged record of successful government, above all successful economic development, the one-party state can also count on the surplus benefit of activating the culturally ingrained belief that those who have conquered the country have a prima facie title to govern it.[14]

What all this means is that if China is to develop from the proto-liberal-democratic society it clearly has already become into a full-fledged liberal democratic society, this must be a change that the Communist Party has a strong vested interest in bringing about or at least acquiescing in. There does not seem to be any such interest, even though it is not entirely precise to speak of the Communist Party as if all of its powerful members have exactly the same interest. Nor is it true, to move from political to cultural factors with a significant bearing on our subject, that all Chinese share the same cultural values that incline or disincline them, as the case may be, to favor the emergence of a liberal democratic society. But it would be hard to deny that there are considerable cultural forces, such as the recent rise of political Confucianism, that stand opposed to the liberal way of life and the democratic form of government.[15] For my purposes there is

---

[14] For recent articulations of this belief by scholars, see, for example, Fang Ning, "Zhongguo minzhu zhengzhi jianshe he zhengzhi tizhi gaige de bage guandian" (Eight Propositions Regarding the Building of Democratic Politics and Reform of the Political Structure), *Lilun redian bianxi* (Sorting out Hot Theoretical Issues) (Beijing: Hongqi chubanshe, 2010), pp. 16–22; and He Qing, "Yong 'weimin' duideng xifang de 'minzhu,'" (Pitting "For the People" against Western "Democracy"), in Pan Wei and Ma Ya, eds., *Renmin gongheguo liushinian yu Zhongguo moshi* (Sixty Years of the People's Republic and the China Model) (Beijing: Sanlian shudian, 2010), pp. 346–49.

[15] Jiang Qing is the most influential advocate of political Confucianism as an alternative both to Chinese-style socialism and to Western-style liberal democracy. See his *A Confucian Constitutional Order: How China's Ancient Past Can Shape Its Political Future*, ed. Daniel A. Bell and Ruiping Fan, trans. Edmund Ryden (Princeton: Princeton University Press, 2013).

Democracy as Unmistakable Reality and Uncertain Prospect 179

no need to go into detail or be more precise here. My brief mention of political factors and even briefer reference to cultural factors are simply meant to make clear why my claim about the proto-liberal-democratic character of China today must be limited essentially to Chinese society as distinct from China's political system and from Chinese political and broader culture.

For a sober and balanced idea of what the foreseeable future of China holds for liberal democracy, we must attend not only to the internal dynamic of Chinese society but also to the vested interests and constitutive fears and inertias that make up the political structure, and we must keep firmly in the background the more elusive yet far from negligible influence of cultural factors. At the risk of serious oversimplification, I see the future of China as depending, above all, on the tug-of-war between an already proto-liberal-democratic society and a still one-party-led political structure, between two constellations of interests and two views of what people are like as social and political beings and how politics ought to be structured accordingly. A schematic approach to this defining conflict yields three possibilities. One possibility, at least in theory, is that of society getting the better of the political structure, in which case we will see China follow through on the normative implications of its current proto-liberal-democratic character and develop into a full-fledged liberal democratic society. This is no doubt a prospect that people of a broadly liberal persuasion are keen to promote. But one can also give *conditional* support to this prospect in the belief that the social changes that have turned China into a proto-liberal-democratic society are here to stay, even though one does not warm to this fact, and therefore moral and practical consistency, especially the need to keep to a minimum the endemic ills and injustices of this kind of society, dictates conditional support for the prospect of a liberal democratic society. This position is not without its dangers, in that the establishment of full-fledged liberal democracy means the entrenchment of a state of affairs that would be more open to change in other, potentially more auspicious directions if Chinese society were only proto-liberal-democratic. A second, reverse possibility, which some on the so-called Maoist left seem to relish, is that of the political structure getting the better of society.[16] This may involve adjustments to the

---

[16] For a brief account of the "Maoist" left, see Qian Liqun, "Huigu 2010 nian" (Looking back on the Year of 2010), in *Sikao Zhongguo de weilai xueshu huiyi lunwenji* (Collected Papers for the Academic Conference on Thinking about the Future of China), Chinese University of Hong Kong, November 2011, pp. 2–41 at pp. 14–17.

political structure, too, as regards, say, the increasingly functional character of the ruling party, but the fundamental change is supposed to occur in society, the kind of change that will bring society in line with the existing political structure with its lingering potential for mass mobilization and quasi-revolutionary populism. Neither of these possibilities seems to represent a realistic prospect, at least for the foreseeable future, as neither seems to have really powerful political forces with a strong vested interest in promoting it or really desperate broadly based social forces ready to take large and sustained risks for it. The second is even more far-fetched than the first. What is much more likely is a third scenario, a prolonged stalemate between society and the political system, and this means essentially a continuation of the status quo. Unless we are presented with strong indications to the contrary, we have reason to believe that the same political motivations that have led to the transformation of Mao's China into a proto-liberal-democratic society will stand in the way of the further transformation of this society into a full-fledged liberal democratic society. Likewise, we have reason to believe that the same political forces that had the power to bring about the first transformation now have the power to prevent or at least to delay the second.

How stable and durable this stalemate will be is by no means certain. By far the most important determinant is what will happen on the front of social justice. To the vast majority of people who think of democracy as a possible remedy of China's problems, nothing looms larger among these problems than the spread and escalation of social injustice. Runaway corruption, staggering inequality, the sheer helplessness of the poorest and most disadvantaged members of society, and, above all, the massive scale on which officials at various levels of power mistreat and abuse people at their mercy and routinely get away with it – all this is fast destroying the basic social and psychological conditions of relatively benign forms of human life and human association. Although it is by no means certain that more democracy will bring more social justice, there is little doubt that it is the cumulative discontent with corruption and inequality and abuse of power, coupled with the not unreasonable belief that at least part of the solution lies in placing checks on those in positions of power, that fuels the pressure for political reform and, in the absence of political reform, could lead to major social unrest. The Communist Party has a strong enough hold on power and boasts an impressive enough record in economic growth to ward off the pressure and keep social unrest under control for now and perhaps for some time to come. But it can count on its ability to do so indefinitely into the future only if it finds a way of drastically reducing social injustice. The challenge, in its terms, is how to succeed in such reduction without, given the Party's interest and agenda, the kind of political reform that may put China on the slippery slope leading to full-fledged liberal democracy. It is not hard to see what a tall order this is. Thus, although a prolonged stalemate between a proto-liberal-democratic society and the one-party-led political system is the most likely scenario for the foreseeable future, it is nevertheless a scenario that is full of contradictions and uncertainties. If the Communist Party succeeds, it will have effectively answered the call for democracy, for, as we have seen, the desire for democracy in China today is first and foremost the desire for social justice. But there is no guarantee that it will. The future of China, not just its political future, depends on how the contradictions inherent in the current stalemate will play out.

9

Freedom's Unfinished Task

I

Freedom, as understood and discussed in this book, does not mark the so-called end of history, with all that this admittedly elusive yet by no means vacuous concept implies. It only marks our place in the modern world – or brings us into it. To be free is the only way to be human under modern conditions of life. But what exactly are modern conditions of life? Do *they* not signal the end of history, a very symptom of the end of history? Do they not have a history that foretells what modern conditions of life can mean or amount to, and that forestalls or forecloses whatever possibility for substantial and meaningful agency we may think is open to us with our newfound freedom? Questions such as these are unavoidable given freedom's ambiguous track record and its ambiguous relation to the good, and they add up to the imperative to treat freedom not as the panacea it is often so complacently taken to be but as a question – as perhaps the most important question for the modern human being.

But why must the modern human being confront this question in the first place? Or, what does it mean to say, as I have done, that to be free is the only way for us to act and to be under modern conditions of life?

Human beings act in human ways, and in so acting they become and remain all that is distinctively and variously human. Action makes possible not only the preservation of the self as a biological being but also the formation of the self as a distinctively human being. Corresponding to these ends, humans need both objective and subjective room for maneuver. Objectively, they must be able to do what it takes to achieve the goal of self-preservation. Subjectively, they need something extra, for the formation of the self as a human being, or the acquisition of an identity, cannot be accomplished without a significant measure of willing and active participation of the self. Unlike self-preservation, self-formation is a task whose completion requires subjective involvement, and this involvement places its special condition on the room for maneuver. The subjective room for involvement is a matter of degree, so is the objective room for action, and both can vary along numerous dimensions of culture and material reality. But there is little doubt that both kinds of room are necessary, and they are in principle jointly sufficient, for human action and being.

This is a claim about human agency under all conceivable conditions. What is distinctive of men and women under modern conditions is that the two generic requirements of human agency can be adequately met only under some explicit description of freedom as a value. Thus, while human agency always requires considerable room for maneuver coupled with a reasonable degree of willingness of participation, under modern conditions of life it lays down an especially stringent condition – that one must, above all else, be a consciously and affirmatively free agent, the kind of agent who thinks oneself free and entitled to be so.

Freedom thus understood is, for modern men and women, not only a condition for action but also, in a deeper and more comprehensive sense, a condition for being. Therefore, the question of freedom is nothing less than a question of being, and it would be superficial, to say the least, to regard the latter question as settled by individual choice, by the very practice of freedom, and to be concerned with freedom only or chiefly as a matter of action. For the conscious affirmation of freedom as the foremost precondition for agency under modern conditions of life raises profound questions about the nature and place of the good in human life and about the relation of freedom to this good.

Liberal democracy, in practice and even in theory, does not provide thorough enough or deep enough answers. It takes a certain understanding and codification of freedom largely for granted. It stands in a parasitic relation to Christianity and the capitalist organization of production and consumption, among other things, when it comes to what count as good and meaningful exercises of freedom. It maintains, in principle and arguably also by default, a virtual silence or agnosticism about all the large and fundamental questions of human life in the context of which alone the good of freedom or the relation of freedom to the good can be comprehended and appraised. And thus it leaves to helpless individuals, and in this way leaves completely unanswered, the question of "freedom to what ends" and, even more importantly, the prior question of "freedom of or for what kind of human beings." Not only do these belong among questions the Chinese would be well advised to ponder in their new quest for freedom, they also have a strong claim to the status of questions, just as urgent if less unfamiliar, in those places where the problem of freedom has long been thought to have been resolved in principle in what therefore must be considered the highest and final form of human society. In its very lack of deep engagement with these questions or its retreat into a comfortable pluralism, liberal democracy leaves the door wide open for frivolousness or nihilism as the upshot of freedom.

2

This is the "state of the art" as far as the mainstream, liberal understanding and practice of freedom are concerned, and this is where we in China will end up, if we are lucky, unless we can imagine a better freedom and create the conditions for its real exercise. But this is not what we can settle for if we really care about freedom and care about it in a way that is responsive to the reality of China.

It is worth emphasizing that we are raising the question of freedom in a specific context, that of a post-communist China in the depths of a moral crisis. This context gives our quest for freedom its unique meaning, rationale, and impetus. It indeed suggests that the unfolding story of freedom in China follows, in part, a rather different logic – regarding the need for freedom and the freedom needed – from that which informed what one might otherwise be tempted to view as its predecessor in the West. If in early modern Europe the rise of liberty was part of a process of neutralization in response to fatally conflicting (religious) values, what we have seen in China for the past three decades is an increasingly expansive need for the value of freedom as a condition for subject-formation in the face of a moral vacuum. This vacuum, as we have seen at many points in this book, resulted from the collapse of a mode of subject-formation in which the human need for agency was satisfied under the description of a collective project rather than individual freedom.

One hugely important upshot of this difference between early modern Europe and present-day China – a difference we may one day see fit to capture in genealogical terms – is that in the two distinct historical contexts, freedom stands in different, even opposed relations to the good. In the case of Europe, liberty, or negative liberty to be more precise, was largely a matter of fleeing evil – fleeing the evil of life-threatening conflict by desisting from intense and belligerent attachment to one conception or another of the good.[1] We catch a glimpse here of the original rationale for what is now called the priority of the right over the good, which is in effect the priority of liberty over the good. In the case of China today, freedom is needed for a different kind of problem, not intractable conflict between different conceptions of the good held with equal intensity but rather the hollowing out of what used to be a shared conception of the good and of the kind of self embedded in it. This means that, instead of shying away from the good, freedom must serve as a way of reconstituting the capacity for seeking the good and making it one's own and ultimately the capacity for self-formation. If the kind of freedom thus needed is not exactly positive freedom in the customary sense, it is definitely not purely negative freedom, either. Whatever else it may be, it must be so conceived as to form a symbiotic relation with the good that alone can help overcome nihilism rather than carry it forward in another form.

As a matter of fact, the latter possibility, that of freedom serving as a vehicle of nihilism, is already looming on the horizon. Even before freedom is allowed to emerge as a value in response to the protracted moral crisis, the rapidly proliferating de facto freedom has created a crisis of its own: a veritable crisis of freedom in the absence of any full-fledged value of freedom, as manifest in a prematurely weary and jaded existence in the midst of so much de facto freedom. We see here the makings of a new wave of nihilism, affecting as it does mainly the younger generations born after the start of the reform, as distinct from the earlier wave of nihilism directly caused by disenchantment with communist values. To neither of these two waves of nihilism, let alone their combined impact, does the elevation of de facto freedom into a value provide by itself an adequate response. As an escape from nihilism and moral crisis, freedom alone, even as a full-fledged value, cannot do the trick. Thus our task is cut out for us: we need to valorize freedom as the condition for a new moral subject and new moral culture, we need to overcome the formidable political obstacles against such valorization, and we need to make sure that we come up with the right kind of freedom, that is, a freedom that stands in the right kind of relation to the good. A tall order indeed!

But even in the midst of this huge challenge, from where we are, it is not simply a question of catching up. For one thing, as we have seen, the nature of our need for freedom and the kind of freedom we need

---

[1] See Pierre Manent, *The City of Man*, trans. Marc A. LePain (Princeton: Princeton University Press, 1998), chap. 1.

are deeply rooted in our situation. For another, our lack of experience of freedom, while an undeniable disadvantage and an incentive to learn from the historical accomplishments of other societies, also means that we are not saddled with all the ideological and institutional baggage that has so often put freedom in chains. This freedom from predetermined freedom cannot but be an asset in a world in which thoughtlessness about freedom is one of the most insidious threats to freedom. But this asset too is fragile and promises nothing but a measure of openness, however transitory, to the future. It is in this moment of openness, and in the spirit of openness, that I shall, in the next and final chapter, offer some very tentative general thoughts about our unique quest for freedom in China and about the nature of the modern world that frames this quest.

10

China's Space of Moral Possibilities

I

This book could with good reason have ended with the last chapter. In that briefest of chapters I argued for approaching freedom in the spirit of a question, especially regarding its relation to the good, after having tried to show, in previous chapters, why freedom must be an important part of any solution to China's moral crisis and, by implication, to many of its other problems. But I cannot quite resist the temptation, in this afterthought of a chapter, to make a modest beginning in taking up the question of freedom beyond arguing for its necessity. This is a rather different undertaking from what has been pursued in all the previous chapters and, for this reason, the attempt must be judged somewhat independently. While this final chapter obviously presupposes and builds on the main steps of argument in the previous chapters, it should not be deemed to weaken any of the latter if the *further*, tentative steps it takes do not constitute good enough answers to questions raised in the earlier. In this spirit, then, I shall pursue an idea about freedom that I should like to think is both definite and appropriately open, and I shall do so by taking some care to situate the question of freedom within the space of broader moral and political possibilities in the foreseeable future of China.

But I must first take a long detour devoted to reflections first on human nature and then on modernity. I see no better way to give a glimpse of the need for this detour than with reference to Marx's cautionary methodological remarks directed at Jeremy Bentham, although utilitarianism is otherwise of no concern for my purposes.

To know what is useful for a dog, one must investigate the nature of dogs. This nature is not itself deducible from the principle of utility. Applying this to man, he that would judge all human acts, movements, relations, etc. according to the principle of utility would first have to deal with human nature in general, and then with human nature as historically modified in each epoch. Bentham does not trouble himself with this. With the driest naïveté he assumes that the modern petty bourgeois, especially the English petty bourgeois, is the normal man.[1]

With the aid of these remarks, I can spell out the rationale for the organization of this chapter more easily. Now, to think normatively yet realistically about the question of freedom for China, we need some understanding of the range of moral and political possibilities to which China is open today. And to grasp these possibilities with the requisite conceptual clarity, we need in turn to situate China in the moral-political landscape of the modern world, and to this end we obviously cannot do without a rough sketch of that landscape, a descriptive and normative account of modernity. But we should be wary of preempting an appropriately historical grasp of modernity by reading too much philosophical anthropology into it or out of it, and therefore we would do well to begin with a brief – indeed all too brief and partial – exercise in the now unfashionable project of reflecting on human nature in general and somewhat ahistorical terms. Thus I devote an extended discussion first to human nature and then to modernity before finally bringing China into the picture.

2

In trying to make sense of any aspect of human life and society, it is impossible entirely to avoid invoking some notion of human nature, if only obliquely. Even if one believes that humans have no nature (or no "essence"), there is a sense in which this lack of nature is still nature, that is, something that can be stated positively, say, in terms of plasticity or malleability – all the more so if one believes that this plasticity or malleability is not unlimited and so humans do not exactly lack nature.

Any attempt today to piece together something that can be provisionally called human nature for explanatory purposes must meet one condition (among others): it must be capable of accommodating all the forms of human life and society that have ever existed, or put negatively and more judiciously, it must not leave outside the scope of its hypotheses

---

[1] Karl Marx, *Capital*, vol. 1, trans. Ben Fowkes (New York: Vintage Books, 1977), pp. 758–59n51.

any form of life and society which, to the best of our knowledge, humans have invented and sustained for a reasonable length of time. This means that our account of human nature must be suitably thin and general, in keeping with the hugely varied and complex phenomena of human life and society as we know them. Only in this way can we, first, do justice to the increasingly insubstantial and pluralistic conception of human life in our modern world and, second, leave room for the fact that various premodern or non-modern forms of human life and society are vastly different from ours. To this end, I propose what I will call a bare notion of agency.

By agency I mean a distinctively human way of being in which action is performed by, and in the service of, a self or subject. To capture this notion of agency in a formula, we can think of agency in terms of action organized as subjectivity, or subjectivity achieved through action.[2] According to this notion of agency, what is at stake in human action is not only self-preservation, individually and collectively, but also, for each individual, the acquisition of a certain identity as a specific kind of human being embedded in various significant human groups, and, for each group, the construction of a collective identity embedded in turn in a yet larger social setting, and so on. All human action requires a certain amount of room – objective freedom in a generic (as distinct from a liberal) sense. This room could be all that is needed for self-preservation. But what makes human action distinctively human is the other stake in it, that which involves self-making, where the self may be individual or collective on various scales. For self-making to be accomplished, whatever the self in the making happens to be like and to whatever degree this self may lack initiative or self-consciousness, the self has to participate with a significant degree of willingness – subjective freedom in a generic sense – if not initial voluntariness. One cannot acquire a self or an identity, with all its meaning and spirit, without some active and willing involvement of oneself, and, of course, this involvement in turn requires room. This involvement is a matter of degree, just as the room available is a matter of degree, but no one can altogether do without either. Thus, given its goals and stakes,

---

[2] In his exposition of Nietzsche's notion of the will to power, Mark Warren coins the phrase "power organized as subjectivity"; see his *Nietzsche and Political Thought* (Cambridge, MA: MIT Press, 1988), p. 59. As noted before, I have found Warren helpful in developing my own account of agency, as is obvious from my adaptation of his very useful phrase. The observant reader will notice that in a departure from my usage in earlier chapters I am experimenting in this chapter with a terminological shift from "power organized as subjectivity" to "action organized as subjectivity."

human action needs both more or less room and more or less willingness of participation. We need a much more complex account than I can provide here in order to understand how these needs are negotiated, contested, and constantly reshaped. But one thing already seems quite clear: room for action and willingness of participation are the only necessary conditions of human agency as such, as distinct from any particular, culturally specific configuration of agency, and they are jointly sufficient for human agency.[3]

If there is one thing that stands out above all else in the notion of action organized as subjectivity, it is the plasticity of the human agent: almost any action will do, and any subjectivity, as long as the action is such that it can be organized as subjectivity.[4] Of course, certain conditions will have to obtain for such organization to take place and persist over time. But none of these conditions places limits on what action one performs, nor on what subjectivity one thereby acquires or maintains. Any action organized into any subjectivity, or any subjectivity achieved through any action, is sufficient for agency, which in turn is sufficient for human being.

Insofar as human agency is plastic in this sense, it precludes definition in terms of anything substantive, whether it goes by the name of the good or virtue or nature or anything else, and to a corresponding degree it resists critique in terms of alienation. All of these are optional normative extras, if you like, in terms of which human agents may be uplifted, tamed, deluded, or fittingly or unfittingly taken to task. But they do not count among the necessary conditions for human agency. For the latter, *any* action organized as *any* subjectivity will suffice.

If we take a historical view, it may be said that it was only after modern nihilism – only after the good, virtue, and nature had all come to be perceived as human constructions, however useful or laudable – that the plasticity of human nature came fully into view. To a large degree, the plasticity of human nature is precisely the independence of this nature from the good or virtue, from anything higher or more demanding than action organized as subjectivity. Anything beyond this has its place in human life and society only as one possible way among others of giving shape to human agency out of the plasticity of human nature.

---

[3] For a more substantial account, see my "Evaluating Agency: A Fundamental Question for Social and Political Philosophy," *Metaphilosophy* 42 (2011): 261–81.
[4] See Friedrich Nietzsche, *Daybreak*, trans. R. J. Hollingdale (Cambridge: Cambridge University Press, 1982), aphorism 204, and *The Gay Science*, trans. Walter Kaufmann (New York: Random House, 1974), aphorism 360.

If we understand human nature to be, largely, human plasticity, then what Pierre Manent (following Leo Strauss) thinks of as the relation between law and nature turns out to be the relation between law and plastic human material. Thus, it is not so much that "law modifies, transforms, or orients nature"[5] as that law gives shape – a particular shape out of innumerable possible shapes – to human material that is largely without a fixed nature or whose nature lies chiefly in its plasticity. But Manent is entirely right about the *authoritarian* nature of all law as law. Law exists to give shape to what is otherwise without shape, and shape-giving is *imposition*, the overcoming of all resistance. Even the most painless shape-giving – that which follows the path of least resistance (which implies that plasticity is a matter of degree and thus mixed up with "substance") – is imposition as regards its intent and its operation.

Imposition is not sufficient, however, for agency understood as action organized as subjectivity. For that which is imposed can give shape to plastic human material only on condition that it is more or less willingly accepted and incorporated by those at the receiving end. In other words, for imposition to be successful, it must happen as a process in which those at the receiving end actively participate, thereby turning imposition into self-imposition. This active element we may call *mimesis*, meaning that imposition as the external force of self-constitution can lead to the emergence and continuation of a self only when it is completed by the internal force of positive imitation of, or identification with, what first comes from the outside. In this sense, *the subject has a mimetic structure*: a subject comes into being by entering into a mimetic relation with preexisting, socially available models or figures of the subject. There is thus an inherent tension within subjectivity – between the moment of imposition and the moment of initiative. Mimesis represents the successful synthesis of these contradictory moments through the self playing the roles at once of imposer and material. Given that mimesis relies on the active element of self-constitution, it must happen in such a way as to be compatible with and conducive to a sense of personal involvement and initiative, at least not to produce consciousness to the contrary. That is why the subject as subject, while mimetic, abhors imitation except under the description of the good (as in the ancient regime) or choice (as in the modern regime). The subject in the making (as it always is) incorporates what is external in

---

[5] Pierre Manent, "The Modern State," in Mark Lilla, ed., *New French Thought: Political Philosophy* (Princeton: Princeton University Press, 1994), pp. 123–33 at p. 131.

the first instance and is able to do so willingly and actively only when it is either drawn to a pre-given figure of the subject unquestioningly accepted as good or else left to choose a figure of the subject of its own free will. In both cases imposition remains at work but is divested of any perceived presence of the sheer will of a personal force stronger than oneself. Thus happens something miraculous: the subject is bent into shape because it is not bent against its will.

3

Even so, imposition is bound to encounter resistance insofar as it gives form to what is otherwise unformed or formless. It will elicit resistance of a different sort when it gives form, a new and different form, to what has already been formed in another way, for habit, acquired vested interest, and sheer inertia can all stand in the way of change. But the really interesting resistance is of a kind that causes one to suspect exceptions to the general rule of normal plasticity. When imposition meets the toughest resistance, in thought or action, and does so from those of whom it cannot be said that age or habit has robbed them of their flexibility, it may be reasonable to infer exceptional limits to plasticity. It looks as if such unusually recalcitrant or independent-minded people somehow have a more predetermined nature than the common run of human agents do. More predetermined, say, by a more exacting sensitivity or a deeper and more inaccessible inwardness, or by what one may call a certain spiritual cleanliness or rigor, either innate or acquired in the first few years of life. Or perhaps by overabundant strength, if we are to follow Nietzsche, a kind of strength that indicates a "higher nature" disposed to think in terms of "good and bad," and hence free from resentment, rather than "good and evil."[6] Or, in sum, by any number of all those traits, discussed in Colin Wilson's fascinating account, that make for "outsiders" who must, at whatever cost, give shape to themselves from their innermost nature and for whom to be shaped by custom and convention is merely to "drift through life."[7]

Such speculation, far from gratuitous, is necessary and of undeniable consequence. For significant limits to plasticity are presupposed by

---

[6] See Friedrich Nietzsche, *On the Genealogy of Morals* (and *Ecce Homo*), trans. Walter Kaufmann and R. J. Hollingdale (New York: Random House, 1967), first essay, esp. sec. 16.

[7] Colin Wilson, *The Outsider* (New York: Tarcher/Putnam, 1982).

certain important and widely held values. Behind the endless protests against homogenization in modern mass societies is an idea well captured, for example, in Hannah Arendt's notion of action as made possible by plurality – the idea that "we are all the same, that is, human, in such a way that nobody is ever the same as anyone else who ever lived, lives, or will live."[8] For Arendt, action presupposes plurality, and plurality in turn covers every human being so that, as Arendt's notion of natality has it, each birth marks a new and novel beginning. Whether as articulated thus by Arendt or in other ways, the belief that everyone is different from everyone else in some deep or significant sense underlies the widespread fear of homogenization, which is seen as an offence perpetrated against intrinsic human diversity. It is possible that this fear is exaggerated because the underlying belief is exaggerated in its assumption that everyone is equally unique, that is, equally an exception to what must therefore be a totally misconceived general rule of normal plasticity. But this much remains true, that where and to the degree that such values as freedom and pluralism make genuine sense and are seriously applicable, strong limits to plasticity are presupposed. The stronger the limits, the more necessary will be the values defending them, and the greater the offence that is possible with imposition.

For this reason, we must distinguish between imposition and domination. Imposition, the giving of form to more or less plastic human material, is a condition of human life and human society, and there can be nothing intrinsically objectionable about it as such. But what if the plastic material in the case of some human beings is not so plastic after all – not so plastic by virtue of being more predetermined (as explained earlier)? What if a form is imposed on such human beings that goes against the grain of their more predetermined nature and that cannot but provoke strong resistance, in thought or feeling or action or all of these, from deep within their nature? When imposition happens under such circumstances, it becomes *domination*: one set of people imposing a form on another who are so different as to constitute a "species apart." Thus *domination is defined in terms of exceptions to normal plasticity*. If such exceptions did not exist, there would be no reason to speak of domination and all we would have is imposition, which can be carried out in better or worse ways but is in principle unobjectionable. Domination is qualitatively different from imposition, or we may think of it as a unique

---

[8] Hannah Arendt, *The Human Condition* (Chicago: University of Chicago Press, 1958), p. 8.

and singularly violent kind of imposition. It is not imposition as such but the imposition of a form on (some) people *against their nature*.

Imposition by its very nature involves an unequal relation – between those who impose a form and those who have it imposed upon them. Domination is an unequal relation in which the imposition does a high degree of violence to the nature of those at the receiving end. Even in the (hypothetical) absence of domination, that is, even within a society whose members have come to share the same overarching framework of values through imposition on uniformly plastic human material, there is bound to be inequality of a different kind: some people will fare much better than others and receive much higher degrees of recognition than others by the standard of their shared values, whatever these values may be. This condition of inequality – hierarchy or social inequality among those who belong to the "same species" in terms of values – is distinct from domination and is objectionable, when it is indeed so, for entirely different reasons (say, social injustice, or even gross social injustice) than apply to the inequality in domination.

Accordingly, we must distinguish between the *struggle for recognition* – the competition for higher standing in a hierarchical structure (such as the mobile hierarchy in a modern society) – and the *struggle for domination* – the competition among sets of people with radically different values for the preeminence of their values, that is, for the imposition of their values on society.

The struggle for domination is a struggle over values, as opposed to relative standing within a given framework of values, and as such, it is of an altogether higher order of importance and consequence than the struggle for recognition. (The importance of the defunct communist movement depends, for example, on whether it is regarded as a struggle for domination or recognition.) The latter can involve conflict in values, concerning, say, what should count as fair rules of cooperation, but the values in question come into conflict only within a shared horizon of more important values. It is over the most important values, those that make up the moral horizon of a society, that the struggle for domination is waged. Those who have carried the day (at any given time) are the real "makers of history," the determiners of the nature of their society (at any given time).

Just as imposition need not take the form of overtly beating the plastic human material into shape, for seduction (as in consumerism) is often just as effective or more effective, so the struggle for domination does not have to take place in the form of any visible contest, nor need there be hanging over the struggle, as it were, an express aim of domination as we would normally think of domination. What defines the struggle for domination is rather that only one set of highest-order values can achieve preeminence in a society at any given time (exclusiveness), that there is no higher stake than which set of values achieves preeminence (importance), and that the process whereby preeminence is established is unavoidably one of rivalry or contestation (struggle), however subtle and seemingly far removed from violence.

The struggle for domination is at its most invisible when the agents of successful imposition are more or less diffuse and (seemingly) unorganized and do not go about their business remotely in the spirit of shaping society with a set of values. Even so it will not be difficult to identify a class of people, however loosely connected and disparately located, who benefit most and flourish best in a society informed by a prevailing set of values, who stand to lose the most from a reversal of those values, who have the strongest vested interest in maintaining the status quo or its development according to its internal momentum, who wield the greatest power to act on this vested interest, and who can be counted on to act on this vested interest, with class consciousness and full awareness of the stakes, whenever it comes seriously under threat. Given all the subtlety and complexity that mark the genesis and evolution of values, what more do we need to see this class of people as imposing its values on the rest of society and winning the struggle for domination over those who lack the common plasticity to adapt to the prevailing values and who must struggle for their replacement or else languish? That they flourish best in a society shows that their nature is most compatible with the preeminent values of that society – so much so that, even if they were not actually responsible for the invention of those values, they would happily have made that invention given the opportunity. That they are poised to defend these values and the society informed by them shows that even if they were not directly responsible for the first imposition of these values, they would have unhesitatingly carried out the imposition given the occasion. That they have both the largest vested interest in maintaining the preeminence of these values and the greatest power to act on this interest marks them out as playing a leading role, as the movers and shakers behind the preeminence of certain values rather than others in their society.

Their soul is the soul of their society. Their spirit is the spirit of their age. And thus it is to them more than to anyone else that we must attribute credit or blame whenever we have good or bad things to say about the society or the age. A society comes to be the way it is through the imposition of values and the struggle for domination, and, for better or for worse, it is shaped in the image of the victors in that struggle.

Human nature, then, reveals itself in the open-ended series of forms that has been successfully imposed on the plastic human material. It is the record of paths of least resistance (success) and paths of most resistance (failure or short-lived success). It is the story of people who over centuries and millennia have yielded to one after another of the dominant forms. It is also the story of those, always a tiny minority, whose lack of ordinary plasticity has prevented them from yielding so readily or not at all and who with their recalcitrance and their suffering must be recognized as a "species apart," as exceptions to normal human plasticity. It is above all because of this tiny minority that "the human problem, that of the relationship between nature and law, remains intrinsically, naturally, and therefore perpetually insoluble."[9] If we take this minority duly into account, then it may be said that what the history of successful impositions reveals is not so much human nature as *mass* human nature – the nature of those who possess ordinary plasticity and therefore whose nature, including both its malleability and the limits to that malleability, can be traced in its paths of least as well as most resistance.

4

We can think of modernity, or the modern human being, in terms of a distinctive second nature and think of this second nature in turn in terms of a distinctive set of constraints on the struggle for domination and, within an established order, on the struggle for recognition. If such constraints are limiting in the sense just described, they are also enabling and, as such, are more appropriately thought of as values that make up the horizon of a distinctively modern way of life. In speaking of constraints, then, I do not mean to make light of their positive dimension as values but only to bring out the fact, which is important for my purposes, that one crucial role of such values is as parameters within which, and indeed sometimes over which, the struggle for domination or for recognition takes place.

The first such constraint involves a decisive shift in our approach to hierarchy. Since hierarchy is a feature of human society that has its source in human nature, it is not surprising that it has not disappeared despite all

---

[9] Manent, "The Modern State," p. 132.

the talk of equality, even of equality as a "sovereign virtue." But hierarchy is deemed just, or at least acceptable, no longer as a matter of ascribed status but only on the basis of competition. Competition imparts legitimacy to a mobile hierarchy when it is supposedly free, inclusive, and fair; all the more so if the inevitably unequal outcomes of competition are so adjusted as to leave the worst-off with a measure of material well-being and even of dignity. Such morally regulated competition, understood especially in terms of equality of opportunity, places a distinctively modern constraint on the production of hierarchy and gives a distinctively modern twist to the perennial struggle for recognition.

At a deeper and less visible level, the modern value of equality, in combination with that of public reason, also places a constraint on the struggle for domination. The struggle over fundamental values has by no means ceased in modern times, but all values, in the face of opposition, require justification in order to gain preeminence, and such justification must be addressed to all.

This constraint is all the more powerful when it works in tandem with a cognate constraint whose source is the modern value of liberty. If we distinguish between a generic notion of freedom and the modern notion of freedom and understand the former as the room for action and initiative that all human beings need in order to be human, then we may say that the latter represents an essentially liberal conception – by now a firmly reified conception – of that room in terms of *individual* agency and of the need to safeguard that agency in terms of *rights*. Under the constraint of this modern notion of freedom, the authoritarian character of all imposition of values must express itself in the form of *authorization* rather than injunction,[10] in the form of rights rather than obligations. This means that, if a set of values is to have a reasonable chance of gaining preeminence among modern people, the content of these values and especially the mode of their imposition must be consistent with people *not* feeling imposed upon, that is, with their feeling free, whether or not they really are free. Thus, under modern conditions, the struggle for domination can be won only when the hand that imposes values is able to render itself invisible.[11]

---

[10] See ibid., p. 131.

[11] By the same logic, the best way for paternalism to work is to make itself invisible by presenting itself as libertarian. See Richard H. Thaler and Cass R. Sunstein, *Nudge: Improving Decisions about Health, Wealth, and Happiness* (New York: Penguin Books, 2008).

Modern liberal society provides the paradigm example of how the invisible hand works: "By subtle, indirect but infallible means, authorization comes ever more to resemble an injunction and has the same effects. The law permits the citizen to be indifferent to all the goods that have been the object of the human pursuit; and little by little it orders that indifference. How is it possible to believe that what the law, which is naturally awe-inspiring, allows is truly wrong?"[12]

If the struggle for domination seems to have quieted down, especially after the end of the Cold War, it is chiefly because the two modern constraints upon it – the equality constraint and the liberty constraint – have virtually been cast in stone, amounting to a new metaphysics. Indeed, the progressive hardening of these constraints marks crucial victories (meta-victories, as it were) and signposts in the struggle for domination. Together, the two constraints have tilted the battlefield decisively in favor of certain outcomes and turned all efforts aimed at achieving other outcomes into an uphill struggle. At times it may even seem that the struggle for domination is so predetermined by the combined force of these constraints that the struggle for recognition is the only game left in town.[13]

Another decisive outcome of the struggle for domination that ushered in the modern world and has since hardened into a constraint upon all further struggles is even more profound and sweeping than either equality or liberty. It is nothing less than the irrevocable loss of any basis – cosmocentric, theocentric, or anthropocentric – for openly imposing a unilaterally chosen set of values on human plasticity. This loss first took the form of what Nietzsche calls European nihilism.[14] What constitutes European nihilism is not only the devaluation of the highest values but also, even more consequentially, the understanding for the first time of the highest values *as values*, and moreover as values posited by human beings as conditions for the will to power. Since Nietzsche, we have learned to think of all morality in terms of values and of all morally informed

---

[12] Manent, "The Modern State," p. 131. See also Pierre Manent, *The City of Man*, trans. Marc A. LePain (Princeton: Princeton University Press, 1998), pp. 180–81.

[13] It is quite revealing that Axel Honneth, an heir to the Frankfurt School, should approvingly see the contemporary "location of critical theory" in this way. See his *Disrespect: The Normative Foundations of Critical Theory* (Cambridge: Polity Press, 2007), esp. chap. 3.

[14] On "European nihilism," see Friedrich Nietzsche, *The Will to Power*, ed. Walter Kaufmann, trans. Walter Kaufmann and R. J. Hollingdale (New York: Random House, 1967), bk. 1. On "original nihilism," in contrast with which "European nihilism" is defined, see bk. 2.

human relations as relations of power as if it is the most natural thing in the world to think in this way. In this we are all schooled in European nihilism.

The "death of God" did not prevent modern people from positing very elevated human values, as distinct from the highest values, whether or not these consciously humanly posited values were in fact parasitic on the highest values, in the manner of what Nietzsche calls "incomplete nihilism."[15] On the contrary, European nihilism made the conscious positing of human values not only possible but also necessary, and, in due course, on the ruins of the highest values were erected human ideals of progress, with either the nation-state or the proletariat as the agent of that progress. Thus the highest values may have died, but high human values were born, and the latter values made possible the citizen subject and the class subject in place of the believer in God. This new round of value-positing, very different from "original nihilism" in its relative lack of psychological innocence, nevertheless created the possibility of a further nihilism after European nihilism: the devaluation of the elevated though consciously humanly posited values.

This possibility is now amply realized. Neither the nation-state nor the proletariat is any longer viewed as an agent of progress, and indeed the very idea of progress has suffered a fatal blow and, with it, the distinctively modern subjectivity in the shape of the citizen subject or the class subject. Thus European nihilism was followed by a distinct, brand-new nihilism: the devaluation of high human values (after the earlier devaluation of the highest values) and the so-called death of the subject (after the earlier death of God). Insofar as this new nihilism signals the exhaustion of the moral and intellectual resources of modernity, we may perhaps call it *postmodern nihilism*, meaning by it the ending of modernity on an

---

[15] Ibid., sec. 28. Nietzsche describes incomplete nihilism in terms of "attempts to escape nihilism without revaluing our values so far." Heidegger provides a useful gloss on this laconic statement. Incomplete nihilism, says Heidegger, does indeed refuse any longer to believe in God as the highest value, but it does not hesitate to assign to whatever (new) values it posits "the old position of authority that is, as it were, gratuitously maintained as the ideal realm of the suprasensory." See "The Word of Nietzsche: 'God Is Dead'," in Martin Heidegger, *The Question Concerning Technology and Other Essays*, trans. William Lovitt (New York: Harper & Row, 1977), pp. 53–112 at p. 69. To put it more simply, one still believes in God without knowing it. Or: one still believes in the position that used to be occupied by God even though one no longer believes God can or should occupy that position. It is this *position* – what we may call the God-position – that is not revalued, and until it is revalued we unknowingly continue to give our values, whatever they are, the strong epistemic status that we seem to disavow when we claim we do not believe in God.

anticlimactic note. Whatever psychological innocence was still a part of consciously human idealism, as was manifest first in a comprehensive Enlightenment rationality and then in its bifurcation into the bourgeois and proletarian versions of progress, is now dissipated, and the loss of any basis for overt imposition or domination is virtually complete. This fact is perhaps the most profound and sweeping constraint on all further struggles to give shape to human plasticity.

Against this background, equality and liberty take on a meaning rather different from that of their counterparts in the more idealistic climate immediately after European nihilism: they have turned postmodernist, as it were, shedding their idealism in keeping with the skeptical and ironic epistemic and moral tendencies of the latest nihilism. With the collapse of all ideals that are not viewed as mere objects of individual preference and choice, liberty has come to mean, above all, freedom from the good – from aspiring to the good, from any obligation to pursue the good as viewed independently of what individuals themselves may happen to desire, and hence from any imposition of the good that is at variance with individual and especially popular desire. Likewise, equality has come to mean, above all, the absence of any point of reference that could render individuals morally unequal in the light of their desires and, given this lack, the equal right of all individuals to seek the satisfaction of their desires as they themselves see fit within the limits of the legally permissible.

In this way, nihilism, first European and then postmodern, has made it possible for modern people finally to become autonomous, and equally so, but the role of nihilism in this process of "enlightenment" also means that this autonomy or maturity will not be placed at the service of the perfectionist ends that Kant, for example, sees as constitutive of human nature.[16] Indeed, freedom from the guidance of another is achieved at the same time as, and indeed through, freedom from the good. And what freedom from the good makes unnecessary and impossible is any distinction between genuine autonomy and apparent autonomy, between autonomy as a normatively appraisable condition and autonomy as merely the

---

[16] See, e.g., *Groundwork of the Metaphysics of Morals*, trans. and ed., Mary Gregor (Cambridge: Cambridge University Press, 1997), 423, 430. It is important that what Kant has to say in answer to the question "What Is Enlightenment?" be understood, in its comprehensive import, in conjunction with his perfectionist view of human possibilities and the self-regarding duties to which they give rise. In this regard, the early Marx, especially of *The Economic and Philosophic Manuscripts of 1844*, ed. Dirk J. Struik, trans. Martin Milligan (New York: International Publishers, 1964), is quite Kantian and has suffered the same blow to his perfectionism in our time of postmodern nihilism.

psychological state of not feeling imposed upon or unfree. This psychological state is all that matters, and all are equally entitled to it. A vulgar Kantianism reigns in our day.

5

With each passing century since its inauguration, the modern world has become more purely or terminally modern, and it is not implausible to see the state of the world today as the relatively enduring outcome of the struggle for domination under the three constraints constitutive of modernity. There is little doubt that liberal democratic capitalism, with neoliberalism as its latest incarnation, has so far turned out to be the form of human social life whose imposition has apparently found the path of least resistance.

Liberal democratic capitalism has met the equality constraint through a bifurcation of recognition into a supposedly equal respect based on citizenship and a regime of unequal esteem determined by competition in the private sphere, and through the redemption of unequal esteem in turn via an equality of opportunity that at its fairest can perform the magic of turning highly unequal outcomes into entirely acceptable ones, especially when supported by a safety net for the least well-off.

It has met the liberty constraint by shaping behavior through economic necessity rather than openly political coercion, by valorizing negative freedom at the expense of full-blown positive freedom, by taking on board certain human rights of a moderately positive kind that go beyond negative freedom, and by accomplishing the shift from a production-centered to a consumption-centered economy that is both good for profit and conducive to the feeling and appearance of individual choice and initiative. And it has done so, above all, by placing the most powerful determinants of human life more and more in the economic rather than political sphere, with the result that power, increasingly wielded by capital rather than more personal agents, has become more and more diffuse and disincorporated, to a degree that is not possible with political power even in the most democratic of societies.

And, finally, liberal democratic capitalism has met the nihilism constraint without even trying, as a liberal capitalist regime centered on consumption has no need for elevated human values, still less the highest values, and is able to shape the plasticity of human desire through seduction and temptation and, for the first time in history, to create the appearance of pandering to the plasticity of human desire instead of shaping it. It is almost as if human plasticity is left to its own devices, with no need for imposition, not to mention domination.[17]

Liberal democratic capitalism has encountered a lot of resistance on the way to its dominance today, undergoing many transformations along the way, and there is no guarantee of the indefinite continuation of this dominance. But it is difficult to imagine, for the foreseeable future, significant weakening of the three constraints on all struggles for domination. That the values of equality and liberty carried the day and hardened into constraints on all further contestation meant a decisive triumph of the moderns against the ancients. The subsequent struggle within the ranks of the moderns between capitalism and (so-called) communism ended in an equally decisive victory of capitalism, and part of this victory involved establishing certain ideological interpretations of the values of equality and liberty – of equality in terms of opportunity rather than outcome and of liberty in predominantly negative rather than positive terms. In the past few decades, especially since the end of the Cold War, these interpretations have become increasingly entrenched, along with an unprecedented leveling of all values toward a global consumerism and hence a nihilism more thorough and complacent than ever before.

It is against this background that neoliberalism came to preeminence. For the ending of the Cold War meant that for the first time capitalism could become truly global, and so it was a matter of time before the "great transformation" first attempted in the Anglo-Saxon model of capitalism was able to spread itself all over the world through an increasingly deregulated regime of mobile (industrial and especially financial) capital and global free trade.[18] This second "great transformation" – the globalization of the first – represented an internal victory, as it were, a victory within the capitalist order of one (Anglo-Saxon) model of capitalism over another (say, the Rhenish), turning the relatively modest and benign institution called the market economy into nothing less than a market society or a market order. Thanks to this victory, and as part of it, the liberal

---

[17] Central to this development is the generalization of the fashion form throughout society. See Gilles Lipovetsky, *The Empire of Fashion: Dressing Modern Democracy*, trans. Catherine Porter (Princeton: Princeton University Press, 1994), part 2. As Lipovetsky writes in the introduction (with more approval than ambivalence), "individual autonomy develops through the heteronomy of seduction." For a more critical view of the impact of consumerism on human freedom, see Zygmunt Bauman, *Consuming Life* (Cambridge: Polity Press, 2007).

[18] On the "great transformation," see Karl Polanyi, *The Great Transformation: The Political and Economic Origins of Our Time* (Boston: Beacon Press, 2nd Beacon pbk. edn., 2001).

interpretation of equality in favor of opportunity has been stretched, until nearly breaking point, to accommodate ever greater inequalities of outcome (in both wealth and power), and the liberal notion of freedom as noninterference and individual choice has been reinterpreted to mean above all the freedom of capital (through deregulation) and of the consumer. Thus, the victory of neoliberalism is won both by successfully operating within the constraints of modernity and, more importantly, by successfully giving new interpretations to the values of equality and liberty.

All these changes in our modern world, not least the rise of neoliberalism, have left a deep mark on the evolution of the modern subject. In my brief general account of the mimetic structure of the subject, I have said that the subject as subject abhors sheer imposition as going against the very grain of its subjectivity and that therefore the subject can accomplish its mimetic self-constitution only under two conditions: either more or less willing subscription to a pre-given conception of the good or more or less free choice from among available conceptions. It is easy to see that the first of these conditions belongs to the ancient model of self-constitution. This model is no longer available, ruled out as it is by the equality constraint. Under the equality constraint, people who hold different conceptions of the good must be treated equally, and therefore imposition can no longer be made compatible with mimesis by appeal to any single pre-given conception of the good. What has taken the place of the defunct, ancient model of self-constitution is a modern one based on free choice among divergent conceptions of the good, and this is precisely what is dictated by the liberty constraint as well. According to this constraint, instead of any pre-given conception of the good commanding voluntary submission, it is the act of free choice that turns into the good whatever is freely chosen. Once mimetic self-constitution is filtered through these two constraints, not to mention the ethically deflationary effect of nihilism, what comes out is bound to be *democratic mimesis* – voluntary imitation under democratic pluralism. Small wonder that the consumer subject has gradually taken over from figures of the subject centered around the nation-state or a class, for the figure of the consumer subject best disguises imposition and is most compatible with democratic mimesis. Indeed, thanks to the consumer subject, we encounter for the first time a form of imposition that looks like its exact opposite when all supraindividual figures of the subject have made way for the competitive seduction of the consumer. Inasmuch as the element of imposition in self-constitution takes the form of seduction and the mimetic element takes the form of unimpeded response to such seduction, the consumer subject can be forgiven for living under an illusion that we may call auto-mimesis. In auto-mimesis, pluralistic seduction seems to bring one into the closest contact with one's true desires and thereby to set in motion a mimetic process in which what one imitates is to all appearances none other than one's true self. And since the elimination of mimesis from subjectivity is impossible, auto-mimesis may even seem the closest one can get to the semblance of sovereign agency.

If one deplores any of these developments regarding the modern world or the modern subject, especially those initiated by neoliberalism, one should deplore even more the increasing tendency for ideological victories to be won with such near irreversibility that, as in the case of the demise of communism and then of the rise of neoliberalism, once one side has won or lost, a space of values is all but closed. This narrowing of moral and political possibilities (as reflected in Margaret Thatcher's slogan "there is no alternative") is the worst legacy of the triumph of neoliberalism and its ideological appropriation of the ending of the Cold War. All attempts to reverse this state of affairs must confront neoliberalism on the site of its victories. And this means, first and foremost, the need to see the battlefield for what it is – a battlefield of values – and to constantly undo in consciousness and institutions the hardening of political or ideological victories into taken-for-granted fixtures of modern society. Thus, in my view, the most important criterion for judging the adequacy of modern normative theories of society is how far they go in leaving the battlefield of values open. By this criterion, Chantal Mouffe's explicitly agonistic conception of democracy as a stage of irreconcilable conflict between minimally mutually respecting adversaries comes off much better than Habermas's in terms of communicative action, which is in turn more open-ended than Rawls's in terms of fully substantive principles of justice.[19]

When I consider next the prospect of freedom in the context of moral and political possibilities in the foreseeable future of China, then, I shall treat as of equal importance both how well China can respond to those

---

[19] The views of Habermas and Rawls in this regard are too well-known to need referencing. See, however, their exchange in Jürgen Habermas, "Reconciliation through the Public Use of Reason: Remarks on John Rawls's *Political Liberalism*," *Journal of Philosophy* 92 (1995): 109–31, and John Rawls, "Reply to Habermas," *Journal of Philosophy* 92 (1995): 132–80. Chantal Mouffe's relevant works include *The Democratic Paradox* (London: Verso, 2000), *On the Political* (London: Routledge, 2005), and *Agonistics: Thinking the World Politically* (London: Verso, 2013).

of its problems for which freedom is an important part of the solution and whether in developing its response China will help enlarge the range of plausible moral and political possibilities for itself and for the world at large.

6

One of the most striking features of China today is a gap between a new material condition of life coupled with a gradually emerging set of values, on the one hand, and old institutions, entrenched power structures, and remnants of an outmoded ideology, on the other. If we take a close look at the internal dynamic of China's transformation in the past three decades, we cannot but notice an inexorable movement in the direction of equality, liberty, and nihilism in a radically changed condition of life in which these values make obvious sense and perform an intelligible function. Yet it is equally noticeable – and consistent with the largely unchanged political reality of a one-party political system – that these values have not been allowed to run what one might consider their natural course given the socioeconomic reality on the ground. This is true especially of liberty and nihilism while the progress of equality finds its chief obstacle not in any inherent logic of one-party rule but in the rapid growth and entrenchment of vested interests that the party in power could have done more to keep in check instead of taking up the lion's share of such interests. Given this complexity, we need a careful spelling out of where China stands with regard to what I have identified as the three principal values of modernity.

With regard to equality, it is undeniable that China has acquired an altogether new tolerance of the gap between rich and poor since the start of the economic reform in the late 1970s and has seen an especially alarming widening of this gap in recent years. Yet it is no less true that this huge inequality is seldom justified in public by appealing to anti-egalitarian values, least of all by China's leaders. The farthest one would go by way of defense or explanation of the status quo is to counsel patience and leave it to the passage of time and economic development to allow the less well-off to catch up or at least move closer. It is revealing, in this connection, that on one highly important issue inherited from Mao's time, namely, the rigid and systematic inequality between the city and the countryside, egalitarian sentiment has noticeably grown in recent years. The moral tide has decisively turned against the complacent acceptance of this gross inequality, although it will take nothing less than a profound change in the economy and a revolution in values (to the point where city-dwellers no longer find it conscionable to live with the privileges they have come to take for granted) to get anywhere near the goal of actually eradicating this inequality.

The major shift in moral reaction to the city-countryside divide is accompanied by an equally significant change in political relations. There is little doubt that the relationship between the leaders and the people is now conceived, though not to the same degree conducted, in much more equal terms than it was even a decade ago, let alone in Mao's time. This new relationship has come about as part of a larger process that also includes the renunciation of class struggle and of the category of people known as class enemies. The result is a situation, unthinkable in Mao's time, in which all people are supposed to enjoy the same basic political and legal standing. Whatever equality may be taken to mean in China today, its reach is wider, in principle, than it has ever been.

The central event of this larger process is the momentous, though unannounced, abandonment of the communist future and hence of the need for any vanguard allegedly superior in consciousness and revolutionary virtues to the masses. What has followed from this decisive event is the gradual, and by now almost complete, leveling of values to the mundane concerns with prosperity, enjoyment, and security. As Xi Jinping put it in his first public speech on November 15, 2012 as general secretary of the Chinese Communist Party, "Our people have an ardent love for life. They wish to have better education, more stable jobs, more income, greater social security, better medical and health care, improved housing conditions, and a better environment. They want their children to have sound growth, have good jobs and lead a more enjoyable life." It is very striking, though entirely consistent with China's new political relations, that Xi immediately goes on to say that "To meet their desire for a happy life is our mission."[20] This conception of the good life and of the role of the Communist Party in relation to it is shared throughout Chinese society, and there is nothing in it to justify political inequality or to give legitimacy to social inequality except via the egalitarian value of equal opportunity.

Although reality is yet to catch up with this new conception, it is quite evident that the less well-off are increasingly couching their grievances

---

[20] "Remarks on the Occasion of Meeting with the Chinese and Foreign Press by Members of the Standing Committee of the Political Bureau of the Eighteenth Central Committee of the Communist Party of China" (http://www.china.org.cn/china/18th_cpc_congress/2012-11/16/content_27130032.htm).

and claims in the language of equality and social justice. This language has already acquired a currency and legitimacy that no one dares to deny. More and more, if significant social inequalities, including that of income, are to become morally acceptable and compatible with a stable social order, they must be justified in the language of equality, say, in terms of different degrees of effort and merit under conditions of equal opportunity – or else the already massively pent-up resentment will continue to grow, with all of its potential consequences.

The factors and circumstances that have cleared away virtually all conceptual obstacles to the value of equality have done largely the same for the value of liberty. The desublimation of the collective project of communism under Mao into the individual pursuit of the more mundane goals so well summarized by Xi Jinping, the corresponding devaluation of all other-regarding and especially collective-regarding values, and the depoliticizing transformation of the Party and State from the vanguard and executive organ of the proletariat into institutions of administration and governance, have combined to remove all reasons for imposing restrictions on individual liberty in the name of any higher cause than social stability. As with equality, the lack of conceptual obstacles to liberty is yet to translate into a well-articulated value and, harder still, into a corresponding social reality. But with the higher good of communism out of the way, there is nothing in the realm of values to stop the gradual entrenchment of the sentiment of liberty. Already, even in the absence of any clearly enunciated value of liberty, the threshold for imposing restrictions on individual liberty has been raised to a level unprecedented since 1949.

The raising of this threshold is made possible and necessary, as we have just seen, by the devaluation of collective, future-oriented communist values, values that once commanded wide acceptance and left no place (and arguably little need) for individual liberties. The devaluation of such values is what we mean by nihilism in the context of post-communist China. China did not experience European nihilism, to be sure, or the much earlier original nihilism. But insofar as original nihilism was the precondition of European nihilism, and insofar as European nihilism was the precursor of the later, postmodern nihilism that was to dissolve the idea of progress and all that goes with it, post-communist China fully partakes of the general ethos and fallout of nihilism – the devaluation of Enlightenment values in a broad sense – in which our world is now enveloped. In the speech earlier mentioned, Xi Jinping does not invoke any values higher than the realization of the everyday wishes of ordinary people. Completely gone, and by now no longer conspicuously so, is any pretension to uplift the people, through moral education and political mobilization, to a shared life devoted to noble goals transcending the individual and the present. The idea of a communist future is dead in China, and, with it, everything that belief in this future makes attractive, justified, and imperative.

7

There is one powerful factor, however, that stands in the way of any full and explicit acknowledgment of nihilism, of the devaluation of communist values. This is the all-important political fact that China remains under the exclusive leadership of the Communist Party. Insufficient to prevent or cure nihilism, this fact nevertheless dictates a firm *official* refusal to publicly own up to it. While communist values have suffered an irreversible devaluation, the rationale for the Communist Party's continuing leadership depends on keeping open the elevated, nearly transcendent place that these values used to occupy. The Communist Party must dwell in this place, even if the values that used to define it have lost their appeal and have been quietly abandoned. Thus, the claim to exclusive leadership has come to rest on the sublimation, reminiscent of the erstwhile collective struggle for a communist future, of the mundane goals of individual prosperity and happiness into the semblance of a collective cause of national revival. Thus Xi says in the speech from which I have already quoted: "Our responsibility now is to rally and lead the entire Party and the people of all ethnic groups in China in taking over the relay baton passed on to us by history, and in making continued efforts to achieve the great renewal of the Chinese nation, make the Chinese nation stand rock-firm in the family of nations, and make even greater contribution to mankind.... To fulfill our responsibility, we will rally and lead the whole Party and the people of all ethnic groups in China in making continued efforts to free up our minds, carry out reform and opening up, further release and develop the productive forces, work hard to resolve the difficulties the people face in both work and life, and unwaveringly pursue common prosperity."[21] It is this collective cause – its supposed collectivity rather than its substance – that makes it appear that the service of the Communist Party at the helm is still essential.

[21] Ibid.

With the disappearance of the communist future as the ultimate goal, however, the rationale for the continuation of the Party's exclusive rule is, strictly speaking, no longer that the Communist Party has a certain political (communist) substance but rather that it happens, for historical reasons, to be the only functional party strong enough to perform a task that in itself is not so distinctive but belongs rather in the generic category of modernization and national revival. To rest the case here would be to admit that the Party's claim to leadership is a totally contingent and pragmatic matter and bears no relation to the Party's communist credentials. This surely would be a dangerously delegitimating admission, and yet any explicit invocation of a communist future would be scarcely less inadvisable for the incredulity and cynicism it is bound to provoke. There seems no option left but to stop appealing to communist values and yet to proceed as if these values had not suffered the decisive devaluation that is everywhere evident in Chinese life. The result is a nihilism kept incomplete for political reasons; in other words, *politically incomplete nihilism*.

Given the incomplete state of nihilism, it is only natural that the good, or more precisely the *place* of the good, however substantively vague and at times even vacuous, continues to enjoy a certain structural priority in Chinese life, just as the Party maintains a claim to leadership that is no less insistent for being increasingly generic and abstract. This fact has important implications for the evolution and especially the articulation of liberty as a value. Although people are, as a matter of fact, left free for the most part to pursue their interests and desires as they see fit, it is difficult to see how liberty can emerge as a full-fledged value since the exclusive leadership of the Communist Party is incompatible with the *public* notion of people being able and free to choose their conceptions of the good without the moral guidance of the Party. Whatever de facto freedoms people enjoy, these freedoms must not be so conceived and codified as to dispense with the role of moral guidance that has always been an essential part of the Party's justification of its exclusive hold on political power.

It would be inaccurate, however, to describe this state of nihilism as only politically incomplete. While individual liberties are yet to be fully secured, there is already a widespread sense, most alarmingly among the younger generations born after the launch of the reform, of a moral (and spiritual) vacuum that no amount of liberty could fill. Thus, the place that has been left vacant by the devaluation of communist values is not only artificially preserved for political reasons, as we have noted, but also kept alive by a widespread yearning for the good and the meaningful, beyond liberty and social justice, among ordinary people. In this way, the nihilism is also *ethically* incomplete. If one is tempted to attribute this neediness to the lingering effects of decades of socialization under Mao, especially in the case of the older generations, one should also note that it has even deeper cultural roots in the Confucian tradition. Against the background of these influences, it is not surprising that the ethically incomplete nihilism feeds upon and in turn feeds the politically incomplete nihilism through the simultaneous presence of a yearning for the good and a certain openness, at least among the most innocent or the most desperate, to potential leaders who can provide visions and exemplars of the good. That the yearning is inarticulate and often *negatively* expressed through the painful sense of a moral (and spiritual) vacuum and its myriad symptoms, and that the openness is tempered more than ever by wariness and cynicism based on repeatedly disappointed expectations, do not show that the yearning or the openness is absent or unimportant but only that we are in a situation of nihilism and yet the nihilism is incomplete.

8

For better or for worse, this politically and ethically incomplete nihilism is the soil from which all that is good must grow. What will become of China is a function of what the contending forces will do on this soil within the constraints – equality, liberty, and nihilism – that have come inexorably but incompletely to form the value-infrastructure of Chinese life, and especially a function of what they will do to further modify or shape these constraints. There is no doubt that the most powerful contending force, though itself a complex and dynamic assemblage of forces, is the Communist Party with its overriding interest in maintaining its monopoly of political power. Thanks to this fact, nihilism will be kept incomplete indefinitely into the future, aided by what is left of a culturally ingrained primacy of the good, and this will in turn keep the other two constraints, especially liberty, from running what might be considered a more natural course given the material reality of Chinese life. The resulting inconsistencies and contradictions make for disorientation, but insofar as nihilism, freedom, and equality – or the actual forms they have taken in the modern world – are questionable in one way or another, the fact that they have not been allowed to run their full course in any particular direction leaves room for different possibilities in China. Such possibilities, whatever they might be, will not be made good easily, still less automatically; we cannot even say with any confidence in advance that they truly exist and are both preferable and realistic. But the incomplete nihilism in China is morally ambiguous rather than merely negative or entirely positive, and it behooves those who care about the future of China to ask seriously whether possibilities, both attractive and realistic, exist in what is otherwise a rather disheartening situation.

In addressing this question, our first order of business must be to decide whether to proceed on the assumption that the Communist Party will continue to be the most powerful political force in the foreseeable future. It makes a world of difference whether we think about the future of China with the preeminence of the Communist Party as a more or less durable feature of the political scene or whether we disregard this preeminence for being undeserved or unhelpful or for being irrelevant for purposes of normative theorizing. All political thinking about China in which the Communist Party does not figure centrally has no traction for the present, indeed for as long as the Communist Party remains the dominant political force. All political thinking about China that belongs to the opposite variety courts massive irrelevance once the central political fact on which it is predicated ceases to be true. For my reflections that follow, I prefer to run the risk of future rather than present irrelevance, a risk that is balanced by the likelihood that the shadow of the Communist Party will long outlast its actual rule in that name.

There is a second decision we must make that is a hardly less powerful determinant of how we think about the present and future of China, and that is whether to think against modernity or rethink modernity without attempting to overthrow it. This too makes a world of difference. Take those who are trying to reshape China in the light of Confucian values reconstructed in one way or another. Many if not most among them take the condition of modern life, including the values informing it, more or less for granted and attempt only to change this condition in moderate ways or at most to promote an "alternative modernity," whatever that may turn out to mean. This becomes clear when we compare such proponents of Confucianism with a radical and uncompromising Confucian figure such as Jiang Qing, who seeks to roll back the unfolding of historical time away from the modern, indeed to get out of historical time altogether in favor of a cosmologically grounded order.[22] Jiang does not rethink modernity; he thinks against the very grain of modernity and seeks nothing less than a paradigm shift. He does not allow himself to be subject to the broad constraints – equality, liberty, and nihilism – within which contestation over values takes place among those who think of themselves as moderns. That is why he lays down his blueprint for a Confucian constitutional order but studiously avoids falling into the modern dialogic trap, for the very act of providing arguments in the modern idiom of public reason is tantamount to admitting defeat even before the contest starts. Small wonder, perhaps, that Jiang is often blithely dismissed as "crazy," the symptom being to think almost entirely outside those constraints that make all contestation over values among the moderns a dialogic exercise among participants who are presupposed to be free and equal and shorn of epistemological or moral certitude.

I would be the last to consider Jiang "crazy" on this account, not least because his unabashed championing of the priority of the good can help prevent the common belief in the priority of the right from becoming automatic and ossified. But I cannot but think that Jiang has avoided one trap only to fall into another difficulty no less forbidding. For to think against modernity, as Jiang does, is to run up against the three gigantic obstacles that inhere in the modern condition and in modern consciousness – equality, liberty, and nihilism – and success in such an undertaking depends on showing why these obstacles should be overcome and how they can be overcome. Jiang does not even see the need to take up this challenge, relying instead on a pervasive sense of crisis supposedly afflicting the modern condition and on the unargued force of his alternative, Confucian vision of human life as a way out of the crisis. For better or for worse, I do not see how these modern constraints on contestation over values can be swept aside (just as I do not see how the Communist Party will leave the stage in the foreseeable future in any but the most inauspicious circumstances); nor is it even clear to me that we should want to throw them overboard even if we could. Yet much is wrong with the modern condition, and there is a good deal to be done both within the modern constraints on contestation and indeed to reinterpret and reshape the constraints themselves. Today's China, already irreversibly a modern

---

[22] See Jiang Qing, *A Confucian Constitutional Order: How China's Ancient Past Can Shape Its Political Future*, ed. Daniel A. Bell and Ruiping Fan, trans. Edmund Ryden (Princeton: Princeton University Press, 2013).

society and yet in the grip of deep inconsistencies and contradictions, provides both the occasion and the incentive to rethink modernity – and to do so with what could be the advantage of "backwardness."

I have thus set the stage for thinking about the future of China, first, by placing the Communist Party at the center of the stage and, second, by seeing the stage in terms of three important features of the modern world as they have inscribed themselves on the social landscape of China indelibly and yet incompletely. In so doing, I am actually taking China as I find it, and in thus approaching China, I want to form a disciplined view of the range of possibilities or potentialities given the structure and dynamic of present-day reality, and, on a more normative note, to see what good things we have reason to hope for and what bad things we have reason to fear. Along the way, I will have occasion to bring up aspects of China's reality that are in principle less inflexible than the presence of the Communist Party and the three features of modernity but may nevertheless exert a powerful, if less predictable, impact on the future course of China.

9

Among those countries whose course of development is likely to make a big and enduring difference in the world as a whole, China stands out in the nature and degree of power still wielded by the nation-state, power that can be used to good effect as well as bad. This is due in large part to the position of the Communist Party, but the legitimacy of this very position is in turn based, in the wake of the failed communist project, on the perception of powerful centrifugal forces that require a strong leadership to keep the country together. It is true that the Communist Party has effectively prevented the emergence of any political force that could take its place at the center. But this does not change the fact that until a credible competitor is able (allowed) to appear on the horizon, or until a democratic arrangement is invented that is plausibly deemed capable of creating a sufficient centripetal pull, the Communist Party's self-appointed place at the top caters, however imperfectly, to a deep political and psychological need. And for this reason, unless the Communist Party performs extremely badly, its preeminence is likely to continue indefinitely into the future, supported by a rationale that goes well beyond the Party's own narrower interest.

As long as the Communist Party occupies the political center, it keeps open a *space* for a kind and degree of power that is not available to the typical elected government. We must be careful, of course, not to exaggerate this space. The Party's power is limited not only by the three constraints we have discussed, relatively weak though these are in today's China, but also by the deep involvement of China in the global capitalist order, especially since joining the WTO. The latter fact is largely of the Communist Party's own making, thanks to the economic reform it unleashed in the late 1970s. Whether we think of the results of the economic reform in terms of socialism with Chinese characteristics or capitalism with Chinese characteristics, the important thing is that, at an identifiable and significant level of abstraction, China is playing the same game as other members of the global capitalist order – competing for the same things and informed by the same values. In comparison, the way China goes about playing this game, with regard, say, to the rule of law or the role of state enterprises, is of decidedly secondary importance. Now that China has been playing this game for decades, with ever deeper integration into the global capitalist order, there is no going back, and there may at times seem almost no going forward any other way. For one thing, the erstwhile dictatorial exercise of power, no longer supported by any credible ideology nor necessitated by material or geopolitical circumstances, is not going to make a comeback. For another, the strategy of delinking favored by some radical theorists as an antidote to global capitalism is clearly ruled out by the depth of China's investment in capitalist goals and values. A further, different kind of obstacle that may limit what the Communist Party can do, if less inflexibly, resides in the growth and entrenchment of a complex structure of powerful vested interests, some deep inside the Party itself. This is in turn both reflected in and contained by the mode of collective leadership at the very top as it has evolved in recent years, with its distinctive representative coverage and checks and balances. Given all these limiting factors and more, the Communist Party finds its space for leadership more and more rigidified and narrowed. Indeed, as part of the process of depoliticization and detotalization, the Party has on its own initiative withdrawn from many areas of everyday life or at least kept a lower profile in them, leaving an ever larger (though often carefully limited and supervised) role for the market and civil society.

What remains unchanged, however, is that as long as the Communist Party is in charge it must justify its exclusive claim to power in a way that will not allow it to operate and be perceived as nothing more than a merely functional party. Given its mode of self-legitimation, the Communist Party must keep open in principle a space for strong moral and political leadership well beyond the competent management of the economy and the provision of minimal welfare and social justice. For this space to be credible, it must actually be used to a significant degree, and this means that the kind of exclusive leadership claimed by the Communist Party must always be exercised with a certain excess beyond functionality or at least the distinct potential for such excess. It is especially in this sense that I shall maintain that, despite all the factors that have come to hem in its exercise of power, the Communist Party still has, structurally, more room for maneuver than is available to any political party in, say, a Western democracy, both for better and for worse.

If this excess does not seem to have been much in evidence, except negatively in the nervous pursuit of stability, this is because the excess has been put to positive use, indeed with great excess, chiefly in promoting economic growth, and this invites perception in essentially functional terms, however qualified. This does not mean, of course, that with such single-minded concentration on economic reform the Communist Party has not in truth metamorphosed into a vastly more functional organization than it ever was under Mao or even under Deng. But what is politically most consequential about this transformation is that the Communist Party has come to rely for its legitimacy so much on rapid and sustained economic growth that it has become captive to its own economic success and incurred a new political vulnerability. It finds itself having to continue to use its excess of power for the increasingly inseparable goals of economic growth and political legitimacy, and this leaves it with an increasingly cramped room for initiative when it comes to other social and political goals. Thus, the toughest challenge for the Communist Party, if it is intent on leading China into the future instead of being led by the economic-political dynamic already unleashed, is to remove or at least significantly reduce its dependence for legitimacy on the continuation of rapid economic growth. Whether this precondition for real political initiative can be satisfied will in turn depend significantly on what happens in the space of values.

10

The Communist Party's space for strong leadership, with its built-in excess of power beyond mere functionality, has its moral-cultural correlative in a certain primacy of the good, as we have seen. One way of pinning down what this primacy exactly is or entails would be to say that it is a function of the still considerably incomplete evolution of the three trends of modernity we have addressed – equality, liberty, and nihilism, especially the last two. With regard to nihilism, it is worth observing that the devaluation of high values has gone farther in post-Mao China than perhaps anywhere in the world. In this sense, China's nihilism is anything but incomplete. But what has been kept largely intact is not only a certain place of the good in the conception of political leadership, as we have noted, but also a corresponding place of the good in Chinese moral and political culture. The values of communism are dead, but the place that used to be occupied by these values is still left largely open. That is why there is a pervasive sense of a moral vacuum, and much of this sense is a yearning for the vacant place of the good to be filled and for the good to reassume its commanding role in the life of the nation and of the individual. What we find here is a still vital legacy of the Confucian tradition and indeed of a strand of Maoism, a legacy to which Confucians and followers of Mao are trying to give a new lease of life in one way or another but which is to some degree independent of the substance of Confucianism or Maoism. Balanced against this impulse is a desire, fed by the internal dynamic of Chinese society and increasing exposure to other societies, for civil and political liberties, for a robust constitutionalism and for the rule of law. The tension between these desires or tendencies, sometimes in the same people and sometimes in different segments of the citizenry, still leaves a large space for the good. This space is a battlefield of values, including the priority of the good versus the priority of the right. Although the moral primacy of the good kept alive in this way stands in a symbiotic relation with the political primacy of the Communist Party, the place of the good need not and should not be under the exclusive sway of the Communist Party. Indeed, the Party can put its political primacy to moral use in the wisest and most enduring manner if it sees its main job in this regard as that of helping create the conditions under which the people themselves are most free and best motivated to renew and enrich the place of the good. It is here that those active in the growing if restricted public sphere may have an especially significant role to play. This is indeed a crucial role, not only because the battle over values will impinge on the attitudes of the public and hence on the Communist Party's use of its excess of power but also because, as Tocqueville warns citizens of modern democratic societies, a government by itself is "incapable of refreshing the circulation of feelings and ideas among a great people."[23]

---

[23] Alexis de Tocqueville, *Democracy in America*, ed. J. P. Mayer, trans. George Lawrence (New York: Harper Perennial, 1988), p. 516.

The primacy of the good with Chinese characteristics – or more precisely *the primacy of the place of the good* – is, I would argue, the key to rethinking modernity along the three dimensions we have identified. With regard to equality, the reality on the ground, as distinct from the social imaginary, is depressing. To begin with, the most fundamental systemic inequality – between the city and the countryside – remains largely intact, while the free mobility of peasant labor for certain types of work in cities has created a huge underprivileged class lacking both the recognition and the basic benefits enjoyed by city-dwellers. In principle, this state of affairs goes against the modern sentiment of political equality, a sentiment already reasonably widespread in China, but given the much greater prominence of livelihood issues in the context of the "rise of the social" in post-Mao China, the chief complaint is that of lack of equal opportunity. But then this is a source of growing resentment that extends well beyond the city-countryside divide, with the social causes of unequal opportunity (family background, connections, and so on) compounded by long-standing regional disparities. Both of these problems translate into a third, inequality of outcome, and by any reasonable modern standard China has seen a dramatic widening of the gap between rich and poor since the start of the economic reform. This situation makes a mockery of the political credentials of the party in power as a "communist" party. With or without the deserved embarrassment, the Communist Party has no choice but to redress the politically delegitimating and socially destabilizing rise in inequality it has presided over in the past three decades. How it will go about doing so, with what success and what consequences, depends on whether, in addition to invoking the unquestioned modern value of equality, it will be able to make a credible and effective appeal to some conception of the good that will help limit the desire for inequality and provide an attractive justification for a more equal society. It is not clear that more equality of opportunity, while a good thing in itself, will lead to greater equality of outcome, as opposed to perhaps making inequality more palatable. It is indeed arguable that equal opportunity is perhaps even harder to achieve in China than moderate equality of outcome, given the culturally accentuated importance of the family and social connections with regard to many opportunities, and given the difficulty, again partly cultural, of establishing the rule of law, itself a blunt instrument for promoting equality. Redistributive justice through progressive taxation seems just as remote from ways of thinking about social justice that make relatively straightforward sense in Chinese moral culture. In any case, for either equal opportunity (beyond nondiscrimination) or redistributive justice to connect with popular sentiment in Chinese society, there is no more congenial way than grounding social justice on some conception of the good that is both attractive and plausible. I will not venture to propose a conception myself. Yet I may seem to be presupposing, with no more basis than the still vital primacy of the good in Chinese moral culture, that such a conception can be found. All I assume, actually, is that the *search* for such a conception recommends itself in China today, that such a search would be worthwhile. Were we to come up empty-handed after serious and repeated efforts, the cause of social justice would be doomed, or else solutions must be sought in a moral-cultural paradigm shift to the priority of the right, which seems an even taller order.

The same primacy of the good can make its presence felt when we turn to the question of liberty. The general condition of life in China today makes unavoidable a wide range of liberties, no matter under what description such liberties are made available and defended when necessary. Yet the circumstances under which the Communist Party maintains its exclusive political leadership mean that, whatever description happens to be adopted, it cannot be the right to be independent of the moral tutelage of the Communist Party, even when in reality the power of tutelage is used very sparingly today. Distinct from this politically based tutelage is a culturally ingrained way of thinking in terms of the good that would render popularly unappealing if not unintelligible any overarching understanding of liberties as freedom from determination by any antecedent conception of the good and hence of the good as a function of the exercise of freedom.

From a moral point of view, this may not be a bad thing at all, since in today's world the liberties enjoyed by members of so-called free societies are used in ways that are overwhelmingly shaped by the forces and ideologies of global capitalism. To the extent (which cannot, of course, be taken for granted but must be fought for) that the moral primacy of the good and the political primacy of the Communist Party can stand between individual liberties and global capital, this is at least a mixed blessing. This is not to pass over the fact that Chinese consumers have made their belated entry into the game with a vengeance or the fact that the Communist Party has formed what is at times an all too cozy relationship with global capital. What I am pointing to is not an encouraging reality but a certain space of possibilities for justifying and shaping liberties in terms of the good. That this space is in part carved out by a political force that is in principle distinct from capital and yet whose relation with capital could easily become one of collusion gives one a glimmer of hope as well as strong cause for vigilance. That this space also exists by virtue of moral-cultural resources adds to the sense of guarded optimism, even though the window provided by tradition is shrinking with the accelerated passage of historical time and changes in conditions of life. From a more pragmatic or prudential point of view, it would be difficult to imagine, at least as things now stand, how China could hang together as a society without the moral centrality of the good and its embodiment, however imperfect, in some centripetal political force. It would be just as difficult to imagine, on the other hand, given the general condition of life after communism, how China could do without a wide range of liberties, and it is only a matter of time before these liberties must not only exist but also be recognized and valorized for what they are.

Thus, once again, for the same reasons as apply to the cause of equality, the challenge is to affirm liberty and at the same time to shape and motivate it by bringing it into positive alignment with some shared and unifying conception of the good. Were this attempt to fail or not be undertaken at all, China could well be left with the unsavory choice between a suffocating and precarious stability and a chaotic freedom – probably without even the prospect of a society of "last men" or of a "brave new world," however depressing this prospect might be. The early modern European solution to the manmade "state of nature" caused in large part by conflicting (religious) conceptions of the good was a gradually established priority of the right with the accent on individual rights, first to self-preservation and then to more and more other things. Given the condition of China today and the strengths and weaknesses of the Chinese tradition, a Chinese experiment with the European recipe may well succeed precisely in bringing about the problem, the "war of all against all," to which the priority of the right proved over time to work in Europe as a solution. If there is any plausibility in this fear, both moral and prudential considerations urge us to try to further the cause of liberty while judiciously affirming the primacy of the good.

As it stands now, however, the primacy of the good means little more than a structure of possibilities – a moral and political structure in which the good is supposed to occupy a preeminent place. This place is now largely empty, as we have seen. In the realm of morality, communist values have suffered a wholesale devaluation with no new values so far successfully put in their place. In the realm of politics, the Communist Party has devoted itself with frenetic energy to economic growth and social stability while leaving the moral potential of the place of the good largely unexplored in the moral wasteland of failed communism and ill-regulated capitalism. The result is a nihilism that has proved especially conspicuous and devastating because it is emptying the place of the good in a society where both social order and political legitimacy have for so long depended on a thick and credible conception of the good. That there is now an acute sense of moral crisis throughout society attests precisely to the lingering primacy of the good. But if this sense of crisis lasts too long without significant alleviation of its causes, we run the grave risk of seeing it harden into cynicism not only about particular values, communist or capitalist, but about the place of the good itself. Indeed, one has reason to fear that this is already beginning to happen.

Before the still relatively naïve nihilism escalates into a more sophisticated nihilism that will have no truck with the very place of the good, something urgent needs to be done, first, about those, especially public officials, who are supposed to act as moral exemplars and who have more power to restore trust in the place of the good or to erode such trust even further. Given the crucial role of exemplars in Chinese moral culture, the current moral crisis in China is in large measure a crisis of exemplification. If the Communist Party fails to respond to this crisis of its own making, to put its own moral house in order after so many broken promises, it will have in the deepest sense lost its legitimate title to govern a society in which so much depends on maintaining the integrity of the place of the good.

No less urgently, China today stands in desperate need of disciplined exercises of the moral imagination in order to fill the gaping void in the place of the good. Important as it is to improve the rule of law (without fetishizing it) and other institutions, it is a higher calling to rebuild the place of the good – to cultivate trust in the place of the good and to give attractive and viable substance to it. And this task requires a lot of moral imagination tempered by a sense both of the Chinese tradition and of the conditions of life in China today. Without such imagination, we would be doomed to the sterility of purely institutional reform, even supposing such reform is successful. But such imagination must do its work in the face of the harsh realities of increasingly competitive global capitalism. Is it entirely a luxury to be seriously critical of global capitalism as the most powerful shaping force in the world today when China is doing all it can to thrive and move up the food chain in the new global order, and especially given that, in order to do so, it must massively expand domestic consumption and, as part of this effort, affirm and spread the ideology of consumerism? Whoever answers in the affirmative without qualification thereby commits oneself to the morally impoverished, if economically and politically ambitious, goal of successfully competing in the chief game in town without substantial interest in altering its rules or challenging its values beyond questions of balance of power. But those who balk at this prospect are immediately confronted with the question of attractive and feasible alternatives and must find a way of answering it without falling back into the failed model of a planned economy, not to mention a planned society.[24]

Not so long ago, it looked in some quarters of Europe as if a convivial or postmaterialist vision of life could capture the imagination of a society on the strength of highly advanced capitalist development, in a way somewhat reminiscent of how Marx envisioned the advent of a communist society. This, if true, would be all the more welcome given that in the European democracies the power of the state is limited, and the priority of the right is entrenched. Whether or not this vision has been kept alive in Europe in the wake of the neoliberal onslaught, there is no remotely comparable chance, at least in the foreseeable future, that even small steps in freedom from the materialist and consumerist grip of capitalism will be taken spontaneously in China. Given its level of development and the extreme unevenness of development in such a populous country, among other factors, China will see progress in this regard only through imaginative exploration of the moral primacy of the good and judicious use of the political possibility of strong leadership.

II

If I were to single out one feature as the key to grasping the spirit and dynamic of the modern world as a whole, it would have to be modern nihilism, first European and then postmodern. Modern nihilism signifies the demise of the good as something antecedent to, and therefore fit to guide and limit, human conduct. It is the demise of the good in this sense that allows both modern liberty and modern equality to come into their own – liberty above all as freedom from determination by any independent and antecedent good, and equality above all as the same right to this liberty. What nihilism thus reveals is the fundamental opposition between the (ancient) good and (modern) liberty, between the primacy

---

[24] For a thoughtful consideration of the prospect of socialism in China in the context of the country's increasing involvement in global capitalism, see Arif Dirlik, "Back to the Future: Contemporary China in the Perspective of Its Past, circa 1980," *boundary 2* 38 (2011): 7–52.

of the good and the primacy of liberty (a more accurate concept than the so-called priority of the right, since the right serves not to give ends to liberty but only to regulate it). The sovereign value of the ancient world was the good, whereas the sovereign value of the modern world is liberty, and nihilism – the demise of the good – explains why the good gave way to liberty. Even in the ancient primacy of the good, however, there exists a certain dialectic between the good and liberty, given the very nature of human agency as requiring initiative and willingness. Nor is it surprising that when the good first yielded primacy to liberty in the modern world, something of the old dialectic remained (say, in Kant and J. S. Mill), only with liberty taking pride of place. This was followed by the advent of postmodern nihilism, and what we find in this epoch-making event is the almost complete dissolution of the dialectic so that the primacy of liberty is replaced by a brand-new dominance of liberty that treats the good as little more than a plaything of choice. This is a very unfortunate way of bringing history – the quest for the good that is the heart and soul of human history – to an end.

I do not think, however, that the modern progress of liberty can and should be rolled back. There is no need to think that way, for it is not fanciful to insist on the need to maintain a dialectical relation between liberty and the good under modern conditions of life. Indeed, such a dialectic is exactly what is called for if we are to leave ourselves open to the possibility of good and meaningful lives under modern conditions of liberty. It is of secondary importance, though still very important, whether such a dialectical relation actually unfolds within a framework of the primacy of the good or of liberty. This is a matter of moral and political culture and tradition, among other things, and one should try not to be dogmatic about which framework is superior in the abstract. Given its tradition and its current condition, China's best hope lies in developing a new primacy of the good fit for the modern world, a primacy of the good that, instead of repressing liberty, gives it the form and inspiration it deserves and yet does so with an epistemic modesty made necessary by the nihilism of the modern world. Nothing is more vital for the future of China than a bracing dialectic between liberty and the good – a dialectic that I hope can be renewed in the West (if I can speak of "the West" as one entity at this level of abstraction) within its own framework of the primacy of liberty.

I do not wish for China to join the rush to the "end of history" by jettisoning the good in favor of liberty, nor to resist becoming modern (which it already is) by keeping liberty at bay in the name of the good. A positive future for China depends, rather, on full cognizance of what it means to live under modern conditions of liberty, and such cognizance involves both acceptance of liberty as constitutive of modern life and awareness of its moral and political liabilities in the absence of a dialectical relation with the good. If China succeeds in taking even modest steps in evolving such a dialectic, in conception and in practice, it will have made a big stride for itself and, moreover, a valuable contribution to the world by adding to the moral and political plurality of the family of nations and enlarging what since the end of the Cold War has been a progressively shrinking space for the moral and political imagination. This will not be easy, and we cannot even be sure whether at this historical moment there is a politically realistic way forward for a big developing country like China that is not predicated on embracing the consumption-driven mode of capitalist development. Clearly, if China fails in such an endeavor, or, as is quite possible, does not even see fit to try, it will have cast itself in advance in a largely mimetic relation to the most advanced capitalist countries in the world, except that it may end up being different in some minor respects entirely by default and in others by narrow political design. In such a scenario, China's achievement and its impact on the world, however quantitatively great, will be little more than a function of how close it will come to being a fully rule-abiding member of the liberal democratic capitalist international order, what share of the global economy it will manage to take up, how comprehensively powerful it will become, and so on. Only the future will reveal how China will turn out in these regards, and the impact of these contingencies on China and the world will be very considerable one way or another, but none of this will be of much positive interest to those whose primary concern is with the *moral* future of China and the world.

Index

abuse of power, 75, 180
Acton, Lord, 81
adaptive preference, 112
agency
  alignment of, with material condition, 139, 141–46
  as common denominator of forms of life and moral culture, 7, 38, 88–89, 93, 106, 107
  bare notion of, 189
  configurations of, 7, 10, 55–56, 63, 88, 104, 190
  role of attribution in, 39–41, 90, 92–97, 107
  understood in terms of power organized as subjectivity, 38–39, 90, 93, 94, 134, 189
agency-through-freedom, 93, 95, 97, 98, 107
agency-through-identification, 94, 97–103
alternative modernity, 211. *See also* modernity
Althusser, Louis, 42, 48
altruism, 15, 28, 29, 56, 160
Arendt, Hannah, 177n13, 193
asceticism, 29, 31, 34, 130–34
autonomy, 41, 67, 93, 95, 101n13, 106, 118, 123, 200. *See also* freedom

Bauman, Zygmunt, 202n17
Bentham, Jeremy, 187, 188
Bourdieu, Pierre, 131n10
bourgeois subject, 160

Buffet, Warren, 161

Canetti, Elias, 29
Cao, Jinqing, 146n25
capitalism, 201, 202, 218, 220
  Anglo-Saxon model of, 202
  China's integration into global, 214
  Rhenish model of, 202
certainty, as standard distinguishing knowledge from opinion, 78, 79
charisma, 54, 166
Chinese moral culture, 14, 17, 19, 22, 23, 44, 51, 124, 217, 220
Christianity, 183
civil society, 214
class enemies, 163, 165, 166, 206
class struggle, 163, 206
Cobb, Jonathan, 152n33, 154n37
coercion, 29, 164, 201
Cold War, 68
collectivism, 28, 29, 106, 160
collectivistic societies, 94, 95, 131
communicative action, 204
communism, 17, 29, 54, 55, 114, 131, 159–60
Communist Party, 35, 36, 180, 210, 211, 213–16, 217, 218, 219, 220
  as functional party, 209, 214
competition, 147, 153, 197, 201
conformism, 3, 31, 50, 57
Confucian moral psychology, 99, 101
Confucian tradition, 16, 74, 100, 102, 103, 210, 216

Confucianism, 98, 99, 100, 102, 211, 216
  political, 178
Confucius, 99, 100, 102
Conscience, 110
consent, 49, 164, 165, 166, 167
  form vs. substance of, 165
  tacit, 165
Constant, Benjamin, 151, 170, 173, 174
constitutionalism, 216
consumerism, 30, 35, 55, 194, 202, 220
corruption, 1, 2, 4, 5, 15, 22, 32, 35, 74, 105, 162, 166, 174, 180
crisis of authority, 22, 105
crisis of belief, 18, 25, 30
crisis of exemplification, 22, 105, 220
crisis of good, 17, 18, 19
crisis of justice, 18, 19, 20, 21
crisis of moral self, 22, 105
crisis of spirit, 18, 19
Cultural Revolution, 115, 123, 166
cynicism, 83, 168, 209, 210, 220

Danto, Arthur C., 129–30n8
Dean, Mitchell, 50n13
death of God, 199
death of subject, 199
democracy, 59, 97, 139, 140, 156–59, 167–77, 178, 179, 180
  agency good of, 172, 173, 174, 177
  agonistic conception of, 204
  and social justice, 174, 176
  deliberative, 169
  modern representative, 172
  role of, for freedom, 173
demoralization, 131, 160
Deng, Xiaoping, 131n10
deregulation, 203
desublimation, 26–30, 160, 207
devotion, to leader, 111–15, 118, 119, 120, 124
dialectic of Chinese revolution, 24, 26
dignity, 4, 197
Ding, Xueliang, 168n6
Dirlik, Arif, 221n24
disenchantment, 160, 185
disrespect, 133, 134
distributive justice, 153, 168
domination, 43, 60, 61, 97, 192–96, 200
  as distinct from imposition, 193, 194
  struggle for, 194–95
Dunn, John, 85

Eastern Europe, 16
economic growth, 1, 35, 173, 178, 180, 215, 219
economic reform, 1, 26, 56, 205, 214, 215, 217
Edwards, James C., 80n10
egalitarianism, 83, 84, 169
ego ideal, 110, 116, 117
egoism, 5, 29
elitism, 72
Elster, Jon, 112n7
end of history, 168, 182, 222
epistemic optimism, 70, 72
epistemic-moral optimism, 71
epistemological optimism, 64, 66, 70–72, 78
epistemological pessimism, 64, 66, 70, 78–82
epistemology, 63, 78, 82
equality
  among agents as bourgeois subjects, 161, 166
  of citizenship, 73, 150, 152, 153, 154, 201
  of opportunity, 151, 162, 197, 201, 217
  qualitative (vs. quantitative), 161, 163
esteem, 126, 150–54, 201
ethics, 47, 101, 168
exemplar, 3, 21, 22, 23, 94, 98–103, 104–05, 118
exhortation, 3, 22, 105, 112
external determination, 41, 48, 49, 50

fairness, 150, 151, 172
Fang, Ning, 178n14
Foucault, Michel, 47, 48
free riding, 21
free will, 95, 99, 103, 192
freedom
  agency good of, 171, 173, 174
  and good, 10, 87
  and nihilism, 184
  and social justice constraint, 172
  and social order, 46, 53, 54
  as a right, 45, 51, 54
  as concrete liberties, 54
  as interpretation, 41, 49
  as misrecognition of external determination, 48, 49
  as mode of subjection, 47–52, 53, 54, 56, 57

as moral resource, 45, 46, 51, 54, 56, 57
as precondition for agency in modern society, 125, 183
as value, 38, 41, 42, 43, 45, 176, 183, 185, 209
concept of, 44, 106
crisis of, 185
de facto, 3, 43, 44, 56, 167, 185
epistemological conditions of, 8, 68, 80. *See also* Metzger, Thomas
experience of, 48, 49, 50, 186
framework for exercise of, 59
from good, 82, 84, 200
ideological use of, 61
meaningful, 43
negative, 184, 185, 201
positive, 185, 201
priority of, over good, 87, 173
rise of, in early modern Europe, 184
substantive goods of, 171, 172, 173, 174
Freud, Sigmund, 8, 108–11, 115, 116, 122n17, 123

getting rich first, 163
Geuss, Raymond, 43n6, 58n18
Gilded Age, 16
globalization, 168, 202
good
and right, 17
perfectionist conceptions of, 15
place of, 183, 209, 216, 217, 219, 220
primacy of place of, 217
Gorz, André, 127n3, 134n16, 153n35, 154n37
Gramsci, Antonio, 164n3
Great Leap Forward, 146
group psychology, 8, 108, 110, 111, 116

Habermas, Jürgen, 204
hagiography, 115
He, Qing, 178n14
hedonism, 25, 26, 28, 29, 35, 55, 132
hegemony, 164
Heidegger, Martin, 78n8, 199n15
hierarchy, 145, 149, 150, 153, 154, 194
mobile, 194, 197
homogenization, in modern societies, 193
Honneth, Axel, 150n29, 152n33, 153n34, 198n13
Hsieh, Yu-wei, 98n7

human nature
as mass human nature, 196
as second nature, 196
plasticity of, 190–94, 195, 196, 198, 200, 201, 202
human rights, 140, 201
hypercathexis, 111, 118
hypnosis, 110, 111, 123

identification, 7, 22, 23, 41–42, 58, 59, 61, 88, 101, 106–07, 108, 115–19, 122
identity, 54, 55, 95–96, 99, 183, 189
ideological confrontation, 68
ideology, 25, 43, 54, 73, 76, 169, 205, 214, 220
ideology critique, 59
Illich, Ivan, 128n4
imposition, 190–96, 197, 200, 202, 203
indisputables, 69, 78
individualism/individuals
as distinct from individual agency, 93
atomistic, 4, 33, 160, 161, 162
possessive, 4
individuality, 50
individualization, 3
inequality, 132, 143, 147, 150, 151, 152, 154, 180, 205, 206, 217
between city and countryside, 145, 205
quantitative (vs. qualitative), 161, 163
internalization
as distinct from identification, 117
of leader, 120
of parental authority, 121
of social forms of authority, 121
two degrees of, 116
introjection, 8, 108, 116, 117, 121, 122, 123, 124
inwardness, 192

Jiang, Qing, 178n15, 211–12
Jiang, Zemin, 131n10
justification, 197

Kant, Immanuel, 96n6, 200n16, 222
Kierkegaard, Søren, 40
Knight, John, 145n22
Kupperman, Joel J., 100n10, 101n12

legitimacy, 35, 36, 139, 141, 167, 177, 213, 220
and economic growth, 215

Li, Shi, 145n22
Liang, Xiaoyan, 128n5
liberal democracy, 9, 168, 169, 173, 174, 179, 181, 184
　democratic component of, 172
　liberal component of, 171
　precedence of liberalism over democracy in, 174
libertarianism, 169
liberty. *See* freedom
Liu, Zhifeng, 12n1
Lu, Xun, 16
Lyotard, Jean-François, 80n10

MacIntyre, Alasdair, 100n11
Mandate of Heaven, 95
Manent, Pierre, 50–51n14, 185, 191, 196, 198
Mannheim, Karl, 73, 74n4
Mao, Zedong, 33, 112, 115, 119, 166
Maoism, 16, 74, 216
Maoist left, 179
Marcuse, Herbert, 51n14
market economy, 202
market society, 202
Marx, Karl, 187, 188, 200n16, 221
materialism, 24
meaning in life, 55, 160, 175
memory, 31, 34, 40, 91
Mencius, 15, 99n9, 103
Metzger, Thomas, 8, 63–87, 106, 107
Mill, John Stuart, 81, 222
Miller, David, 154n36
mimesis, 191, 203
mobilization, 54, 164, 166, 180, 208
modern Chinese political thought, 65, 70, 77, 79
modern Western political thought, 65, 70, 79
modernity, 11, 196, 199, 201, 203, 205, 211, 217
moral authority, 14, 22, 104, 105, 118, 119, 123
　external, 103, 121
moral change, 89, 107
moral crisis, sense of, 16, 220
moral culture, 93, 95, 97, 98, 101, 106–07, 108, 185
moral education, 119, 168, 208
moral leader, 3
moral optimism, 71, 72, 76

moral vacuum, 6, 25, 30, 184, 216
morality
　leader-centered, 8, 108, 111, 112, 117–20, 124
　superego-centered, 8, 108, 111, 120, 124
Mouffe, Chantal, 204

national revival, 33, 208, 209
nationalism, 160
neoliberalism, 201, 202, 203, 204
Nietzsche, Friedrich, 38, 39, 40n4, 78n7, 79n9, 91n1–2, 95, 190n4, 192n6, 198, 199
nihilism
　effects of, on equality, 200
　effects of, on liberty, 200
　ethically incomplete, 210
　European, 198, 199, 200, 207
　incomplete, 199, 211
　original, 198, 199, 207
　politically incomplete, 209, 210
　postmodern, 199, 200, 207, 222
nondisputables, 69, 77, 79
normal agency, 139, 140, 142, 144, 149
　and middle class, 148, 149
normal agency range, 139
normal normative discourse, 157, 159, 169
normative reasoning, 156, 167
nostalgia, 32, 33

oligarchy, 72, 177
optimism, about elites, 72, 75, 76
optimism, about human nature, 72
outsiders, 192

paternalism, 112, 197
personality cult, 115
Pettit, Philip, 44n7
plausibility
　critical, 51, 58, 59, 62
　empirical, 58, 61, 62
pluralism, 81, 154, 184, 193, 203
plurality, as presupposed by Arendt's notion of action, 193, 223
Pogge, Thomas, 127n2, 140n20
Polanyi, Karl, 202n18
political culture, 46, 47, 51, 52, 53, 54, 76, 216, 222
political optimism, 70, 85
political rationality, 85
political reform, 1, 2, 178, 180

Popper, Karl, 70
populism, 162, 165, 180
  moral, 83, 84
  substantive, 165, 166, 177
poverty
  agency poverty, 134, 135–42, 143–51, 154, 155
  as distinct from asceticism, 133
  negative social meaning of, 129
  positive social meaning of, 131
  stakes of, 11, 126
  status poverty, 127–35, 136, 137, 144, 145, 146, 147–50, 152, 154–55
  subsistence poverty, 126–35, 136–40, 141, 143–48, 153, 154, 155
power
  as condition of subjectivity, 135
  as distinct from feeling of power, 40, 91, 92, 113
priority of good, 81, 87, 212, 216
priority of right, 82, 185, 212, 216, 218, 219, 221, 222
private life, 49, 56, 171
Progressive Era, 16
propaganda, 3, 26, 32, 34, 35, 164, 168
prosperity, 35, 56, 57, 130, 132, 160, 161, 162, 163, 165, 206, 208
public discontent, 178
public life, 171
public reason, 197, 212

Qian, Liqun, 179n16

Rawls, John, 81, 85, 204
reciprocity, 21
recognition
  bifurcation of, into respect and esteem, 150, 151, 153, 154, 200, 201
  struggle for, 163, 171, 172, 176, 194, 196, 197, 198
Reformation, Protestant, 103
resentment, 9, 19, 32, 35, 152, 162, 192, 207, 217
respect, 126, 127, 131, 134, 135, 136, 137, 138, 141, 143, 144, 145, 150–54, 201
responsibility, 3, 6, 40, 44, 91, 127, 129
resublimation, 27, 30, 31, 34, 35
Riesman, David, 51n14
rise of China, 178
rise of the social, 177, 217
Rorty, Richard, 80n10

Rose, Nikolas, 47n8, 50n12
rule of law, 168, 214, 216, 217, 220
Russia, 16
Rycroft, Charles, 116n14

seduction, as form of imposition, 194, 201, 202, 203, 204
self-constitution, 135, 153, 175, 191, 203
  ancient model of, 203
  modern model of, 203
self-cultivation, 99, 100, 102, 103
self-denial, 27, 29, 95
self-determination, 41, 48, 171
self-direction, 100, 101
self-respect, 134, 135, 138, 142, 143
self-sacrifice, 27, 160
Sen, Amartya, 127n3, 129n6, 135n17
Sennett, Richard, 152n33, 154n37
Shao, Daosheng, 12n1
Shi, Tong, 132n14
Shue, Henry, 130n9
Shun, Kwong-loi, 101n13
skepticism, 70, 76, 78, 81, 82, 83
Skorupski, John, 81n11, 101n13, 162n2
social exclusion, 128, 132
social imaginary, 5, 163, 164, 177, 217
social justice, 165, 168, 171, 172, 176, 178, 180
social order, 17, 18, 19, 24, 46, 47, 51, 54, 61, 67, 89, 106, 107, 207, 220
social unrest, 180
socialism, 17, 24, 145, 178, 214, 221
socialization, 42, 58, 77, 97, 210
Socrates, 78
solidarity, 4, 54, 113, 131
Song, Lina, 145n22
state of nature, 219
Strauss, Leo, 191
subjection, as condition of subjectivity, 41, 42, 49, 50
subjectivity
  inherent tension in, 191
  mimetic structure of, 191, 203
sublimation, 26, 27, 28, 29, 30, 31, 34, 45
superego, 108, 109, 110, 112, 116, 117, 120, 121, 122, 123, 124
Surin, Kenneth, 68n2

teleology, 95
Thatcher, Margaret, 204
Tocqueville, Alexis de, 216

tolerance, 81, 205
totally administered society, 60
transition, 6, 16, 24, 27, 56, 108, 121, 123, 130
trust, 9, 21, 220

Übelhör, Monika, 98n8
United States, 64, 65, 66, 67–68n2
universal suffrage, 92
utopia, 73
utopianism, 25, 26, 28, 73, 74, 75

values
 as valorizing interpretations, 113
 leveling down of, 162
 objectivity of, 81, 82, 83

Walzer, Michael, 134n13, 149n27, 150n30, 154n36
Wang, Xiaoying, 12n1
Wang, Yangming, 101, 102, 103
Warren, Mark, 38n1, 106n15, 189n2

West, the, 63, 64, 65, 68, 86, 106, 184, 222
Westernization, 170
will to power, 39, 113, 114, 189, 198
Williams, Raymond, 149n26
Wilson, Colin, 192n7
Wollheim, Richard, 116, 117, 118n16, 123n19
WTO, 214

Xi, Jinping, 206, 207
Xu, Xiao, 128n5

Yan, Yunxiang, 12n1, 15n2

Zeng Zi, 100
Zhang, Shuguang, 146n25
Zhang, Xiaobo, 146n24
Zhao, Wenqing, 15n2
Zhou, Baosong, 169n7
Zhou, Guanghui, 166n4
Zhou, Yongping, 128n5
Zhu, Xi, 102